the ultimate
Fly-Fishing
guide to the
Great Smoky Mountains

the ultimate

Fly-Fishing

guide to the
Great Smoky Mountains

Don Kirk
and Greg Ward

Menasha Ridge Press
Birmingham, Alabama

The Ultimate Fly-Fishing Guide to the Great Smoky Mountains

Copyright © 2011 by Don Kirk and Greg Ward

All rights reserved

Printed in the United States of America

Published by Menasha Ridge Press

Distributed by Publishers Group West

First edition, first printing

Library of Congress Cataloging-in-Publication Data

Kirk, Don, 1952—

The ultimate fly-fishing guide to the smoky mountains /Don Kirk,
Greg Ward.

p.   cm.

Includes Index.

ISBN-13: 978-0-89732-691-9 (pbk.)

ISBN-10: 0-89732-691-1 ()

1. Fly fishing—Great Smoky Mountains National Park (N.C. and Tenn.)
I. Ward, Greg. II. Title.

SH456.K45 2011

799.1'10976889--dc22

2011007749

Menasha Ridge Press

P.O. Box 43673

Birmingham, Alabama 35243

www.menasharidge.com

Cover painting: Jim Gray. The image is available in three sizes as a limited edition giclee print on canvas from Jim Gray Gallery in the Arts and Crafts Community in Gatlinburg or online at **www.JimGrayGallery.com.**

Cover design: Scott McGrew

Text design: Annie Long

Photo credits:

Pages 29 and 33 courtesy of the Tennessee State Library and Archives

Page 86, Dreamstime

All other photos courtesy of the authors

table *of* contents

Acknowledgments

Where to start?

Born a military brat, I would like to acknowledge the good sense of my father, Don Ward, for moving us home to my mother's native east Tennessee; thanks to my mother, Joan, for letting me spend so much time in the mountains and for taking me there whenever I wanted before I learned to drive. Thanks and much appreciation to my loving wife, Diane, who had no problem with me leaving perfectly gainful employment with the state of Tennessee to pursue my dreams of opening a fly shop and starting a guide service. Thank the good Lord for giving me the ability to write with no formal training except for what my high school English teacher, Donna Cantrell, and my English major wife, who's always my first editor, have managed to drum into my stubborn head. Thanks to my daughters—Crystal, Lauren, and Sara—for being such great fishing and hunting buddies over the years. Thanks to my brother Don for teaching me how to fish with explosives. And many thanks to my Uncle Tom Norton for taking me fishing and hunting every chance he got after my dad passed away in 1976 (the keys to the Ranger bass boat and Toyota Land Cruiser helped a great deal as well!). I owe a lot to my late Uncle Gene Lawson and all those nights on Douglas Lake listening to whippoorwills. The many deer camps in Lower Alabama with Uncle Gary, Tommy Joe Norton, Taylor, and Uncle Tom have a special place in my heart.

Thanks to my great friends from the shop and all my fishing buddies, especially Chris Johnson; Brandon Ogle, who is the closest I ever got to having a son; Cory Smith and Jesse West for taking care of trips while I worked on this book;

authors like H. Lea Lawrence, Wilma Dykeman, Dave Whitlock, Mel Krieger, and Tom Rosenbough. I always wanted to be Dave Whitlock when I grew up.

Special thanks to Don Kirk for his great stories, numerous phone calls, and hours on the water—and for trusting me for up-to-date knowledge and material. Kudos to Molly Merkle with Menasha Ridge Press and Keen Communications for putting up with me and my lack of computer know-how.

And last but not least, thanks to Jim and Chris Gray for such a perfect cover for a book on the Smokies.

*T*HINGS HAPPEN FOR A REASON.

As I was loading a couple of suitcases into my SUV for a weekend over the mountain to celebrate my 22nd wedding anniversary, my cell phone rang. It was Don Kirk asking me to go look at some photographs of the Smokies and get permission to use one for the cover of our book. I was thinking of using a Jim Gray painting instead, which I must have thought out loud because within moments Don said, "Go to **www.JimGrayGallery.com** and pull up *Sanctuary*." *Sanctuary* is a painting of two men doing what they love most: Chris Gray fly-fishing Ramsey Prong, and his dad, Jim, painting a picture of the beautiful scenery of the Smokies with his son in the middle of it. The Grays have been long-time friends of my family, and within minutes I emailed Chris to get permission to use his dad's painting for the cover of the *Ultimate Fly-fishing Guide to the Smoky Mountains*. Jim said it would be an honor—and just like that Sanctuary became the cover of our book.

Things happen for a reason.

—GREG WARD

the ultimate
Fly-Fishing
guide to the
Great Smoky Mountains

Introduction

THE GREAT SMOKY MOUNTAINS NATIONAL Park offers one of the last wild trout habitats in the eastern United States. Annually, millions of Americans visit this natural wonderland seeking recreation and a chance to enjoy the outdoors. Among these visitors are thousands of anglers eager to test their luck against the stream-bred trout of the park's famed waters. Most of these anglers lack the needed information and are confused by the seemingly endless number of streams available.

Some time in the early 1970s when my children where young (as was I), the idea of writing a trout fishing guide to the streams of the Great Smoky Mountains National Park first crossed my mind. It took a few more years of fishing, then several years of work before that book was published in 1981. Since that time, *Trout Fishing Guide To The Smokies* has been a raving success that has been revised and reprinted many times. Few endeavors have netted me so many compliments as that little guidebook.

Many things have changed over the last three decades in the Great Smoky Mountains National Park. Regulations have changed radically, and fishing pressure on many streams has increased dramatically. Guide services available to anglers wishing to sample park waters were virtually nonexistent when my book was first written, as were fly-fishing shops within 50 miles of the park. That also has changed. Both the shops and guide services are now very common around the Smokies. The city of Gatlinburg even promotes fishing for trout, something that was unheard of only a few decades ago.

1

This book is designed to help both experienced and novice anglers select waters that suit their tastes and abilities. You will find a chapter on each of the major streams in the park. Listed with each stream are such valuable data as its location, fishing pressure, species of trout found in that particular watershed, both auto and trail access routes, campsite accommodations, and other information. Also included are chapters covering the early history of fly-fishing for trout in and near the park, information on the aquatic insects most abundant in the streams, proven dry and wet nymph patterns, tips on gear, and other aspects of fly-fishing.

In the Great Smoky Mountains National Park, we have some of the finest trout fishing anywhere. And although the trout are wary, even a beginner can expect to catch a few. The Great Smoky Mountains National Park has long been one of the country's most popular fly-fishing destinations. This book represents at least the sixth attempt by an ardent angler to provide fellow fishermen with information on how and where to catch trout from these streams. The first book written exclusively on fishing in the Smokies was penned in 1937 by then park ranger, Joe F. Manley. Manley, who was employed by the National Park Service for only two years before accepting employment in Gatlinburg as chief of their water works department, was an avid fisherman. His 80-page, hardbound book was vanity published once—3,000 copies, according to Manley, whom I spoke to last in 1990 at his home in Gatlinburg. This rare and little-known book is unknown to most anglers, but was brought to my attention in 1987 by noted Smoky Mountain angler Eddie George of Louisville, Tennessee, who could rightly be termed the best fly-fisherman to ever cast these streams. In fact, the copy of Manley's book I have was given to me by George. According to Manley, shortly after his book, *Fishing Guide to the Smokies,* was printed, he agreed to guide an editor from either *Field and Stream* or *Outdoor Life* magazine (he could not recall precisely which). During the course of their fishing trips, Manley shared information on his book with the Northerner, who bought and took home his entire printing. Only a few dozen of these books were ever sold locally. Over two decades after talking with Manley, I discovered that the purchaser of his inventory of books was Ben East, legendary editor at *Outdoor Life.*

Manley's book contains interesting information on the streams of the Smokies and is about equally split between trout and bass fishing. One of the most interesting photographs in the book depicts Manley at the Sinks on Little River holding up a stringer of smallmouth bass weighing between 3 and 5 pounds. His favorite fly rod "lure," a Heddon-made Flaptail, can still be found at antique tackle shows at a cost of $40 to $80. Can you imagine how quickly most of us would climb a tree to retrieve one of these costly little jewels? If you can find a copy of Manley's book for less than $200, do not hesitate to part with the cash. It is harder to find than eyebrows on a brook trout. Also worth noting is that Manley remained a well-known fisherman in the park as well as its adjacent waters. He was quite fond of catching big muskie in the then free-floating portions of the Little Tennessee River located to the south of the park.

The second book written on this subject was the effort of Jim Gasque, a somewhat prolific writer from western North Carolina. This title, *Hunting and Fishing in the Great Smokies*, was published by Alfred A. Knopf of New York, who at the same time published other well-known sporting titles such as *Trout* by Ray Bergman, *Ruffed Grouse* by John Alden Knight, and *A Book of Duck Shooting* by Van Campen Heilner. *Hunting and Fishing in the Great Smokies* and Jim Gasque's other, better-known title, *Bass Fishing*, can still be found on book lists circulated among collectors of vintage fishing tackle and associated paraphernalia. Published in 1948, Gasque's book was the first nationally distributed book on fishing in (and around) the Smokies, although Horace Kephart, who also was a great fan of angling these waters, often wrote about it as well as did Robert S. Mason. Gasque's book immortalized the great western North Carolina angler, Mark Cathey. Unfortunately, I was born too late to ever meet Cathey. Written in the folksy, "me 'n' Joe" style of outdoor writing common to the era, it provides more in the way entertainment than information, although the techniques and few flies noted in the book are as deadly on trout today as when the information was penned half a century ago. Gasque's chapters on Cataloochee and Deep Creeks are extremely insightful. *Hunting and Fishing in the Great Smokies* is a gem worth the current asking price of $50 to $100.

The third book written on trout fishing in the Great Smoky Mountains National Park is perhaps the rarest of all of the four titles known to me. Discovered when going through the National Park Service archives in 1979, *Sport Fishing The Smokies* by Joe Manley is an extremely short, but very accurate book on the ins and outs of catching trout in the Smokies. Only 16 pages long, this informative book was published in 1969 and apparently had a very short shelf life. My favorite notation in the book was when the author advised anglers looking for bigger trout to use techniques that took their flies deep along the bottom. How right Manley was.

The fourth book written on fishing for trout in the Great Smoky Mountains National Park was an effort I began in the mid-1970s as a young man with an unquenchable thirst for catching fish from these pristine waters. The first printing of 1,000 books was published by McGuire/Denton Publishers of Dayton, Ohio. It was the first comprehensive, stream-by-stream guide to the 13 major watersheds in the park. This white, blue, and black paperback has become something of a collectible in its own right. I own only three copies and can only guess what the publishers did with the remaining inventory or what became of that pair of Yankees, may God bless them.

In 1984 with my assistance, Menasha Ridge Press of Birmingham, Alabama, acquired rights to that book, *Trout Fishing Guide to the Smokies*. It was revised, with chapters added to include the waters in the Cherokee reservation located east of the national park, as well as the five lakes that border the southern portion of the Smokies. Now known as *Smoky Mountains Trout Fishing Guide*, this book has been extremely well received. It went through a dozen printings before my fly-fishing-only book took its place on bookstore shelves.

Naturally, other books have been written that include considerable information on fly-fishing in the Great Smoky Mountains. My close friend and mentor, Charley "Chum" Dickey (who is from my hometown), wrote a book with Freddie Moses (a noted fly-fishing attorney from Knoxville, Tennessee) titled *Trout Fishing*. Published by Oxmoor House, this tough-to-find title from the 1960s is one of my most cherished possessions. Now deceased, Chum was my mentor for many years and is sorely missed by all. He told me to go places besides the Smokies so I would not look like a total hillbilly. I did what he suggested. I've fished and hunted around the world a couple of times (enough that I don't care to any more), although I still do not like wearing shoes.

Chum has been gone a while, but like Cathey and Manley, Charley Dickey was an icon to fly-fishing in the Smokies. Along with his fishing pal, Fred Moses of Knoxville, they not only fished the streams of the park like possessed fiends, but also traveled widely, fly-fishing and hunting. Moses, a star running back on General Neyland's Tennessee Vols football teams in 1933–1934, was rated by his long-time partner, Chum, as the best caster to ever ply the waters of the Smokies. Moses might also be the boldest too, as the following excerpt from *Trout Fishing: Basic Guide to Dry Fly Fishing* reveals. Charlie later told me that this incident occurred at Big Creek.

Not long ago, Fred and Charley were fishing a small river in the Smokies, poking along with Charley fishing the forehand side and Fred the backhand. They alternated honeyholes and ambled along side by side, fishing the few flat stretches. As they rounded the turn, there on a huge boulder lay two young ladies without clothes, basking in the sun. They did not hear the approaching anglers above the roaring water and may have been sleeping.

Charley was deeply worried that they might get sunburned, but Fred was concerned with ethical behavior on a trout stream; should the anglers fish past the sunbathers without saying anything, or should they ask permission to move ahead?

After a lengthy debate, the anglers decided to wade quietly past the sunning lasses lest a sudden awakening frighten them. The trout fishermen pulled in their lines and pushed slowly up the difficult current, passing the boulder where the sleeping beauties languished. The fishermen would be around the next turn in a few seconds and could go back to their routine casting.

At the last moment Fred could stand it no longer. He removed the Cahill on the end of his leader and replaced it with a hookless spinner. Then he stripped out line and began to false cast until he had just the right amount of line out.

Then he stripped line on one of the girls and dropped the spoon, cold out of the water, right on the most logical part of her anatomy. The target turned over, took one look, and let out a scream which drowned out all of the cascades and waterfalls in the Smokies. There was a scurry of sunburned flesh scampering through the laurels as the two anglers turned and continued upstream.

When Fred and Charley returned to their vehicle after dark, weary and sore, the air in all four tires had been let out!

$$\Longrightarrow\Longleftarrow$$

OTHER PRE-1996 PUBLISHED BOOKS YOU MIGHT WISH TO LOCATE ON this subject include *Papa Was A Fisherman: Memories of the Great Smokies* by Joe B. Long (1969), *Twenty Years Hunting and Fishing in the Great Smokies* by Sam Hunnicutt, and *On The Spine of Time: An Angler's Love of the Smokies* (1991) by another personal friend and neighbor in Homewood, Alabama, Harry Middleton When I left Tennessee for Alabama to start magazines, I lived only a block away from Middleton for over a year before running into him at the Piggly Wiggly. I am not sure which of us was the most surprised. I wish I had met him sooner.

Since my GSMNP fly-fishing book appeared in 1998, a bevy of latecomers have appeared. Longtime fishing pal and fellow Morristownian (as was Davy Crockett), H. Lea Lawrence wrote *The Fly Fisherman's Guide to the Great Smoky Mountains National Park* (Cumberland House, 1998). Lea was another valuable friend and mentor, and without question the most talented conversationalist ever to make a living in the outdoors business. Ian Rutter was the next to publish a guidebook, and this young fellow did a splendid job. I predict Smoky Mountains fly-fishermen will read Rutter's prose for many years to come.

The most recent book on fly-fishing in the Smokies was penned by North Carolinian Jim Casada, whom I have known for many years. When I launched *Southern Sporting Journal,* its fly-fishing column was written by my close friend, Jim Bashline, former editor at *Field & Stream.* After only a couple of issues, Jim passed away unexpectedly. I was fortunate enough to get fly-fishing expert Casada to take over the publication's fly-fishing column. Casada is knowledgeable of park waters in North Carolina. His book also does an excellent job of providing information on fly-fishing guides to the Smokies. I wholeheartedly recommend it.

The only complaint I have received about my previous books is that they revealed too many formerly secret fishing spots to interloping Yankees. In that respect I believe I also have misgivings, but from the many letters I have received over the years, I think I did more good than bad with my efforts. My first book on fishing in the Smokies was the beginning of an outdoor writing career that has spanned five decades. In the late 1980s when I was still keeping track of such things, I had sold over 10,000 articles and columns.

Becoming an editor in the 1990s, I started more than two dozen sporting titles (plus one on NASCAR racing and polo). Some of them, such as *Whitetail Journal,* remain in publication.

During the last 20 years I have dedicated well over half of my effort to ghost writing for so-called celebrity hunters and fishermen. It's a quick buck, no hassles with young editors, and I don't have to kill or catch every damned critter that I write about under the names of others. Additionally, I have hosted a number of television shows, my favorite being Bassin' Mexico, which we did for four years. It took about six weeks of fishing in Mexico per season of television. On one morning trip there between 9:00 and 11:00 a.m., Wild Bill Skinner and I caught and released over 40 bass that topped ten pounds. The largest exceeded 16 pounds. There is a clip on YouTube of Wild Bill wrestling what was surely a new-world-record largemouth bass. I can be seen behind him. The guide knocked the fish off the bait at the side of the boat. The last time I looked, that clip had over 200,000 views.

Over the years I have hunted and fished everywhere from Alaska and Africa, to Chile and Scotland. I have fly-fished for Atlantic salmon with Ted Williams on the Miramchi River, bowhunted with Fred Bear at Grouse Haven, hunted caribou and mountain lion with Bob Foulkrod, and drank whiskey around campfires since I was 12. For a while I was not as ever-present in the Smokies as I was in the old days. However, everywhere I went, I measured it against these mountains. My epitaph will read, He went there, did that, and sold the T-shirt on Ebay.

When it came to being a topnotch fly-fisherman or archer, I even disappointed myself most of the time. I have grown as accustomed to being told, "I thought you could fish or shoot better than that." When it comes to fly-fishing in the Smokies, I apply the same reasoning that I have long used for sex. It is less consequential to be the best angler, so long as I get to go as often as I am physically able to do so. Fishing is fun. Writing this book is fun. Neither requires the brilliance of a rocket scientist, or for that matter, even the ability to rebuild a carburetor.

One last word. Insofar as I have outlived most of the people I acknowledged in my past fishing books on the Smokies, I have decided not to list any this time. Greg Ward can repay his debts via that bit of print.

Tight lines,

DON KIRK
Montevallo, Alabama
(*it's a damned state . . .*)
2010

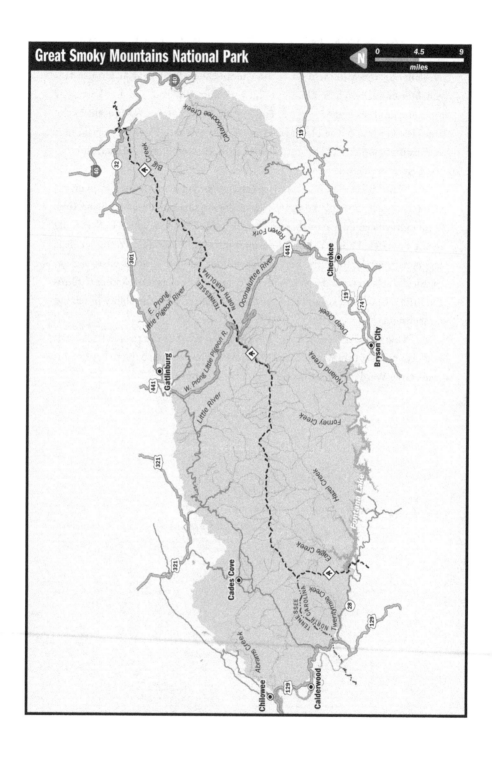

chapter 1

Smoky Mountains Trout and Bass

$\mathcal{T}$HE MAJESTIC GREAT SMOKY MOUNTAINS National Park is a rugged half-million-acre wilderness sanctuary located on the border between Tennessee and North Carolina. Encompassed in the park are several steep, tree-lined ridges, separated by deep valleys. There are more than 1,000 miles of cool, crystal-clear streams.

One of the most diverse biospheres on earth, the Smokies range from an elevation of 850 feet at the mouth of Abrams Creek to 6,642 feet on Clingmans Dome. The flora are incredibly diverse, with several trees reaching their record growth in the park. There are 13 major watersheds in the Smokies, as well as a number of smaller ones. These streams range in size from the largest, the Little River and Oconaluftee River, which during periods of normal flow are big enough to float a canoe down, to an almost endless number of small headwater rills. Living in these streams is a wide spectrum of aquatic insects and invertebrates, as well as more than 70 species of fish, including darters, suckers, dace, shiners, chubs, sculpin, bream, bass, and the native brook trout. Since the turn of the century, two other species, the rainbow trout and the brown trout, have become part of the ecosystem of the Smokies, although they are considered "exotics" by fisheries biologists.

The Brook Trout *(Salvelinus fontinalis)*

THE BROOK TROUT, known affectionately to the mountain folk of the Smokies as the "spec," is not a true trout, but a char. The world's trout—salmon, grayling, and whitefish—are members of one homogeneous group. The trout, in turn, are divided into two technically separate groups, the true trout and the chars.

This classification is arrived at principally through skeletal structure, teeth, and scale differences. This is of little importance to anglers, as the more apparent differences in coloration are obvious. Chars always have a dark background color with light spots. True trout, such as the rainbow and brown, always have a light background color with dark spots.

The brook trout is distinctive from other fish with its "worm like" markings on its back (known as vermiculations) and white-edged lower fins. The brook trout, like all chars, spawns in the fall. The brook trout of the Smokies are most closely related to lake trout, Dolly Varden trout, and Arctic char. They

Brook char, or speckle trout, are the only native cold-water game fish in the Smokies.

are the most handsome of all of the trout found in the park, in coloration and appearance. Only the ruby-flanked Arctic char that I've caught in the rivers and lakes of Quebec, Labrador, and the Northwest Territories are more visually stunning (and more tasty).

I grew up boulder-hopping headwater streams for brook trout. In 1978 I caught my largest brook trout in park waters. It was a 15-inch specimen taken while fishing with Vic Stewart at Meigs Creek. I have chased brook all over the South and Northeast as well as western waters where these bejeweled fish have been introduced. Once while caribou hunting along the Leaf River in Quebec, we fished the quarter-mile-wide river where every cast resulted in latching into a 5-to-7-pound brook trout. The first day of this was fun, but after catching and releasing scores of these leviathan brook trout, it occurred to me that it was far greater fun to ambush an 8-inch brookie in a rivulet in the Smokies.

In the Smokies, the brook trout feed on numerous forms of aquatic insects, including stone flies, mayflies, and caddis flies. Terrestrial insects are also an important part of their diet, and include bees, wasps, beetles, ants, jassids, flies, and grasshoppers. Crayfish are important daily fare, as are minnows. The brook trout is capable of digesting a stomach full of food in less than half an hour, a fact that prods the brookie to constantly look out for almost any edible morsels.

The brookies of the Smokies were "marooned" here after the glacial epoch. Originally an ocean-dwelling fish from the Arctic, the brook trout migrated down the eastern seacoast, fleeing the freezing onslaught of the ensuing Ice Age. When the rivers had cooled sufficiently to offer suitable habitat, the brookies moved upstream and established themselves. As the rivers began to warm, the brook trout were forced to retreat into the cool mountain headwaters.

The brook trout was once abundant in the Smokies. Accounts of fishing trips made into the mountains prior to 1890 tell of fish being caught by the hundreds. Large-scale logging operations came into the Smokies in the late 1890s. Whole watersheds were logged out, dams were erected on the streams, railroad lines were built up alongside many streams, and fires fed on the slash left behind by the timber-cutting operations: these were but some of the devastating problems the brook trout faced. All logging operations ceased in 1935 (approximately two-thirds of the Smokies were logged during this period), and better land management helped heal the wounds left by the previous forty years.

Estimates of the total amount of original brook trout water are speculative, but most agree that it was between 400 and 440 miles with the present boundaries of the park. There is reasonable documentation that when the park was officially established that brook trout had disappeared from over 150 miles

Brook trout have made a remarkable
comeback in the national park.

of their former range. By 1980 these fish are believed to have lost an additional 130-to-140 miles of stream.

Rainbow trout were introduced into every major stream in the Smokies prior to the creation of the park, and were periodically stocked in these waters thereafter into the 1970s. Massive stockings of as many as 400,000 rainbow trout were continued through 1947. The brook trout, which lost over half of its original range to the loggers, is now losing additional territory to the rainbow trout. Why the brook trout cannot regain its lost range where habitat conditions have returned to near-normal, and what part the rainbow trout plays in this drama, are not fully understood. Several explanations have been offered, and research into the dilemma continues. A moratorium was placed on the killing of brook trout in the park in 1975. Scores of headwater streams were closed for almost three decades to protect the remaining brookies. In 2002 a number of formerly closed brook trout streams were opened to fishing. In addition, several other brook trout streams that had never closed to fishing amended regulations, allowing anglers to keep brook trout of 7 inches or longer.

Considerable debate remains not only over the future of the brook trout in the streams of the Great Smoky Mountains National Park, but also whether these fish are indeed a unique subspecies of brook trout. It has been the subject of more federally funded research projects than the money spent to land on the moon. Reams of research on the brook trout subject has failed to settle the issue to everyone's satisfaction. In the world of zoology there are two schools of classification: One group lumps barely indistinguishable subspecies such as the yellow-rumped warbler and Myrtle's warbler into one subspecies. Conversely, the other school splits things to infinity, noting that the Myrtle's warbler has tail feather vane lengths of 5.6cm, while the yellow-rumprd warbler has a tail feather vane length of 5.4cm. Need I say that this school of zoology is known as the "splitters."

After exhaustive, incredibly expensive research, there is general consensus that the brook trout of the Smokies (in fact, southern Appalachian brook trout found south of the New River in Virginia) are genetically different than those same fish found north of this dividing line. Since the 1990s a number of studies are in general agreement that brook trout of southern Appalachia are indeed genetically unique. Pure southern-strain brook trout do exist, and in some locales are doing remarkably well. Where northern brook trout have been introduced, and in the Great Smoky Mountain National Park this covers nearly all watersheds, northern-strain brookies and southern-strain/northern-strain hybrids are common. According to some sources, it is not uncommon for northern- and southern-strain brookies to occupy the same waters.

In an ongoing effort to make sure confusion rules supreme in Bedlam, the latest DNA detective work supposes that not only are the specs of the south unique, but that indeed some streamsheds in the Smokies have brook trout populations different even within this microcosm. There is considerable debate regarding just about everything in connection with the future of the southern brook trout. Their average life expectancy is three years or less, which does not work to their advantage. Whether or not they are being assaulted more these days by factors such as acid rain and global warming, two suggestions I personally do not buy into, is a matter of enlightened conjecture. Pressure from rainbow and brown trout is the primary problem. Citing their desire to save the brook trout of the Great Smoky Mountains National Park, the National Park Service may ultimately need to take more aggressive management approaches.

The Rainbow Trout *(Oncorhynchus mykiss)*

THE VERY NAME OF THIS FISH rings out with a surge of raw energy and beauty. The rainbow trout is well known for unsurpassed fighting ability, arching leaps, and superb eating quality. A powerful downstream run by one of these fish that rips the line from your reel will make you feel as if your heart is trying to bypass your Adam's apple.

The rainbow trout's original range extended from California to Bristol Bay in Alaska. This fish prefers fast, oxygenated water. Recognizable by its silvery flanks slashed with scarlet and its greenish back, the rainbow trout is a beautiful fish. Predominantly an insect eater, particularly in the streams of the Smokies, the rainbow will, however, strike spinners and minnow imitations with gusto.

Rainbow trout from the Sierra Mountains of California were shipped to Michigan in 1878. In a few years the adaptable Western natives were providing blue-ribbon fishing in a number of Michigan rivers. Anglers from across the eastern part of the country sought the highly touted rainbow to replace the quickly diminishing brook trout. Rainbows are easily reared in hatcheries, but they were discontented in small streams when suitable habitat in larger waters was open to them. The wanderlust problem is of little concern to fisheries personnel in the southern Appalachian Mountains, where fish are confined to small streams and rivers (except for the existence of a few high-elevation impoundments).

Rainbow trout spawn in spring, with runs normally in February. An interesting change has been observed recently in southern rainbows, with a few fish spawning in the fall. I have caught rainbows from the West Prong of the Little Pigeon in October and early November that were decked out in dark spawning hues and full of roe.

The exact date and site of the first stocking of rainbow trout in the Smokies is not known. There is some contention that landowners stocked them in Abrams Creek in 1900, though no records were kept. At least a portion of the original stock of rainbow trout came from California. However, from where, by whom, and when rainbow entered individual watersheds in the Great Smoky Mountain National Park is at best enlightened conjecture. Today, the rainbow trout is the dominant game fish in the park, having extended its range into every stream system.

Most fish average 7 inches in length and generally do not top 9 inches. However, an occasional 12- to 16-inch rainbow is taken. On rare days, 3- to 4-pound fish are caught. Spawning runs from impoundments (Fontana, Cheoah, and Chilhowee Lakes) often bring large fish upstream for short periods of time, but this usually occurs from late December through February. While it is a misnomer, some locals call this a "steelhead" run, similar to the famous one during the 1950s and 1960s up Doe Creek from Watauga Lake over 100 miles north of the Finger Lakes of the Smokies.

Rainbow trout are the most-often sought game fish in the Smokies.

It is a bit ironic that a century ago the spunky little stream trout brought here saved sport fishing in the Smokies but is now reviled by the NPS as an unwelcomed interloper exotic species. As much as I love the specs, the 'bow is still welcomed by me.

The Brown Trout *(Salmo trutta)*

THE BROWN TROUT was brought to this country from Germany in 1883. Eggs shipped across the Atlantic arrived at a New York hatchery, where they were hatched and planted in local waters. Brown trout stock from Scotland arrived the following year. Fish from the German strain were called German browns or Von Behr trout, and those from Scotland were known as Loch Leven browns. For a number of years, records listed the two fish individually. Today, however, all Salmo trutta in this country are referred to as simply brown trout.

Brown trout were introduced into the Tennessee Valley in 1900. Browns in excess of 25 pounds have been caught in this region; the largest brown known to have been taken in the park was a respectable 16-pounder. A 32-inch 15-pounder was taken in October, 2009 by a client angler, according to Steve Claxton, whose guide service is based out of Bryson City. Although browns were never officially stocked in the Smokies, downstream waters were stocked by both Tennessee and North Carolina fish-and-game agencies in the 1950s. Browns began to appear in the waters of the park as early as the 1940s, and by the 1970s brown trout occupied more than 50 miles of park waters.

Brown trout are primarily insect eaters, with adult mayflies being their favorite food. Frederic M. Halford, the famous English angling writer, wrote of the feeding habits of the brown trout: "The nymphs are the brown trout's beef, and the adult mayfly his caviar." A carnivorous creature, the brown will use everything in a stream, from tiny plankton to an occasional brother or sister. In park streams, larger members of this clan are nocturnal feeders. The best time to tie into a big brown in the Smokies is at dusk or dawn, or immediately after a rain.

The brown trout can be distinguished by its generally brownish-yellow color with orange spots on the sides—although a few are sometimes a silvery tan with dark brown spots. Brown trout prefer slower water than do rainbows, but have been taken in fast waters up to 4,500 feet in elevation in park streams. They spawn in fall.

There is a simple reason brown trout grow larger in the waters of the Great Smoky Mountains National Park. The secret is their habitat preference compared to that of a rainbow trout. Browns are predators, more comparable to a large snake or lion, and feed only on large items. After feeding, they then retire to digest their prey while remaining inactive. Rainbows are like chickadees, constantly flirting with the current for food, eating only slightly more than it takes to sustain their bulk. The energy saved by the brown trout is channeled to growth, not day-to-day survival.

The Smallmouth Bass *(Micropterus dolomieui)*

RIPPING, CARTWHEELING SURFACE antics are Mr. Smalljaw's calling card. This well-muscled fish's strength is overshadowed only by its courageous determination to be free and its no-nonsense, aggressive disposition.

The smallmouth bass is a member of the Centrarchidae family of sunfish. Among the thousands who identify themselves as "bass fishermen," this fighter is their passion, the thing from which sweet dreams are made. The lower reaches of many streams in the Great Smoky Mountains National Park are prime bronzeback country. Recognizing this, the legislature made the small-mouth bass the official fish of the state of Tennessee.

The controversial, world-record smallmouth bass, which weighed 11 pounds, 15 ounces, was caught in Dale Hollow Lake in Tennessee in 1955. Actually, the fish was caught so close to the Kentucky state line that both states claim it. Being a good Volunteer State resident, however, I'll go with the home team!

The presence of smallmouth bass in the streams of the Great Smoky Mountains National Park comes as a shock to many, including a few lifelong trouters in the region. However, these marvelous game fish, as well as rock bass and even a few largemouth bass, are found in these streams. It is a bit ironic that most fly-fishermen frequenting these streams ignore the brown bass, as it is a far better fighter than any of the trout occurring here.

Part of the reason many fly-fishermen do not pursue the great smallie angling opportunities found in the park is the mistaken impression that these fish can only be caught on hardware such as spinners and small crankbaits. However, nothing could be farther from the truth. Smallmouth bass can be enticed to strike a variety of flies, ranging from streamers to nymphs. For the most part, all of the bass in the Smokies are most common in the lower reaches of the largest streams, such as Deep Creek and the East Prong of Little Pigeon River.

During the early years of the park, fly-fishing for smallmouth bass was almost as common as for trout. Lack of shade on many reaches of water (that are now canopied at least half of the year) resulted in prime smallmouth bass habitat. During those days, fly-fishermen used what was known then as fly-rod baits. In most instances, these were scaled-down versions of proven plugs such as Heddon's Flaptail or South Bend's Bass Oreno. These bantam-sized plugs were too light to be cast with any tackle of that era other than a fly rod. Modern ultralight tackle will cast these dainty offerings, which are now highly sought after by collectors of vintage fishing tackle.

The smallmouth bass is a member of the black bass clan, the toughest branch of the scrappy sunfish family. They resemble their larger cousins, the largemouth bass, as well as the Kentucky bass. The most notable differences are in body shape and coloration. Smallies are more streamlined and sport amber-to-bronze coloration. Their flanks have vertical bars, or "tiger stripes," and their eyes are reddish.

Adult smallmouth bass prefer rock- or gravel-bottomed feeding stations, which characterizes most of their habitat in the Great Smoky Mountains National Park. Three- to five-pound smallmouth bass are trophies from these waters, while a 12-inch rock bass is a true "eyepopper." Each season, a few larger bass are taken from park waters. In the loosely knit world of black bass fishing, rock bass are often referred to as the "brook trout" of this far-flung clan of alpha sunfish.

Crawfish, which are common to park streams, are key prey items, along with small fish such as darters and sculpins, spring lizards, insects, and other invertebrates. These fish are slightly more meat-conscious than trout, although they will take small flies.

Fly-fishing specifically for smallmouth bass is a challenging sport, but their abundance in the park makes it worthwhile. I could easily devote an entire book to this subject, as the various techniques and awesome array of fishing situations take years to master.

Experienced park smallie fly-fishermen agree that more consistent results are obtained with light tackle and relatively small baits. I like two- to four-pound test tippets, but some fly-fishermen advocated the use of six- to eight-pound test tippets. On occasion, it is possible to use heavier tippets, but because big bronzebacks are so easily startled, the odds are stacked against success.

Favorite smallmouth fly patters include Muddler Minnows, Joe's Hopper, large stone fly nymphs, and the Wooly Booger. Presented to the rear of pools, these fly patterns are deadly.

One reason many fly-fishing trouters fail to catch smallmouth and rock bass from the streams of the Smokies is they fail to recognize the distinctly different habitat preferences of the sunfish clan. Trout, and especially rainbows, are far more likely to be caught in modestly swift runs. Smallmouth bass shun fast water, preferring to "lay up" in the rear of pools in shaded areas.

Winter is a fine time to fish for brown bass in the park. December water temperatures and normally abundant rainfall help keep these cool-natured fish active. Streamers cannot be beat during this time, when the metabolism of the fish slows down. Streamers worked slowly over dropoffs, saddles, and bars can bring surprising results. Even during the dead of winter, smallie fishing in the streams of the park can be excellent.

Around late February, smallmouth bass begin getting active, and wander. Bottom fly-fishing rock dropoffs with streamers is an old-time tactic that still works.

March and April are exciting months for tangling with Smoky Mountain brownies. In most streams, they can be found shallow in the slow runs. Two- to four-foot depths are not uncommon. Streamers and nymphs retrieved at a brisk pace are met by violent strikes.

Spawning action can be located along sloping gravel- or rock-bottomed areas. Plastic streamers and nymphs bounced through likely bedding cover can net an irate parent fish or two. Following the spawn, the fish spread out along rocky-bottomed areas. During the May-through-August period, great smallie action is available at Abrams Creek and Little River.

Some of the best smallmouth bass angling is found in Fontana Lake, an impoundment with a national reputation for producing lunker-class brownies. Using hair bugs and poppers, surface action is respectable during the spring and early summer months, especially early in the morning and late evening. Using high-density lines, you can expect brisker action on subsurface offerings than at other times of the year.

The West Prong of the Little Pigeon downstream from Gatlinburg to its mouth at the French Broad easily rates among the country's top three or four smallmouth bass fisheries.

chapter 2

Smoky Mountains Angling:
A Historical Overview

$\mathcal{T}$HE STORY OF TROUT FISHING in the Great Smoky Mountains and the surrounding region has been largely ignored in print. Whether for sport or sustenance, fishing has long been a favorite American pursuit. Trout fishing in the crystal-clear waters of the Smokies has occupied a special place in the fabric of mountain life since before the arrival of the settlers.

The Cherokee were perhaps the first people to encounter the local brook trout. The Cherokee name for these colorful little fish was "unahnvsahti," according to my old friend Adam Smith, a tribal member who often showed me roots and herbs when I frequently visited the reservation. Some sources believe that the Cherokee also called the native fish "adaja." At best it is a wild guess, which is noted here merely to add to the overall confusion.

What is known, though, is that for the Cherokee, fishing was not a recreational pastime, although it was not altogether an arduous affair. Like all eastern tribes they used bone hooks and choke stones. Brook trout served as trail fare for Native American travelers crossing the rugged mountains. A favorite and very effective method of getting trout was to sprinkle a pool or two with poison made from local plants, such as the bark of the black walnut tree. After being stricken by the poison, the fish, which were usually stunned, floated to the surface and were easily gathered. Additionally, ground-up yellow buckeye nuts and goat's rue (also called devil's shoestring) were used. These nuts contain the compound aesculin, which attacks the nervous system of trout. The rootstock of

Brook trout were unable to withstand the late-19th- and early 20th- century assaults of civilization.

the goat's rue contains rotenone, although not so concentrated as the NPS used to gut Abrams Creek in the 1960s.

The use of a weir was another fishing technique employed by the Cherokee. A "V" of rocks was positioned in a stream. At the point of the "V," a weir was fastened down. Fish were driven downstream to be caught in the weir. This sort of effort was often a cooperative undertaking by several families or even an entire village and typically occurred on larger streams. A community fish fry usually followed. White settlers took possession of these stone weirs and used them for generations. Today most have been dynamited by game wardens, but I know the location of at least one on the Nolichucky River.

Early settlers arriving in the Tennessee Valley found the cloud-covered peaks mantled in the most diverse hardwood forest in the world. Preferring to carve a living out of the many rich river bottoms, most settlers bypassed the Smokies. Those who chose to live in the isolated mountains picked the rich coves and scattered bottomlands. As the population grew, some settlers moved westward, while others moved farther up the slopes of the mountains in search of tillable land. Travel was difficult, and hard cash was scarce. The region became a backwater area in America's great western movement of the 19th century. It developed its own distinct culture, independent and self-reliant; the area's color-ful lifestyle flourished for almost a century.

Like the Cherokee, the mountain people looked upon the brook trout as a dependable source of food rather than a form of sport. Referred to as "specs" by these mountaineers, brook trout originally prospered in all waters above an elevation of 2,000 feet. The hardworking mountain people must surely have enjoyed fishing for these little fighters. Early accounts repeatedly speak of daily catches of hundreds of fish. Fishing methods such as poisoning and weirs were adopted from the Cherokee.

One favorite method commonly used in this region was known as "chok-ing." Store-bought fish hooks were out of the reach of the economically de-pressed mountain people, but their resourcefulness sidestepped this problem neatly. A suitable bait was tied to a length of string and dropped into the water. When a trout would take the bait, the trick was to quickly jerk the fish out onto the bank before it had a chance to expel the bait. According to old-timers, many a meal of fresh trout came to the table as a result.

While visiting Catluche River (Cataloochee) in the 1880s, Wilbur G. Zei-gler and Ben S. Grosscup, who authored *The Heart of the Alleghanies or Western North Carolina: Comprising its Topography, History, Resources, People, Narra-tives, Incidents, and Pictures of Travel Adventures in Hunting and Fishing,* en-countered a young boy who had caught a "mess" of brook trout using a snare made of horse tail hair that was very effective when the little streams were a bit riley. The lad explained to them that he made a running noose in a long horse hair or two or three of 'em tied together on the end of a pole. The boy would watch the water behind a log until he spotted a big trout. The boy would then drop the noose over the head of the fish, and with a quick jerk, snake the trout free from the stream. Sounds like fun.

Logging in the Smokies prior to the 1880s was insignificant compared to what occurred in the next 55 years. The abundant forests of the southern mountains had not escaped the attention of the growing nation's appetite for wood. Large-scale logging operations descended upon the southern Appalachians near the close of the 19th century. The shrill sound of the narrow-gauge locomotives laboring up steep grades could be heard from northern Virginia to Georgia. The Smokies, situated in the middle of this widespread activity, yielded over 1 billion board feet of lumber by 1935.

These cuttings devastated the land and the wildlife. The brook trout, which require unpolluted, cold water, could not cope with silt-choked streams, high water temperatures, dams, and other factors. Concerned fishermen shipped in rainbow trout in the early 1900s. The adaptable rainbow prospered. Anglers of that era contend that fishing during the first 30 years of the 20th century was the best ever seen in these mountains. The streams were free of overhead cover

During World War II, catches such as this
are said to have been common in the Smokies.

that now shades most of them. Many forms of aquatic insects prospered in the sunlight to a greater degree than they can today in the shaded waters. Open glades, then common alongside many streams, were alive with grasshoppers, the favorite summer bait of that time. Trout were said to have averaged more than a pound each.

Walter Cole, a resident of Gatlinburg was born in the Sugarland and roamed the Smokies before the arrival of the logging companies. At the time I knew him, he was in his late 90s, and he shared these memories with me one morning in 1980.

> As I remember, I was 7 years old when my father and older brother allowed me to come along when they crossed over Blanket Mountain, by the Huskey Gap Trail, to fish for trout in Little River. We packed in our cornmeal, skillet, lard, coffee, blankets, ax, and gun. We had our crop laid in, with harvesting time still a ways off. In those days, anybody could just go up in the mountains, build a shelter, and stay as long as they wanted, huntin' and fishin'.
>
> The logging people hadn't come yet, and the creeks were swarming with speckle trouts, thick as gnats. It was always dark as sundown, fishin' for them, with the big hemlocks and poplars shading out the light. It was easy to catch all the 10- to 14-inch fish you wanted then. I've even caught a few that were a tad longer than 16 inches.
>
> We set up camp and gathered enough stickbait to last all day, then cut us a good birch sapling for a fishin' pole. We started up the creek, stringing our catch on a stick till it wouldn't hold another fish. We set it down in a deep pool to keep it cool, moving on upstream doing the same until we had caught all we wanted. On the way back to camp, we collected the hidden fish, fried them whole in hot grease, and ate them with nothin' except cornbread. That was the best eatin' I ever had. We would do that every summer, sometimes staying for weeks living on fish and game we'd sometimes shoot. Come frost, we'd be sure to be home to get in the corn and cut wood."

Cole later went to work for the Little River Logging Company, where he did a bit of everything. He recalled the riotous living in the Elkmont camp, where moonshine, gambling, fast women, and fishing were as much a part of living as sawdust and splinters.

> *I was there when the first rainbow trout came into camp from Michigan. They raised them up in a run next to Little River. When they were ready to release them in the creeks, they turned half of them loose in Little River and hauled the others over Huskey Gap, by a mule-pulled wagon, in rain barrels, to the West Prong of the Little Pigeon. I believe the year was 1911. The fishery people have been trying to figure out what has driven the "specs" off. I can tell you in one word—rainbow. The brook trout's time has passed. Someday I figure the rainbow may have to give way to the brown trout, just the same way.*

For years it was assumed that sport fishing in the Smokies was almost solely a local endeavor and that it was pretty much rudimentary bait fishing with pole and line. This is hardly the case, though, as modern fly-fishing as it's practiced today found its way to these waters almost as quickly as it did to the Catskills.

During these early years of fly-fishing, the Smokies attracted the attention of serious anglers. Some were sport fishermen whose lines were tipped with a feathery fly; others preferred to cast dynamite into a pool.

The American angling scene, which during the late 1880s had seen the introduction of brightly colored flies for trout, was undergoing a change of its own during these times. An angler from New York, Theodore Gordon, was experimenting with a new technique for taking trout. Correspondence between Gordon and F. M. Halford, an Englishman dubbed the "father of dry fly-fishing," led to Halford's sending Gordon a sample of English dry flies. From this beginning, the sport of dry fly-fishing spread from Gordon's home waters in the Catskills down the Appalachian range. In the southern Appalachians, however, it was not nearly as quickly embraced as in many other regions, but the time lapse is far shorter than was once assumed.

Most early anglers of the South used the old "buggy whip" style rods or a simple cane pole from cane breaks such as those still found along Hesse Creek. The buggy whip rods were sometimes homemade from such materials as ash, birch, hickory, or cherry. Hair from the tail of a stallion or gelding was used to make fishing line. (Many experienced fishermen shunned the use of hair from a mare or filly because it was believed that contact with urine weakened the strength of the hairs.)

Of course, those who could afford it used silk fly line that had to be greased before each fishing trip. If you fished until noon, it often was necessary to unspool the fly line to be put in a butter-churn-looking spindle to dry in the sun. Store-bought gut leaders were equally inconvenient. When you bought them, they were almost as stiff and brittle as uncooked spaghetti. Soaked overnight in a tin leader box between layers of damp felt, they became much like the leaders fly-fishermen would recognize today.

Most Appalachian trout fishermen lacked the funds to purchase the $5 Charles F. Orvis fly rods or even the $1 bamboo rods pictured in the large mail-order catalogs. There was at least one local rod builder located in Pigeon Forge. The Ramsey Rods, built completely from scratch, lacked the exquisite craftsmanship of those from the shops in the East; yet they exhibited a fine feel and were affordable. Those that remain today are treasured by their owners.

I met Ernest Ramsey around 1973. At the time Ramsey had long ago stopped making split-cane bamboo rods, but he still tied flies. His pattern selection consisted of perhaps a dozen different flies, the most exotic being a single dun wing Royal Coachman. The flies were dirt cheap in 1970, $3 a dozen, and if you looked closely at them you might easily have guessed they were a bit overpriced. However, they caught trout—and lots of them—on a consistent basis. They were also tough as nails, taking more abuse than any flies you could order from Vermont in those days. He always offered us a sip from a fruit jar whenever we made a stop by his home on Middle Creek. Smooth, no; but warming, yes.

Ramsey's fly-tying business was more of a sideline, as he was perhaps Sevier County's best-known trainer and fighter of gamecocks. To say he had a never-ending supply of fresh hackles would be quite an understatement. Ramsey showed me his rod-making gear once and offered to sell it to me along with a big armload of Tonkin bamboo in the raw. I was perhaps 20 years old then and way too smart to waste money on those dust-encrusted contraptions.

Each little community had its own group of devoted hunters and anglers. They spent an enormous amount of time hunting bear or raccoon, and fishing. Having a reputation for being in the mountains at all hours was also useful to those making moonshine. The phrase "going fishing" often implied one was going to brew "corn squeezins." I sometimes wonder if trout, which are fond of sweet corn, did not develop this taste during the days of moonshine making, when mash was commonly dumped in the streams!

Trout fishing gradually became a form of recreation with the locals and the ever-increasing stream of tourists coming to explore the Smokies. The use of bait slowly gave way to the use of artificials. In those days, each streamshed of the Smokies had a few men who worked as guides for fishing, hiking, or hunting, as the era of the traveling hunter/fisherman was becoming popular nationwide.

The earliest published writing on recreational fishing dates to 1883 when coauthors, Wilbur G. Zeigler and Ben S. Grosscup, published *The Heart of the Alleghanies or Western North Carolina: Comprising its Topography, History, Resources, People, Narratives, Incidents, and Pictures of Travel Adventures in Hunting and Fishing.* Avid anglers who were particularly fond of the Cataloochee, they devoted an entire chapter to trout fishing. "With Rod and Line" opens with:

> *Streams, from which the angler can soon fill his basket with trout, are not wanting in these mountains. It is the cold, pure waters, that spring from the perpetual fountains of the heights, that this royal fish inhabits. Show me a swift and amber-colored stream, babbling down the mountains slope under dense, luxurious forests, and, between laureled banks, issuing with rapids and cascades into a primitive valley, and I will insure that in it swims, in countless numbers, the prized fish of the angler.*

Robert S. Mason, in his now out-of-print book, *The Lure of the Smokies*, published in 1927, devoted several pages to fishing in the Smoky Mountains. He listed the names of guides who were available for hire, flies that were most effective, and comments from a number of long-time anglers of the region. Among Mason's favorites was Matt Whittle of Gatlinburg.

Whittle, a horticulturalist by trade, fished the streams of the Smokies all his life, and prior to the creation of the park was perhaps the best-known angler on the Tennessee side of the mountains. His roots in the region go back to the earliest settlers in the Little Pigeon River drainage. John "Bullhead" Whaley sold to Whittle brothers some 800 acres in what became Cherokee Orchard. Located in the shadow of the western flank of Mount Le Conte, it was a prosperous business. When the NPS acquired the Whittle property in 1933, the brothers were tending to about 6,800 apple trees, representing some 47 varieties. They also commercially grew Virginia boxwoods, eastern hemlocks, azaleas, andromeda, and other nursery stock. The NPS gave the owners of the nursery 30 years to abandon the orchard in increments of one third of the land per decade. Each season the fruit was picked and shipped to market until the last tract of orchard was relinquished in 1963. The once-thriving fruit trees and other ornamentals have been overtaken by weeds, vines, and finally the forest itself. If you know where to look, you can still find gnarled apple trees producing small, tasty apples.

Dubbed the "Izaak Walton" of the Smokies, Whittle understood the habits of his quarry as few have on either side of the Smokies. Going against the common belief of his day that indicated matching the hatch when fishing with flies, Whittle felt it was of no real importance what kind of fly you used, but how you fished with what you were using, and how the fish were feeding. Whittle often left his orchard-and-shrubbery business to guide "Yankee" fishermen up the streams of the Smokies. Well-known angler George La Branche is said to have been among those who accompanied Whittle into the Smokies.

In the 1990s when I spent considerable time with Joe Manley, he recounted frequently going fly-fishing with Whittle, whom he credited with showing him where and how to fish the streams of the Smokies. Manley says that he was introduced by Whittle to such famous anglers as Ben East and Joe Brooks of *Outdoor Life* as well as Ozark Ripley. Manley described Matt Whittle as the most knowledgeable angler and expert of local flora of the Smokies.

According to Manley, one of Whittle's favorite stories involved fishing with George La Blanche, the noted Yankee fly-fishing expert of his era. George La Branche, along with Theodore Gordon had property (it is now inundated) along the Neversink River in New York. La Branche pioneered fishing dry flies on fast water, something new to the sport in the early 1900s. According to Manley, Whittle had a acquired a copy of La Branche's book, *The Dry Fly and Fast Water Fishing with the Floating Fly on American Trout Streams* (Charles Scribner's Sons, 1914). Whittle initiated correspondence with La Branche, which resulted in the then most famous fly-fishermen in the country visiting the Smokies.

> *"Matt told me that George La Branche had the most delicate fly presentation he ever saw," noted Manley. "He schooled Matt in the importance of checking the fly in the air to get a delicate delivery. A powerful caster, La Branche was skillful enough to whip his silk fly line so that the fly stopped motionless in midair only an inch from the water at the head of a plunge pool. His flies were on the surface before his leader or line touched the surface. Matt said he owed a lot to what La Branche taught him."*

I am of the opinion that Manley's footprints in the lore of fly-fishing in the Smokies are not only largely unknown, but by some presumably scholarly

Ben East of Outdoor Life *photographing Joe Manley fishing in the national park during the 1940s.*

sources, virtually ignored. Manley and I met and chatted on numerous occasions. In the 1940s and 1950s he was perhaps the best-known angler in the state, knowing outdoor writers and editors of sporting journals from many locales. Along with taking Ben East of *Outdoor Life* fly-fishing in the Smokies on several occasions, he also accompanied Charles N. Elliott, a Georgia native who was also an editor at that well-known New York-based sporting publication. Elliott befriended me in the mid-1970s when we first met at an outdoor-writer's conference. Ironically, at the time I was putting together my first Great Smoky Mountains National Park trout fishing guidebook.

Perhaps the most respected fly-fishermen in the South at that time, Elliott did not believe that a detailed guidebook on the remote waters of the Great Smoky Mountains National Park was a good idea. He thought it should be carefully considered because of the increased fishing traffic that might follow. An entire book could be devoted to Charles Elliott's contributions to fly-fishing for trout in the southern Appalachian Mountains. He was a forest ranger for many years, and then later he was the longest-serving editor at *Outdoor Life*, from 1956 to 1974. His home waters are the the Cohutta Wilderness Area in northern Georgia, but he frequented the streams in the Great Smoky Mountains

National Park when he had the opportunity. The more you learn about Elloitt, the more interesting he is to the lore of fly-fishing for trout in the Smokies. For example, *Mark Trail* is a newspaper comic strip created by cartoonist Ed Dodd in 1946 and loosely based on the life and career of Elliott, who died in 2000. The Mark Trail strip centers on environmental and ecological themes. In 2006, King Features syndicated the strip to nearly 175 newspapers. Among Dodd's efforts with the Mark Trail character is the book *Mark Trail in the Smokies!: A Naturalist's Look at Great Smokey Mountains National Park and the Southern Appalachians,* which was published in 1989.

In the 1930s when Elliott worked at the *Atlanta Journal Constitution,* he told me that he was befriended by a promising young writer named Margret Mitchell. She had written her first and only novel, *Gone With The Wind,* when she was struck down by a motorist in downtown Atlanta.

Manley also told me that Matt Whittle also fished with Ozark Ripley, one of the best-known outdoor writers of the early 1900s, who had moved from Missouri to Chattanooga in the 1930s. Ozark Ripley was the colorful pen name for John Baptiste de Macklot Thompson (generally referred to as John B. Thompson), who was educated in France prior to World War I. An avid fly-fisherman, Ripley lived in east Tennessee where he continued his passion for float fishing for smallmouth bass he had engaged in while operating out of the Ozarks. Perhaps the most interesting of all Smoky Mountains fly-fishing lore lies in this man and his relationships with Ernest Peckinpaugh. Many fly-fishing historians credit the invention of the popping bug to Ernest H. Peckinpaugh of Chattanooga, Tennessee, prior to World War I. The legend of Peckinpaugh's invention was recounted by Robert Page Lincoln (Bloody Abe's boy) in 1952:

> To E. H. Peckinpaugh, of Chattanooga, Tennessee, belongs the honor of having invented the cork-bodied bass bug. . . . According to Peckinpaugh he had accidentally dropped a cork bottle stopper on the stream which he was fishing and as it floated away with the current he was suddenly struck with the idea of making a floating bass bug out of cork. As a result he ran the stem of a hook through a cork . . . . Instead of feathers he used a pinch or two of bucktail hair, tying in the thatch at the head of the fly as it were. While this initial lure was quite crude, Peckinpaugh was amazed at the fish that it took . . . . All this took place in the year 1907.

Quite the marketer, Peckinpaugh entered into agreements with well-known anglers of the 1900s to have their names associated with special bugs and flies in his diverse line. Along with Ozark Ripley, the list includes Zane Grey and Dr. Henshall. Here's where the story gets interesting though. Long before migrating to Chattanooga or meeting Ernest Peckinpaugh, Ripley had been in contact with none other than Theodore Gordon, the Fly Father. According to Ozark's published remarks, a letter Gordon wrote to him in 1903 indicated that the Wizard of the Neversink was making dressing popping bugs prior to this time. I'm still searching for the still-missing parts to this mystery, but Whittle's association with the country's first fly-fishing icons raises many questions that are still unanswered for those who seek a truly accurate account of the history of fly-fishing in the Smoky Mountains.

Fly-fishing for trout also has roots on the North Carolina side of the park, although by comparison they're pretty vanilla. The Hazel Creek area was one of the most developed regions of the Smokies prior to the formation of the National Park. It was also the stomping ground of Colonel Calhoun and the well-known Hazel Creek Fishing Club. From their lodge, which was located on Hazel Creek near the present-day Calhoun backcountry campsite, members hunted boar, bear, and deer during the winter, and fished for trout during the summer. During the tenure of the Hazel Creek Club Fishing, much of the water was private fishing, complete with a club warden to prevent any of the 600 people living in the Hazel Creek valley from fishing these waters, which had been stocked with rainbow trout by "Squire" Granville Calhoun of Bryson City. Despite the fact the adjacent slopes were denuded and splash dams had been a determent to the stream, in surprisingly short order Hazel Creek gained a reputation as the finest trout stream in the East. Tales of the exploits of these rough-and-ready men and their favorite hounds are still the subject of lively discussions among locals.

One of the most famous duos of the mountains included two North Carolina men named Samuel Hunnicutt and Mark Cathey. Natives of the Bryson City/Deep Creek area, they were said to have been inseparable companions from the turn of the century through the 1920s. Deep Creek, which they considered the best fishing in the country, was a favorite haunt of both. Cathey occasionally guided fishermen into the Smokies. He accompanied Horace Kephart up Deep Creek on a number of Kephart's many trips. Kephart, aside from being one of the earliest outdoor scribes to give accounts of the Smokies and an outspoken advocate for the formation of the national park, was fond of trout fishing in these mountains. Cathey took considerable satisfaction in allowing his guest to watch him bewitch trout using his "dance of the fly." Using a long cane pole, he would dabble the fly over the water in a figure eight, enticing even the most wary and sullen trout into a vicious strike.

Cathey was born on Conley Creek near Whittier in 1871 and lived most of his life on Indian Creek, a feeder stream to Deep Creek. He died of an apparent heart attack while hunting during mid-autumn in 1944. On the afternoon of his death, he left his sister's cabin on Hughes Branch to get a mess of squirrels. Cathey did not return and was later found stone cold with his back against a large oak with his rifle in lap and his loyal Plott hound lying beside him. His tombstone epitaph in a Bryson City cemetery simply reads: "Beloved Hunter and Fisherman was himself caught by the Gospel Hook just before the season closed for good." Doubtless Cathey was well known on the North Carolina side of the Smokies, but his fame was far less than that of Matt Whittle.

Born in 1880, Samuel Hunnicutt grew up on Deep Creek at the mouth of Bumgarner Branch just upstream from Indian Creek, approximately a mile north of the Deep Creek Campground area. Never rightly accused of having a bashful bone in him, from this youth onward Hunnicutt was known for announcing his approach with a loud yodel-yell, which he noted was "perfect." Aside from being a fisherman, he was a much-heralded bear–and–coon hunter, with a perfect love for Plott hounds, a sporting breed developed in the Smokies. Hunicutt's three best-known hounds were Dread, Jolly, and Old Wheeler. When he was age 46 in 1926 and the region was abuzz with efforts to create the national park, Hunnicutt published *Twenty Years of Hunting and Fishing in the Great Smokies* (Knoxville: S.B. Newman & Company). A 216-page, soft-covered book, that contains numerous photographs of hunters and fishermen, their camps and hounds. In 1951 Hunnicutt published a second edition that consisted of 188 pages.

Hunnicutt and Cathey would spend weeks at a time on the upper reaches of Deep Creek. An amusing tale concerning one of their trips tells of the two leaving camp one morning at the forks of the Left Prong and the mainstream of Deep Creek. Cathey was to fish the Left Prong until supper, and Hunnicutt the Right Prong. Hunnicutt found the fish less than cooperative, and returned to camp empty-handed. Cathey had not yet made it back, so after waiting for a while, Hunnicutt decided to try his hand up the Left Prong and meet Cathey on his return trip. He'd fished approximately 300 yards of the creek, creeling eleven nice trout along the way, when he rounded a bend and saw Cathey, who had 90 trout strung over his shoulder. Hunnicutt asked Cathey if he was mad about his coming to meet him. Cathey's reply was short and rather stern, as he eyed the eleven fish at Hunnicutt's side: "No, but had you not come to meet me, I would have had a hundred trout when I reached camp."

During the late 1960s and early 1970s while researching my various books on fishing the Great Smokiy Mountains National Park, I encountered a surprising number of old men who shared their stories of Uncle Mark. They are too numerous to note here, but the zeal with which each one of these old-timers told me their Cathey recollections was as telling as was their tales. Doubtless he

Cherokee Chief Carl Standing Deer was not only an expert archer, but also the best-known tribal fly-fisherman of his day in the 1940s.

was a dashing daredevil of an old bachelor, who as a youth rode logs bareback down the shoots, and later in life chased bears over the ridges so long as the baritone bays of his Plott hounds could be heard.

Carl Standing Deer of the Qualla Reservation was perhaps the best-known sport angler among the Cherokees during the early years of the park. Standing Deer, whose greatest claim to fame rested on his deadly aim with his hand-built bow, proudly referred to himself as the grandson of Suyetta, the revered Cherokee storyteller. Standing Deer was a dyed-in-the-wool traditionalist, who used horsehair lines after gut and even nylon lines were available, and scorned flies, preferring stickbait and wasp larvae. Standing Deer considered Deep Creek to have the finest fishing in the Smokies, and was occasionally available as a guide. He often posed in his chief attire along the main thoroughfare of Cherokee, and one can only wonder how many kids from my generation had their photos taken with the war-bonnet-wearing chief by an old Browning Hawkeye camera for the modest charge of 25 cents.

After the national park was formed, the fishing changed. Gradually, bait fishing became illegal in all park waters. Creel and size limits were imposed. Auto access to many streams became a thing of the past. With the building of Fontana Dam, the park grew as the Tennessee Valley Authority turned over much of the land it had acquired from residents who would have been isolated as a result of the impounding of the Little Tennessee River. The power from Fontana Dam was funneled into the nation's atomic research center at Oak Ridge. The Smokies were the site of some secret road-building practice for the Army Corps of Engineers and of other experiments for the military.

Until 1947 the streams of the Smokies were annually restocked with large numbers of both brook and rainbow trout, in an effort to provide park visitors with "quality" fishing. Rearing stations were operated at the Chimneys, Tremont, Cades Cove, and on Kephart's Prong. Today, the Smokies offer fine sport fishing for rainbow and brown trout. Fishing for brook trout was sharply curtailed in 1975 when a large number of brook trout streams were closed to all fishing, and it then became illegal to kill a brook trout.

This area is rich in tradition and fishing tales. When tramping down the banks of these streams, it is always interesting to wonder what happened along these trails in previous years.

chapter 3

About Those Creeks

T HERE IS NO SUCH THING AS A TYPICAL POOL, run, or glide in the Great Smoky Mountains National Park, much less a typical stream. One of the truly great things about fly-fishing here is the virtually infinite variety of angling challenges and opportunities found among the 733 miles of fishable streams in the national park. Frankly, that variety has astonished every one of the hundreds of anglers I have guided on fly-fishing trips over the last quarter of a century.

Streams in the Great Smoky Mountains National Park can be broken down into five general categories, with single streams often containing all categories as they progress from their headwaters to their ending points, or where they leave the park. The five are small rivers; medium-size, low-gradient streams; medium-size, high-gradient streams; small, high-gradient streams; and "brush" creeks.

The park has several small, river-sized streams. These include the lower reaches of the Oconaluftee River, Little River, and Abrams Creek. These differ dramatically from headwater rills. Gradient and flow volume are the key differences, although, as a rule, the farther downstream the pH of a stream is measured, the higher it is, thus the more fertile it becomes. Flow rates vary from season to season, and especially during exceptionally rainy weather or dry weather. For example, the average flow rate of Little River is 200 to 400 cubic feet of water per second. During rainy weather this can more than double, while in droughts such as were experienced in 2007 and 2008, dwindle to 70 cubic feet of water per second.

Small river-like streams in the Great Smoky Mountains National Park share several common characteristics. They are wide in many places; these flows spread out shallowly in areas up to 200 feet wide over river slicks and bedrock. These spots are dotted with pocket waters that usually hold trout throughout the year, and in most instances hold smallmouth bass and rock bass. These streams also hold the largest percentage of long, slow pools with bottoms of fine gravel and sand that appear to be custom-made for fly-fishing the last hour of the day, when duns are most common. These waters also boast a sprinkling of plunge pools, with examples of the most extreme being Abrams Falls and the Sinks on the Little River. Another characteristic of the park's small rivers is that the trees found along each side of these flows rarely meet to form a complete canopy over the stream. Solar energy striking the streambed is conducive to the productivity of stream-borne insects and to the food chain in general.

A significant portion of the largest trout and bass found in the Great Smoky Mountains National Park populate these small river reaches. This is usually because these streams provide larger trout with more "elbow room," and they also offer a greater quantity and variety of forage than smaller, higher-elevation streams. These large streams also provide fly-fishermen with the greatest opportunities to use a variety of techniques to catch trout and bass. Casts of 100 feet or longer are possible on some stretches and pools; although, to be honest, the short-line method of fishing is usually more effective than "gold medal style" distance casting.

The medium-size, low-gradient stream covers the lower reaches of streams such as Eagle Creek, Hazel Creek, Hurricane Creek, or Panther Creek. These streams resemble scaled-down versions of the previously mentioned small rivers. They average 14 to 30 feet wide, and more often than not the overstory of trees meets over the creeks to form a shading canopy during summer. Medium-size, low-gradient streams usually have pH levels very comparable to those of the low-elevation small rivers. The average pH in these waters is 7.2 to 7.8. These streams typically host outstanding populations of caddis flies and mayflies, but in many instances are not the best producers of stone flies.

Medium-size, low-gradient streams offer their best fly-fishing for trout in winter and spring. These streams tend to warm during the summer, and early-autumn trout will migrate upstream where higher elevations provide cooler habitat and the faster flow increases the level of dissolved oxygen. During hot weather, though, many of these streams offer outstanding, but largely overlooked, opportunities to catch smallmouth bass on a fly rod by using hair bugs.

In the Great Smoky Mountains National Park, medium-size, high-gradient streams comprise a significant portion of my favorite fly-fishing waters. This type can be in the upper reaches of the two previously noted classifications of water, or it can be a major watershed such as Big Creek. In terms of size, these streams are nearly identical to the medium-size, low-gradient streams, although it is far more common for these waters to constrict to a mere few feet when they wash between large boulders. One of the biggest differences fly-fishermen will note is the high rate of flow in these waters, which often feature staircase-like series of plunge pools connected by swift, shallow runs that occasionally terminate in large, deep pools.

Such fast-flowing waters usually have heavy overstory canopies. More often than not, these streams tumble rapidly over massive "graybacks" (a nickname given to stream boulders by the locals) as they rush down the steep sides of the Smoky Mountains. The best time to fly-fish many of these waters is from late spring through early autumn, when many trout migrate upstream to take advantage of the cooler temperatures and the higher levels of dissolved oxygen the rushing ripples and cascades inject into the water.

Average pH levels on medium-size, high-gradient streams vary considerably, from 6.8 to 7.4 (7.0 is neutral) on some streams, to a low 6.0 to 6.4 on a few others. In the Great Smoky Mountains National Park, these streams are fairly decent producers of prime trout foods such as mayflies, caddis flies, and stone flies. Some of the best hatches of the eastern salmonfly (*Pternarcys*), the largest stone fly found in park waters, and the giant golden stone fly (*Aconeuria*) occur on these waters. Mayflies are also common in these waters, especially those such as the *Epeorus* (which includes the Quill Gordon), which demand unpolluted, highly oxygenated water to thrive.

Fishing quality is good to excellent on virtually all of these streams. Rainbows are the primary quarry found here, but large brown trout often rule large pools, and brook trout are not as rare in some waters as many might have you believe. My all-time favorite method of fly-fishing streams in the Great Smoky Mountains National Park (standing in a downstream plunge pool and fishing the pool immediately above it at eye level) can be practiced with the consistency of daily sunrises on many stretches of the medium-size, high-gradient streams.

Small, high-gradient streams are scaled-down versions of the aforementioned larger, high-gradient flows. Examples of this type of water are Walker Prong, Ramsey Fork, and the upper reaches of Eagle Creek. These streams include the upper reaches of the majority of the primary streams noted in this guidebook. Primary differences include less flow volume, and, in many instances, lower pH levels, which result in lower fertility. The latter translates to fewer pounds of trout per surface.

With the exception of the deep plunge pools that are found periodically along these streams, the depth of the water is rarely more than knee-deep. Stream widths vary from 4 to 20 feet. Flow rates are "super charged," with long, slow pools rarely being found, although they do occur. Quarries in these streams vary from the primary species, the rainbow trout, followed by the brook trout as well as a few brown trout.

Small, high-gradient streams offer trout cool sanctuary during hot weather, but this is also when they are at their lowest flow volume. These waters can be difficult to fish when flow levels are low, as trout tend to stack up in placid pools that not only require precision casting under often difficult-to-negotiate, dense forest canopies, but also demand delicate presentation. Spring is a great time to fly-fish these waters. Another outstanding time to "go high" is during the summer, when rainy weather has made downstream reaches in the park difficult to fly-fish. Rain runoff occurs quickly in the Smokies, and the first water to hit ideal flow levels is always the headwater streams.

Fly-fishing tactics for small, high-gradient streams are similar to those noted for medium-size, high-gradient streams. Like many other fly-fishermen, I like to downsize my tackle for these waters, usually opting to use a 6.5-foot Orvis Flea designed to cast a 2-weight fly line. A trick for catching trout from these waters during times of low flow, which was taught to me by a friend from Waynesville, North Carolina, is to use boulders along and in the stream to aid in fly presentation. Picture a run of water emptying into a pool as quietly as if you were pouring tea from a pitcher. Dropping a fly delicately enough to avoid spooking trout located near the entering water is tough. However, if you cast so your fly line never enters the water (that is, it lands on streamside gravel and rocks), you will draw a strike. The same principle can be used on other slow flows, where midstream boulders and rocks can be used for temporarily "parking" fly line, while upstream only the leader, or even just the tippet, comes down on the pool.

The brush streams, while abundant in the park, actually are a relatively diminutive group of streams few users of this guidebook are ever likely to fly-fish or find interesting. On the other hand, insofar as I have always been a "small creek freak," I am compelled to include them. These are the smallest fishable (and in some instances semifishable) flows in the Great Smoky Mountains National Park. At high elevations, many of these waters were closed to fishing during the brook trout moratorium of 1975. Since 2000 many of these waters have been reopened. These often are so-called branches, which, during very dry periods, all but dry up.

Size and canopy are the biggest differences separating brush creeks from most other streams. In most instances, brush creeks are slightly to significantly smaller than any of the other waters found in the park. Examples of brush creeks include the upper reaches of Little Cataloochee Creek, Beetree Creek (a tributary of Deep Creek), and Bee Gum Branch (a tributary of Forney Creek). Average widths are 2 to 10 feet. As the name implies, brush creeks are usually heavily overgrown on at least enough of their courses to make travel along the streambed a taxing adventure even to the stoutest souls.

This is not to imply that portions, often even large reaches, are not brushed over with steel-tough tangles of rhododendron and laurel. Plunge pools, and occasionally large trout, are the secrets these trickles can reveal to those willing to fight the streamside greenery.

Rainbow and brook trout are the primary quarries on these waters. Early spring and during the summer after or during rain are the only truly good times to make trips to any of these waters. Fly-fishing is tough on all but the most open sections of a brush creek. Tactics are largely the same as outlined for medium-size waters. One interesting variation is dabbling, which is often more effective when done downstream. The trick is to allow just enough tippet to extend from the tip of your rod to permit you to negotiate getting a fly into a pool, which many times has only a few inches of clearance between the surface and the top of the overhead bushes. Sure, you will get a strike doing this. That is the easy part. What takes practice is setting the hook and, once you have accomplished that, working your catch out of the hole without getting everything tangled in the brush. That is a skill one must master.

chapter 4

Where to Find Fish and Why

ANGLING FOR TROUT IN THE SMOKIES is not limited to expert fishermen. Trout can be caught on a $2 cane pole, or on a $2,000 fly rod. Fine fishing tackle is a joy to use, but by no means is it a prerequisite for success. The name of the game is having fun.

Several important bits of information will aid in catching trout. Anglers increase their chances if they know where their quarry prefers to "hang out" and what morsels are most tempting to its palate. Other important keys to success include mastering a stealthy approach to the stream and being able to place your offering in a spot where it will not alarm the fish.

Each of the three trout of the Smokies tends to occupy slightly different water when feeding, although any one species may occasionally be in any given spot. Trout in the wild have established feeding spots, or stations, where they position themselves to await food coming down with the current. Size and aggressiveness determine how good a feeding spot a trout is able to defend and keep.

Understanding where trout position themselves in the stream is one of the most important bits of knowledge an angler can possess. When surveying a pool or stretch of pocket water for likely fish-holding spots, remember a trout must have cover that shields it from the current, and offers at least limited shelter during times of danger. A typical pool starts with a noisy waterfall. The water rushes over smooth, gray boulders, falling into a carved-out plunge pool.

40

Current-loving rainbow trout are right at home in the swift waters of the plunge pool. Large rainbow trout often station themselves at the base of the falls, while smaller members of the clan will gather around the perimeter of the pool or in the pool's main channel. From the depths of the plunge pool, the flow of the stream moves on to the tail of the pool, where the average depth becomes more shallow. It is here you will often find the secretive brown trout. Its favorite lairs are near solitary rocks or submerged tree roots alongside the bank. These fish, particularly the large fellows, often shun feeding during the day, preferring to chase minnows at night. Brook trout favor much the same sort of habitat as the brown trout, though the brookie does not shy away from a sunlit meal. Pocket water, so common to the park, can be treated like a miniature pool.

Where fish are located is important, but knowing their feeding habits is of equal importance. The trout of the park are best termed "opportunistic feeders." The streams of the Smokies and the surrounding mountains are poor producers of food; they are acidic and carry only a limited amount of nutrients (Abrams Creek is the only notable exception). While by no means devoid of aquatic insects, local streams do not support the massive concentrations of the spring-run limestone creeks of Pennsylvania, or Hampshire, England. A typical trout will, in the course of a few hours, consume a combination of mayflies, caddis flies, stone flies, midges, and a terrestrial or two. Close examination of their stomach contents will reveal dominant feeding on the most abundant food, but along with that particular food, a few other tidbits will usually be present. During the late winter and very early spring, Smokies trout feed primarily on the nymphs, but can be caught on dry flies then too.

Spring is a time of brisk activity in and on the streams. As the season progresses, the weather becomes milder, warming the water. Insect emergence becomes more common, along with surface feeding by trout. Such activity peaks by late spring, about the only time local trout can afford to be selective, so fly selection should be considered. Terrestrials quickly become important to the diet of the trout, even in spring.

Summer fishing action is often slow. The remaining insect hatches are small and sporadic. Streams suffer from the seasonal dry weather, often running at little more than a trickle, compared to a couple of months earlier. Water temperatures rise, causing many trout to seek deep, cool havens and to feed at night. Successful anglers often use terrestrial insect imitations, such as grasshoppers, ants, jassids (or leafhoppers), beetles, caterpillars, and bees.

Bigger rainbow trout are more common in the lower reaches of streams where there is more "elbow room."

Fall is an exciting time. The scenery surrounding the streams is at its best. Trees and shrubs are decked out in their brightest yellows, flame reds, spectacular oranges, and regal golds. Trout seem to sense the coming winter and feed with uncharacteristic abandon. Terrestrials are still the cornerstone of their diets, although often overlooked are some interesting hatches of caddis flies. During late fall, growing nymphs and larvae take on increasing dietary importance.

The cold winter months cause trout to become torpid and stay close to the bottom. The cold water slows down a fish's metabolism, reducing the amount of food needed to survive. Anglers feeling the urge to fish during the winter will be pleased to learn that on the mild days, trout move into the sunny areas and do a modest amount of feeding.

Armed with an understanding of where the trout are and what their food preferences are, anglers can use their knowledge on the stream. The importance of a quiet approach and accurate presentation of the chosen lure or fly cannot be overemphasized. Try not to hurry. Stand back for a minute to observe and plan a strategy. The fish are usually facing upstream, into the current. Most experienced Smoky Mountains trout fishermen prefer to fish upstream, thus coming up behind their quarry. Exceptions to this would be in times of high or cloudy water. Unless you are an expert caster, chances are you will not place every cast in the desired spot, but if you can hit the right spot with the right offering often enough, you will catch fish.

One question I am often asked is, "What is the best way to fish the streams of the park—fly-fishing, spinners, or what?" The simplest and least expensive way to have a productive day on one of the creeks of the Smokies is to incorporate the use of a simple cane pole. Use of cane poles was widespread in the Smokies prior to World War II, and it is still fairly common to encounter an old fisherman from Bryson City or Cosby fishing with a 10- to 14-foot cane pole. The mountain folk are deadly with these.

Besides being very effective, cane poles are one of the least expensive routes you can take. An out-of-state visitor who forgets his fishing gear and wants to try his luck in park waters can purchase a pole, a spool of four-pound test line, a half-dozen flies, and a fishing permit for less than fifteen dollars.

A cane pole enables you to stand back from the area where the fly is dropped. Tactics employed when using a cane pole are almost the same as those used when fly-fishing, and the basics are the same for a wet fly, dry fly, or a nymph. Attempt to drop the fly along the edges of waterfalls, allowing the current to carry it to the end of the pool or run. If a strike does not occur the first time, and you feel there is a fish in the area, repeat the drift in a slightly different section of the pool. Keep a tight line the entire time your fly is in or on the water, as a lightning-fast strike can occur at any point.

chapter 5

Casting Tactics and Gear Tips

ONE OF THE FIRST THINGS many fly-fishermen notice when casting in the streams of the Great Smoky Mountains National Park is it rarely is what they expected before they tried. Even accomplished fly casters sometimes experience difficulty adjusting to the low overhead canopies and swift currents of these streams. Classic casting, where the line goes above the head of the caster on the back cast, can be impossible to accomplish on these waters. Personally, I have never liked the surface disturbance roll back casting creates, so I rarely do or recommend this for these streams.

Fly-fishermen find that the biggest obstacle to ideal fishing conditions is the lack of casting room, plus problems with drag. You will find yourself doing a good deal of sidearm casting, especially on some of the small streams. Plan to lose a few flies while angling these canopied waters.

While I do not tout myself as an expert fly-fisherman, I do catch trout and bass from these streams using these techniques. One thing I have learned over the years from fly-fishing here is that what is behind you is just as important as what lies ahead. I am referring to the infernal trees and limbs the National Park Service has shown little inclination to trim to improve my casting ease. It usually happens when I walk up on an extremely inviting run, where I know an eager-to-strike trout is waiting for my challenge. For the last 50 casts I have looked behind me, working my back cast through "keyhole" size openings in the streamside greenery. (This is an art form that those who fly-fish in these streams eventually master.) However, in the excitement of coming up on the best run of the day, I forget to check my back cast. Whammo!—my last No.14 Adams takes up permanent residence 16 feet up a hemlock. Even if I extend the butt of my fly rod into the tree to use the reel as a hook, I am out of luck.

Unorthodox casting techniques are the rule rather than the exception on all but the largest waters in the Great Smoky Mountains National Park. Many times, presenting a fly under a limb hanging a foot above the surface can only be accomplished by sidearm casting. This easy-to-master technique requires two things—knowing what is behind you and deadly casting accuracy. Under these conditions, there is no room for error.

Next to casting difficulties in tight conditions, drag problems are the next thing that surprises newcomers to these waters. How severe the drag problem is depends on the sort of water you are attempting to challenge. If you cast to water that has few crosscurrents, or limit yourself to extremely short casts, drag will be minimal. If you prefer to make long casts across broken pocket water or exposed rocks, you will be forced to mend your line constantly. Proficient fly-casters who attempt long shots into distant feeding lanes across such barriers and who have experience with an ever-constant drag will catch considerably more fish. When concentrating your efforts on short, easy casts, you often risk getting close enough to the fish to alert them to your presence.

One thing I did not discuss in previous books that I should have was the deadly effectiveness of fishing a nymph dropper-style under a dry fly. Two flies are permitted in park waters, and by using this dual-presentation approach, you more than double your odds of a strike. Many fly-fishermen have difficulty detecting light takes on nymphs. The dry works like a bobber, or strike indicator, for those too bashful to admit what they really are. The added benefit is trout also will perfer the dry over your subsurface offering. It's my opinion that dry/nymph-dropper fishing takes a little advantage away from a strictly dry-fly approach, but the tradeoff is pretty handsome.

Several things facilitate dealing with the fast, swirling currents found on many runs in the streams of the Great Smoky Mountains National Park. The instant your fly is on the water, begin mending line. By holding the tip of your fly rod aloft, you can get more line off the water, thus less line is exposed to the current. The result usually is less drag. A leader that is at least 9 to 10 feet long also can reduce the headaches nearly every fly-fisherman experiences dealing with drag on these waters.

Picking an ideal fly rod for the streams of the Smokies is a job comparable to picking the ideal wine. Long fly rods (9 to 9.5 feet) have been the choice of a number of highly successful, long-time patrons of the region; but an almost equal number of noted fly-fishermen prefer extremely short fly rods (6 to 6.5 feet).

Those favoring the long rod say the added length allows them to keep more line off the water, thus helping to eliminate drag. Greater casting accuracy is also cited as a plus for the long rod. Those who favor short rods cite the use of light lines (No.3 to No.4) and maneuverability on the stream as solid advantages. The short rod is easy to work on small streams, where overhead growth can hinder casting.

Regardless of your choice in the length of your fly rod, it should be of good quality. For dry fly-fishing, fly rods should be engineered to cast fly lines in the 2- to 4-weight class. Weight forward lines are recommended on these waters, where you are not always afforded the luxury of traditional, power-building casts. When fly-fishing using streamers, wet flies, or nymphs, heavier fly lines in the 5- to 8-weight class work well on these waters. My personal fly rod is an old, early graphite designed to cast 4-weight line. It is light and responsive, yet extremely powerful. I use it for 90% of the fishing I do. Several years ago, while black bear hunting in New Brunswick, Canada, near Juniper on the headwaters of the Miramichi River, I carried along this rod in the event we might prowl some beaver ponds where brookies are thick as fleas on an old hound in summer.

My host, Frank MacDonald, had taken me fishing for Atlantic salmon there in previous years. On my first trip up there we drove to Doaktown to attend Ted Williams's birthday celebration, and there I met the famous Yankees baseball player for the first time. A couple of days later I fished with Ted on his favorite reach of the Miramichi, and I marveled at this casting ability. At lunch we talked about old fishing tackle. He collected Creek Chub Bait Company (CCBC) dingbats in the musky size, and at the time I had perhaps the largest collection of CCBC lures in the country. Even at that, I only had half a dozen or so CCBC dingbats in the rare musky size.

On two other occasions I fished with Ted, who had the biggest hands I have ever seen, and he was certainly the gruffest person I ever knew. Except for the conversation about old dingbats, he had little say—especially when I refused to gift one or two to his collection. On one particular trip, the regular salmon season had yet to open on the Miramichi, but where the stream passed his lodge in Doaktown, the so-called black salmon season was open.

Unlike Pacific salmon, Atlantic salmon generally survive their upstream spawning rites, and most return to the sea. Some get caught upstream during the winter, where they remain until the ice leaves the Miramichi, and they return to saltwater in late spring. While I was unprepared to fish for salmon on this trip that was predominantly meant for hunting, I certainly did not say no when Frank asked if I was interested in making a trip. The fact that he promised a shore lunch— a washtub full of lobster—was not lost on me either.

Smelt were running the shoreline much the same as gizzard shad do in the impoundments surrounding the Great Smoky Mountain National Park. It was pretty mundane fishing, more or less trolling smelt flies on the outside of their schools, which stretched as far as you could see under the surface in a 5-foot-wide ribbon. I caught a couple of salmon and discovered black salmon are not quite the incredible battlers as their brethren fresh up from the North Atlantic. I had almost nodded off when the fourth salmon struck, but I immediately knew it was a considerably larger fish than those I'd caught earlier.

We engaged in a tug-of-war for a few minutes, and then when I worked the fish closer to the boat, it leaped forth from the water. The salmon was almost 4 feet long and cleared the water skyward at least 10 feet. The closest thing I have ever seen to this was when Spencer Tracy in the movie, *The Old Man and Sea*, first saw his great marlin erupt into the air. For the next half hour I tangled with the leviathan salmon, which took me to the shoreline before I landed it. There must have been 100 people around it while we measured the fish before releasing it.

Without a word, the crowd parted to allow Ted Williams to come see the fish. I was unaware that his lodge was 100 yards behind me. In his typical gruff fashion, he walked over where I was knee deep in the river, and said tersely, "Biggest one caught here in a long time." Without another word, or letting me know if he remembered fishing with me in years past, he turned and walked away. The salmon taped 46 inches long, and we estimated its weight at around 43 pounds. The incredible part of the story is, though, that this fish was landed on the same rod I used a week earlier when fishing Abrams Creek.

The point is, any damned fly rod will work, but in my opinion, the most versatile is a 9-to-9.5-foot rod designed to cast a 4- to 5-weight line. I have a little Orvis Flea rod that is fun to use and is a lot of giggles when you hang into a 12-inch rainbow trout, which will bend the rod all the way down into the bowels of its cork handle. I began fly-fishing up in the Smokies using an old Granger bamboo rod my Uncle Ott Wiscarver had won in a card game in Greeneville late one night. He nearly wore it out on Paint Creek near his home in Greeneville, so with his help we refined the dark cane rod and mended its treads. It worked great until I fell on it at Walnut Bottom. After that I bought a secondhand Browning

Silaflex fly rod, which I used until receiving my first graphite rod from Fenwick in the mid-1970s. If you can paint flies on the surface of a pool with your fly rod, then it is the one to use. Both of my old, retired rods have been requested for inclusion (along with Mark Cathey's hankies) in the Smithsonian's Smoky Mountains Fly-fishing Heritage section scheduled to open in 2014.

Low-range fly rods in the $50-to-$80 range are better than the rods made 20 years ago that cost $400 or more. When writing this book I tried out a number of great rods, all top-shelf models. They are wonderful to cast, but if you break an $800 rod, you are not going to be happy. Your choice of reel is even less important. I like pretty reels that cost a lot more than there is any practical reason to spend. However, I like sports cars too, and I really dig $40 cigars—two moral shortcomings I have that really need to be addressed.

When fly-fishing in the Smokies, the only thing you really need to spend top dollar on is fly line: buy the best fly line money can buy, and the same goes for leader material. I like to think of it like ordering a drink containing tequila—request only the top-shelf stuff. This is not a fly-fishing primer, so get the best to cast the best. It is money well spent.

During the winter months waders are necessary, although I did not know this until I was in my mid-20s when a man told me cold-water wet wading caused arthritis. Neoprene waders in the 3-millimeter range are perfect for not only keeping you warm and dry, but also for helping to cushion the occasional falls you certainly will take in these waters. Neoprene may be the greatest thing to happen to cold-water wading since humans walked upright, but these spongy wonders do have their drawbacks. Walking any distance in neoprene waders is akin to sitting in a sauna. For big guys such as myself, putting on and taking off neoprene waders gives one a new appreciation for what women go through with pantyhose. The proliferation of this material in waters slowed around ten years ago in no small part due to pressure put on the sport by organizations dedicated to saving the neoprene seal.

At this writing, waders such as the Simms G4 Pro chest waders are the rage. These high-tech waders feature breathable GORE-TEX three- and five-layered, thermo-laminated construction with bells and whistles such as built-in gravel guards. One can only wonder what marvels will succeed these high-tech waders. High-tech waders like these are suitable for cold-weather fishing and are also tolerable to wear when it is warmer.

During warmer weather, microthin waders such as those offered by Red Ball, or just wading wet in shorts (my personal favorite) will suffice. This is particularly true if you bleed easy, as I do, so you can keep track of every scrape and skin puncture. From about the middle of May through early October, my standard wading apparel includes shorts, wool socks, and felt-soled wading boots. Wading boots with felt soles; spikes; felt soles with spikes; or slip-on chains are essential for safe wading in the slippery-bottomed streams of the Great Smoky Mountains National Park.

Other gear is helpful. I like to have a little flashlight, three to four full flasks, cigars and disposable lighter, GPS unit, at least eight or nine different flies, toilet paper (and spare toilet paper), my various medications, extra-strength reading glasses, pocket field guide to dangerous spiders, a moral compass, spare tippet material, toe nail clippers (U.S. made), sunscreen, Gideon's Bible, and rations for two days in case I get lost. My fly vest reminds some of Sir Edmund Hillary's backpack.

chapter 6

Weather, Seasons, and Other Factors

FEW PLACES IN THE UNITED STATES frequented by fly-fishermen are more at the mercy of the seasons and weather than the streams of the Great Smoky Mountains National Park. Understanding how weather and the seasons affect trout behavior in these waters can appreciably enhance your enjoyment of angling there, as well as up your odds for success.

Temperature and rainfall are the two most obvious factors, but there are many others. By any standard, annual rainfall is heavy in the Smokies. Along with the Olympia Peninsula, it is the closest thing on the continent to a hardwood/conifer rain forest. Some years the annual precipitation reaches 100 inches, which puts these peaks in the same category as the Amazon River basin. In recent years park highland areas such as Mount LeConte and Newfound Gap received annual rainfall of 85 and 94 inches respectively. Lower-lying areas received about a third less rainfall. For example, the current average for Cades Cove is 63 inches; Oconaluftee gets 59 inches, and the Sugarland gets 60 inches.

As might be expected, some seasons are drier than others. Factors such as hurricanes from the east coast and the Gulf of Mexico historically have resulted in heavy rain and flooding. Flooding and draughts are part of nature's cycle. The trout prefer ideal conditions, and suffer when flooding and draught batter these streams. However, these streams and their trout are remarkably resilient. At least so far, when up against the ropes these trout rebound with renewed vigor when either extreme subsides.

The waters of the Great Smoky Mountains National Park are a year-round fishery where on any given day of the year it is possible to have for a great day astream. Of course, the odds are better at certain times for a magical alignment of the planets, stars, and flow level.

I could fill pages with graphs like those used to track the sale of Maytag washing machines, but it's really a waste of time. Here's the succinct skinny on weather and rainfall in the Smokies. It rains more in the winter, so streams are often high. It is colder in the winter, so be prepared. It rains a lot in the spring, so flow levels vary from high to just right. It can be cold in spring, so bring along a sweater. Summer rain usually comes in the form of thunder showers. If you can predict them, you need to sell that information to someone with a lot of money. The best way to know if a thunder shower is underway is you feel rain and hear thunder. Otherwise, summers are modestly dry. Dress appropriately, but please remember that in western North Carolina there are laws against lewd attire. Fall is much the same as summer—dry. It does rain but most of the time not until the leaves fall. Sweat shirts are popular at this time, but if you are fishing on the Tennessee side of the park, I advise against sweat shirts in crimson that say something like "Roll Tide."

As a know-it-all sprig back in the late 1960s, I encountered an old man on Little River who had drawn up to about 4 feet tall and perhaps would tip the scales at 90 pounds. He was wielding an old bamboo fly rod. Where his thumb rested on the grip of the rod, the cork had been worn away to the cane. Rudely, I splashed up on the run he was fishing. He dropped a fly inches from where my knee met the surface. To my astonishment he instantly was fast into a 16-inch rainbow. He danced the little trout around a moment, his eyes on me rather than the cartwheeling 'bow. With the fish worked to his side, he released it without removing it from the stream.

Humbled, I walked over to ask what fly he was using. We chatted, and, of course, I asked him if he had caught many big trout from these streams. He indicated that indeed he had, especially during World War II when everyone else was too busy to fish. He kept and fried up the fish he caught. His recordkeeping system was simple. He placed every trout of 20 inches or better on cardboard where he used a pencil to draw an outline of the trout. The outline was then cut free, and on its side was recorded the date and place the fish had been caught. At the time he told me he had filled two steamer chests with cardboard trophies.

When asked what the secret to catching big trout in the Little River was, he explained to me that 90 percent of the big trout are caught during a 10 percent window, when their feeding activity peaks. The trick is to be fishing at your best when this occurs. Naturally, I asked how one could possibly know when the trouts' feeding activity peaked. "It's real easy," he said to me. "All ya gotta do is fish all of the time."

Winter Fly-fishing

WINTER FISHING IS RELATIVELY NEW to the streams of the Great Smoky Mountains National Park. Until the mid-1970s, most of these streams were closed to all angling between late October and mid-April. This practice was a carryover from the old fishery management days, when it was believed that wading streams during the winter damaged the trout eggs resting in shallow gravel beds located in the tails of swift runs. Prior to the 1970s, only the West Prong of the Little Pigeon, the Little, and the Oconaluftee Rivers were open to year-round angling where fish creeled had to be 16 inches or better.

Abolishment of closed fishing seasons in the Great Smoky Mountains National Park was, until recently, largely enjoyed by a small cadre of local anglers. Unlike trout streams found farther north in the Appalachian Mountains, the flows in this park rarely ice over, especially in their lower reaches. During periods of warm weather, which are relatively common to winters in the region, exceptionally good fly-fishing, even with dry flies, is the rule rather than the exception.

Aquatic insects hatch all winter, but especially when the temperature climbs above 45 degrees Fahrenheit. This is true even in headwater brook trout streams. The trout found in these waters are not as active during the winter as they are at other times of the year, but their predictable opportunistic feeding habits can still be very effectively used by fly-fishermen. In fact, some of the biggest brown and rainbow trout caught by flyrodders are landed at this time.

Winter fly-fishing for trout can be notoriously inconsistent, while casting for smallmouth bass is a little more predictable. Weather is the key to success. My favorite days are bluebird, low-wind, mild-temperature days, particularly when they are preceded by two days when the temperature gradually warmed and it did not rain. This is largely a personal preference, as is my liking for days when the weather is nice, occasionally reaching 60 to 80 degrees Fahrenheit by mid-afternoon. Such weather guarantees flies will be in the air and trout will

Winter fishing in the Smokies is outstanding most of the time.

not only be feeding in the runs, but also lounging in the tails of long, slow pools. However, it is not the only time trout and bass can be caught in large numbers and size during winter.

Winter flow levels are rarely low, and often too high to fish easily. If there is much snow melt in the streams, they are not typically productive. Approaching cold-front days, those days when the sky is a Confederate gray and menacing, often offer the best winter fishing of the year. Frankly, I do not believe anyone understands precisely what it is about an approaching cold front and the resulting barometric changes that brings out feeding binges in Mother Nature's world. All I know is it happens to everything from songbirds and White-tailed deer, to trout and bass. I recall fishing at Smokemont once when an ice-storm warning had been issued. By noon, the temperature was near 60 degrees Fahrenheit, and by three o'clock it was spitting snow and sleet.

The fishing, though, was phenomenal that afternoon, akin to dabbling salmon eggs in a hatchery run full of starving trout. I nearly got stranded in the mountains because of making "one last cast" too many times that day. By the time I could tear myself away, the roads had become virtually impassable, but I had taken three brown trout over 18 inches, and more 10- to 12-inch rainbows than I had seen in the preceding spring and summer months combined.

That is but one example of the fine winter angling I have enjoyed over the last three decades of fly-fishing in the Great Smoky Mountains National Park. Fly-fishing these streams during approaching cold fronts can be a bit hairy at times, but the pay-off is often worth taking a chance.

One of the nicest aspects of fly-fishing during winter in the Great Smoky Mountains National Park is that the best fishing occurs during what is usually the most pleasant time of the day—late morning through mid-afternoon. For the most part this is when air temperatures are warmest, which triggers fly hatches, which in turn accelerates feeding by trout and bass. As always, exceptions do occur. Most notably this relates to larger trout, especially browns. These fish remain remarkably nocturnal even during the cold weather months. Late evening and early morning fly-fishing for big trout by using a Muddler Minnow, Spuddler, or other streamer can be extremely effective, as is drifting large stone fly nymphs through long, slow runs. However, at this time of the year, when planning your fishing trips to the park, you can sleep late, get home in time for supper, and still cash in on the peak fishing hours.

Another quirk that characterizes big trout during winter in the national park is this is when mature rainbow and brown trout accomplish most of their spawning. While it is true that spawning occurs in autumn, it peaks between early February and the last full moon period in March. Spawning trout in larger streams move to headwater areas, where they can be caught. The most interesting spawning action, though, is found upstream from the mouth of the streams which empty into the lakes bordering the southern edge of the park. Large trout from the lakes make their way upstream, often in surprisingly large numbers, where they spawn in small- to medium-size feeder streams. During its peak, this spawning run at Abrams Creek upstream from Chilhowee Lake offers fishing akin to that found in Alaska. This is the only time I recommend flies that mimic roe.

Just as there are best times, there are also times when you are better off tying flies in front of a warm fire than making a trip to these waters. When snow is falling, these trout and bass are not particularly difficult to entice to strike a dry fly or a nymph. However, when water from melting snow is entering these streams, it negatively affects trout and bass. Much the same is true of when cold rain is falling in the mountains. During winter, trees and other plant life in the Smokies do not use rainfall to nearly the same degree as in spring and summer. The net result is typically a greater flow volume in the streams than at other times. During and following rainy weather, park streams, even the high-elevation rivulets, are often too high to effectively fish, short of using a lead line and heavily weighted nymphs.

Tactics for catching winter trout are simple. The tails of pools often hold more actively feeding trout now than at most other times of the year. Deep ripples also harbor rainbow trout in large numbers, while brookies and brown trout will be found lurking under deadfalls, undercut banks, and the side areas of large- to medium-sized pools. These fish are not as active now as during most other times of the year, but they certainly can be caught almost anytime with varying degrees of success.

Dark fly patterns are the norm, with No.14 to No.16 being the most common. (See the chapters on flies and fly patterns for more information.) Clad in neoprene waders, anglers can withstand the cold water temperatures throughout the day. (I personally wish to thank whoever developed these fantastic waders.) It is often possible to fly-fish these waters with only a wool shirt above the waist, if you top it with a lightweight jacket or shirt featuring W. L. Gore's WINDSTOPPER fabric.

Spring Fly-fishing

ANY FLY-FISHERMAN unable to have a great time on the streams of the Great Smoky Mountains National Park during March, April, and May probably needs to have a new leisure-time activity. If there is a better place in the southern Appalachian highlands for fly-fishermen to be in spring, I have yet to discover it during my travels. However, spring does not occur uniformly throughout the Great Smoky Mountains National Park.

The first signs of spring are evident at the lowest elevations, such as the mouth of Abrams Creek and the lower reaches of the Cataloochee Valley. The changing of the season progresses up the slopes of the mountains in stages, culminating at the crests just above the starting points of the headwater rills.

First-time visitors to the park in mid-May see lush, green foliage at the lower elevations near the Sugarland Park Headquarters; after driving for ten minutes, they are often shocked to discover the same species of trees still budding at Newfound Gap.

Spring progresses in the streams of the park in much the same manner, which is why in my first fishing guidebooks to these waters, I did not include my detailed fly emergence data. A single stream such as the West Prong of the Little Pigeon River could, in the course of a single day in mid-May, experience fly hatches that resemble early spring hatches at the 4,000-foot elevation, and early summer hatches at the 1,500-foot elevation. This, coupled with the incredible diversity of the benthic macroinvertebrate community found in the streams of the Great Smoky Mountains National Park and the highly opportunistic feeding habits of these trout and bass, makes in-depth fly hatch emergence information of limited value. Nevertheless, many fly-fishermen asked for the information, so it is in this volume.

Extended periods of rainfall typically occur during spring, and as you might expect, flow levels are strong, exceeded only in overall volume by those of winter. Actually, it is not terribly uncommon for dry spells to occur at this time, which can shrink some streams back to levels most anglers familiar with these waters normally associate with the dog days of summer. However, for the most part, fly-fishermen are more likely to encounter optimal flow levels at these streams during spring than at any other time of the year. The benefit of good flow levels is more trout are likely to be found in the feeding lanes, and as a result, they have only a short time to examine approaching flies.

Day-long good fishing is a hallmark of spring fly-fishing for trout and smallmouth bass, although your odds of catching a big fish are better very early in the morning and late in the afternoon. The last thing you want to do is cancel a fishing trip on those dreary, overcast days, or even those days when a drizzle, not a steady rain, dominates the weather. Some of the best spring fly-fishing I have enjoyed over the last 25 years occurred on those ugly days when it was not really raining, but the air was permeated with half mist and half rain.

Most experienced Smoky Mountain fly-fishermen split their spring casting efforts between nymphs/wet flies and dry flies, with a few being astute enough to realize the deadly effectiveness of big streamers such as the Muddler Minnow and Spuddler (sizes No.4 to No.8). (Personally, at this time I enjoy great success casting a dry fly in conjunction with a nymph dropper.)

This is the time of year most knowledgeable fly-fishermen carry the greatest variety of fly patterns. Spring is a transitional time, when nymphs and adult aquatic insects not only become more abundant, but they also become larger and lighter in color. The "single-to-10-fly" anglers I know who, for the most part, rely on one pattern, that is, the Adams, carry this single pattern in three to six color variations, ranging from very light gray body with light hackle, to a medium gray body with brown hackle, to an almost black body with dark gray hackle. At the very least, your fly box should contain a good selection of mayfly and caddis fly adults, ranging in color from relatively dark to light.

Spring is a great time to drift nymphs through dark runs and shallow glides. Again, your fly boxes should contain a variety. Caddis fly pupa patterns and mayfly and stone fly nymph patterns should reflect diversity (see the charts in Chapter 7, Stream Insects and Feathery Deceivers), particularly in size and color. If you remember anything in this book about the aquatic insects found in the streams of the Great Smoky Mountains National Park, remember that as winter gives way to spring, the flies and nymphs undergo a transition from black, dark brown, and gray to light gray and tan. The transition continues from spring to summer as flies and nymphs become increasingly lighter and larger. In autumn the cycle reverts back to darker and smaller flies and nymphs, until they are again very small and very dark during winter.

Spring fly-fishing in the Smokies lends itself to a wide array of techniques and tactics. Insofar as the trout and smallmouth bass actively feed now, it is tougher to do something that will not catch fish, than something that will catch them. This is probably overstating the wonders of spring a little, but it is such a wonderful time, particularly the last two weeks of May when caddis fly and mayfly hatches are rarely surpassed.

Admittedly, it is difficult to lump the fly-fishing conditions you will find in late March with those of late May. However, the transition is steady both in terms of the passage of the weeks and the season's changes creeping toward the headwaters of these streams.

Summer Fly-fishing

WITHOUT QUESTION, summertime presents fly-fishermen in the Great Smoky Mountains National Park with more challenges than any other season. Rarely must anglers be more versatile than during the hot weather months of June, July,

August, and early September. Anglers must be on guard against the muggy, often excessively humid heat, as well as tube riders seeking relief from the heat by riding the current. Throw in bloodthirsty mosquitoes and pesky "no-see-ums," and you see this is not a time to toss flies without possible consequences.

The park annually receives more rainfall than nearly any other region of the United States. A sizable portion of the annual rainfall comes in the form of summertime thunderstorms. It is not uncommon for the park to experience thunderstorms daily, or three times a day for week after week during the summer. Granted, a storm may pelt the Cosby area one day, then the next day it will shower at Raven Fork. Most thundershowers occur between mid- to late afternoon, but predawn and early thunderstorms are certainly not uncommon.

Rather than being a bane, rain is a blessing during the hot weather months. Even the most harsh thunderstorms result in better angling than were the same stream to have only enough water to barely trickling along. This is not to say you should fly-fish when lightning bolts are lashing the sky—that would be insane. It also does not mean the initial high water provides prime fishing, although brown trout specialists live to dabble Muddler Minnows along undercut banks when thunderstorms turn otherwise gin-clear streams to the color of chocolate milk.

Rain accomplishes three very important things. It clouds the water, making it more difficult for trout to spot the approach of anglers. Increased flow levels enable trout and bass relegated to pools to move into feeding lanes. Runoff from the rain also washes a smorgasbord of terrestrial insects such as caterpillars, ants, jassids, beetles, grasshoppers, and inchworms into streams. The result is trout and bass feeding frenzies that usually last as long as the conditions that triggered this behavior continue.

It is rare for a fly-fisherman not to catch more and bigger trout and smallmouth bass following and sometimes during the rain. There is little question a majority of the bruiser brown trout caught in the Great Smoky Mountains National Park are landed under these conditions.

Here are sage words of warning regarding thunderstorms in these mountains. In recent years several people have been killed and injured by bolts of lightning. Whenever possible, seek safe refuge from lightning, and never fly-fish under these conditions. Also, it is not uncommon for thunderstorms to occur without your knowledge several miles upstream from where you are angling. As a result, the flow level of the stream may rise rapidly without warning. Classic flash floods are uncommon, but waters rising a foot or more rather quickly are not.

One afternoon I was fishing with my youngest son, Shae, who was then 6 (he has now made me a grandfather). We were in the lower reaches of the West Prong of the Little Pigeon River, upstream from the Sugarlands Ranger Headquarters, when the clear water suddenly turned brown. The sun was shining bright, but it had rained upstream from the Chimneys. We were on the side of the stream opposite the Transmountain Highway, where I had left my car. Putting Shae on my shoulders, I started crossing the stream at the tail of a pool that was thigh deep. Before I could get across the 50-foot-wide stream, the current rose above my waist. A minute after we got out, the stream rose another foot. Not before or since have I seen a stream in the Great Smoky Mountains National Park rise so rapidly with or without warning.

Unfortunately, not every fly-fishing trip to the streams coincides with rainy weather. Often we go fly-fishing on waters during the driest weather. This is undoubtedly the toughest of all times to cast for trout and bass on these waters. As a general rule, the farther upstream you fish, the more pronounced the effects of dry weather are on stream flow and on your odds for catching fish. Of course, it is possible to catch trout in slow, low, very clear water, especially if you fish very early in the morning or late in the evening. However, it requires highly accurate casting, faultless, drag-free presentation, and a lot of patience to catch even small trout from streams when those streams are running well below their normal flow rate.

If there is enough water, high elevation streams offer great respite from often slow fishing action during the day at lower elevation runs. Most hatches occur late in the evening or very early in the morning, which is when many trout do most of their feeding. Naturally, there are exceptions. I still do not understand why nice-size rainbow trout will rise to fly patterns during midday when these offerings are drifted over fast runs. I can understand why these fish prefer swift, well-oxygenated runs at this time when water temperatures are at their highest for the year and oxygen levels are their annual lowest. But what is mysterious is why they shun such offerings in the morning, only to seize them during the hottest part of the day. However, like most Smoky Mountains long rodders, I like to fish to the last legal tick of the clock when surface activity seems to boom in the dwindling light.

In a nutshell, there is no such thing as a typical day of fly-fishing for trout during the summer at these waters. Virtually every type of response you can imagine can occur, and on consecutive days!

Autumn Fly-Fishing

ONE OF MY FAVORITE SEASONS for fly-fishing in the Great Smoky Mountains National Park, autumn is a magical time. In many ways it is the very finest fly-fishing of the entire year. During autumn, these ancient rock piles take on a sur-realistic feeling. Ablaze with spectacular oranges, scarlets, golds, and maroons, these mountains are beautiful against a backdrop of cloudless, azure skies.

It is the only time of the year you can plan a trip to these streams with reasonable confidence that the weather reports from the previous day will de-liver what was promised. It is a time when the mornings are crisp enough to make a sweater feel good, and the afternoons are for fly-fishing in short sleeves. Bluebird skies beckon for day-long fishing trips, something many sane anglers here have forgone since early June.

Even though flow levels are rarely high, the trout are unusually coopera-tive. Fishery biologists say their high rate of feeding is instinctive, an effort to store fat for the oncoming winter. I contend the reason is the bright autumn foliage, which transforms the world above them from greens and blues to every color in the rainbow. In my opinion, the stunning smattering of color throws the world of the trout out of kilter, causing them to feed with abandonment not seen by fly-fishermen in the Great Smoky Mountains since the caddis fly hatches of late May.

Autumn may be the driest time in the national park, but it does rain dur-ing this time. The best single day of fly-fishing I ever enjoyed on these waters oc-curred here on October 12, 1983, a day marked by a steady drizzle. Vic Stewart and I were fishing the West Prong of the Little Pigeon River only a mile upstream from the Sugarland. It was cool, but when actively fishing wearing a raincoat, it was very comfortable.

The stream remained clear all day, and because it was quite low prior to the rain, it never rose high enough to create difficult wading or tough fishing at the fast runs typically resulting from heavy rainfall in the Smokies. We started out using No. 8 Joe's Hoppers, which could have been our luckiest move of the day. I do not believe anything we might have tossed could have matched the incredible results these simple fly patterns fetched.

Starting at eight o'clock in the morning, we fished our way upstream. Within an hour, we had caught and released more than a dozen rainbow trout more than 12 inches long. These fish appeared to be ready to spawn. Females were full of eggs, and males were squirting milt. Their flanks were deep maroon, something I have only seen in these fish at this time of year (although rainbow trout also spawn in the spring and winter in the park).

It is not only the rainbow trout that behave differently at this time. Brown trout, which are noted for their nocturnal behavior, are now commonly encountered feeding with gusto at midstream, or even lying in the tails of streams in water so shallow their backs protrude from the surface. On many occasions I have nearly stepped on these fish, causing both of us quite a lot of excitement when our mutual discoveries were made.

Terrestrial fly patterns are often the rule for the day, but fly hatches also occur with remarkable predictability. Orange spinners work well late in the evening, as do a few Dun Variants. Early morning fly-fishing fun is often supplemented by hatches of the large pale caddis and little yellow stone flies. Even when these are hatching at rates sufficient to attract trout, when stream flow levels are at seasonal lows, anglers must be astute at "far and fine" casting and presentation techniques.

chapter 7

Stream Insects and Feathery Deceivers

*A*QUATIC INSECTS in the streams of the Smokies play an essential role in the diet of the trout. Fly-fishermen have long understood this relationship, fashioning their style of angling around this knowledge.

In many parts of the angling world, timetables giving the site and approximate time of the emergence of a well-known mayfly have been available for a number of years. The streams of the Smokies, however, are not dominated by any particular insect species or order, much the same as the mountainside flora is not dominated by any particular plant.

Aquatic insect populations are low in most cases. These streams are poor producers of food, primarily due to their acidic composition. Acid water is low in nutrients that are necessary for large concentrations of insects to exist. While there are some algae in these streams, they are generally inconsequential to the vitality of the fishery or benthic macroinvertebrate communities. Other problems local insects must endure are acid rain and flash floods that scour the bottom of fragile life forms.

Just about every type of mayfly that occurs in the Appalachians is found in the park. However, the population densities of the aquatic insects are low, usually so low that even during peak emergence, they can sometimes play only a minor part in the trout's feeding habits.

Work done in researching the caddis flies of the Smokies by several noted zoologists has revealed that the Tennessee Valley has one of the world's richest

Choosing the correct fly pattern is half the fun.

populations of caddis flies in the world. There are more than 50 genera of caddis flies found in the Smokies, according to Dr. David Etnier, professor of zoology at the University of Tennessee. It is worth noting that a couple of short-horned sedges, the cinnamon caddis, and little sister caddis are found almost exclusively in Abrams Creek, where their hatch is noteworthy. As a fly-fisherman, what you need to remember about caddis is "green" and "yellow."

Stone flies also do well in the swift, pollution-free waters of the park. The oxygen-rich, cascading streams harbor stone fly nymphs, important to the trout's diet during certain times of the year. These meaty morsels are eagerly seized by big brown trout. The peak time for stone flies to merge is during the spring, but they emerge almost year-round with the exception of the coldest months of winter.

Stone flies typically emerge during the night when they crawl out on streamside rocks where they shed their nymph outer skeletal husk. Most of these seen along the streams are the little yellow stone flies, which are locally known as Yellow Sallies. Like the mayfly, winged adult stone flies return to the water to mate and deposit their eggs. Their return to the water signals some of the best dry fly-fishing in the Smokies. However, if by chance you observe Yellow Sallies ascending from the water, knot on a Yallarhammar so you can join the subsurface circus.

Emerged stone flies have four wings that fold flat atop their thorax, giving the appearance of a single wing when they are not flying. In flight, stone flies often appear bigger than they really are. Stone fly nymphs have two short tails. Their legs are tipped with prominent claws; most have no visible gills, although on some species found in the Smokies, the gills are found under their head or upper body. Stone fly nymphs are typically found on or near stones in the stream, where they move like turtles. Predatory feeders, stone fly nymphs are particularly fond of mayfly nymphs. Even in the pristine waters of the Great Smoky Mountain National Park it's a dog-eat-dog world.

Watch the surface of the water carefully if you plan to attempt to match the hatch. Mayfly adults look like little fairies on the water and typically have clumsy-looking flight patterns. Adults have two, larger upright wings and can, and usually do, have two little ones called hind wings. Freshly emerged mayflies are called dun. Colors range from cream to coffee. Mayfly nymphs have either two or three tails. Their legs end with a single claw, and gill plates on their bellies are easily seen. Mayflies reside in streams in their nymphal form the vast majority of their lives. Depending on the species, it can be a single year or it can be two years. Once they emerge as adults with wings, they live for only for a day or two, sometimes even less.

Hatches of mayflies can be found on almost any day from January through October. During the cold months, hatches usually occur during the warmest hours of the afternoon. The Quill Gordon (sizes #12 to #10) is the most anticipated hatch of the early-spring emerging mayflies, followed by the Blue Quill, which is half the size of the former but twice as abundant. Blue Quill hatches occur far longer than those of the larger Quill Gordon. Often confused with Blue Wing Olives, which are extraordinarily plentiful at nearby tailwater trout rivers, these Blue Quills are not Baetis. Worth noting is the spring hatch of Eastern Green Drakes on Abrams Creek—again, the only stream in the park with sizeable numbers of these mayflies.

Later, during mid-spring, emergences can occur during mid-morning through late afternoon. By late spring, hatches will be encountered in early morning and then in late afternoon. This is when these streams are dominated by emergences of March Brown and Henderickson mayflies, and then shortly thereafter Light Cahill mayflies. During the hot-weather months you will always see tons of microscopic midges going hither and fro. If your vision is as poor as mine these days, you not only need someone to attach them to your leader, you need a ghillie to tell you approximately where your fly is on the water. On some park streams the only summer hatch of mayflies of merit is that of the Isoncychic, or Mahogany Dun. Their showings on the water are as unpredictable as a drunk monkey on a tricycle, but when you hit a slew of them riding the waves, they are almost that much fun.

Summer is a time of limited, often sporadic insect activity, which usually occurs only during the early morning and around dusk. Matching the hatch is sometimes effective; however, presentation to these opportunistic feeders is really the key. Stimulator fly patterns as well as traditional flies such as the Royal Coachman, Adams, Ginger Quill, and the Black Gnat find their way into the fly boxes of local anglers. Probably the most famous fly to come out of the Smokies was the Yallarhammar. There are numerous variations of this fly today on both sides of the mountains. It is basically a peacock herl-bodied wet fly, hackled with a split section of wing feather from a yellow-shafted woodpecker, known locally as a Yallarhammar. It is illegal to kill this bird or to sell flies using its plumage. (Yallarhammar flies are now being made with feathers from other species, dyed the correct shade of yellow—so I am told.) However, the use of this fly is incredibly widespread, although its effectiveness is, in my opinion, no better than that of several other flies I could name. Other regional favorites include the Ramsey

Smallies are suckers for big hair flies.

(it closely resembles a standard brown hackle), My Pet, Forky Tail Nymph, the nationally known Tellico Nymph, the Gray Hackle Yellow, Cotton Top, and the Thunderhead. The Thunderhead is a Wulff-style dry hairwing fly.

Well-known flies such as the Adams, Coachman, Henryville Special, and several other established patterns are also used with great success inside the park. A dry fly that closely resembles a hairwing Adams, the Thunderhead, is the creation of Fred Hall of Bryson City. Hall is one of the greatest Smoky Mountains fly-tiers, and his clients have included such well-known anglers as Joe Brooks. Frank Young, another Carolina fly-tier, added one of the most interesting modifications to this fly that I have ever seen. Young substituted the soft belly fur of an opossum in place of the kip tail usually used in making the Thunderhead. The result is equally interesting, as the fluffy opossum fibers give the fly an added touch of drift as they fall gently on the surface of the water. The addition of the opossum hair makes this an all-hillbilly candidate.

When my original Smoky Mountain trout fishing guide was written in the late 1970s, every effort was made over a two-year research period to locate and interview the "great sages of the long rod" of the region. In my defense, I think I did a fairly good job, but made one glaring error in overlooking one of the true greats, Eddie George of Louisville, Tennessee, whom I interviewed in 1987. The creator of the famous George Nymph (which I mistakenly identified as the Cotton Top), George told me that he grew up fishing these streams prior to the Second World War with the old men of that era. A mayfly-style nymph of his creation, the George Nymph is nationally known as an effective trout taker, and cannot be topped as a year-round offering in the streams of the Great Smoky Mountains National Park.

My Pet, the Ugly Devil, the Quill Tail, and the Near Nuff all originated in western North Carolina. The Gray Hackle Yellow, a delicate dry fly, is said to be the top choice of a number of Cherokee anglers. The Streaker Nymph is another fly of Carolina origin that is overlooked by most modern-day fly gurus. It is very similar to the Tellico nymph, but is more slender and lighter in color. A favorite of many Hazel Creek regulars, it is tied to mock the abundant stickbait found in the flow of the park's creeks.

Unfortunately, space in this volume does not permit me to tell of every noted Smoky Mountain fly-fishing and fly-tying sage. The list would be long, and would certainly include such modern marvels as Marty Maxwell of Robbinsville, North Carolina, and Gary Cown of Knoxville, Tennessee, plus old-timers such as Levi Miller, Claude Gossett, Cap Weese, and Elvin Hayes, to name a few of the many fly-fishermen who have contributed the rich fly-fishing tradition of the Great Smoky Mountains.

Southern trout flies are beginning to become known nationally, as visiting anglers take these patterns home. Traditional patterns will take fish equally well. I know one top-flight dry fly-fisherman who uses a No. 14 Royal Coachman exclusively.

When concentrating exclusively on smallmouth and rock bass fly suggestions, always include the Muddler Minnow (sizes No.6 and No.8), hellgrammite imitations (sizes No.6 to No.4), Olive Wooly Boogers (sizes No.6 to No. 8), and the Green Inch (sizes No.4 to No.8). Dace-style streamers (sizes No.4 to No.8) and crayfish imitators (sizes No.2 to No.6) are also highly effective on these waters.

Starting on page 69 is an aquatic insect emergence table put in this book to cover the tastes and needs of the most discriminating fly-fishermen. It is merely a general guideline that may or may not apply precisely to the time and place you may be fishing in the Smokies. Some streams have superior benthic communities of macroinvertebrates, and hatches may be off as much as two weeks or more due to weather and other considerations.

Aquatic Insect Fly Pattern/Time Recommendations

AS I LABOR HERE AT THIS MOMENT IN TIME, there are 469 species of aquatic insects on the menu for trout and bass in the streams of the Great Smoky Mountains National Park. That number could change as you read this drivel. When I did my first guides to fishing the park waters, I swore that I would not burden anglers with this knowledge. Frankly, it is more productive to know that in 1928 the Tennessee Vols' 13–12 victory over the Florida Gators denied that school their first shot at an undefeated football season. Mom, please forgive me for cluttering the hard drive space on the brains of so many anglers. I have been asked hundreds of times for this information, so here goes.

The streams of the park have 120 species of Ephemeroptera (mayflies), 111 species of Plecoptera (stone flies), 7 species of Megaloptera (dobsonflies, fishflies, and alderflies), and 231 species of Trichoptera (caddis flies). This includes ten species new to science discovered since 2007. Represented in the order Ephemeroptera are the eastern Nearctic species of the Baetidae genera Acentrella, Acerpenna, and Baetis; the Ephemerellidae genera Attenella, Dannella, Drunella, and Ephemerella; the Heptageniidae genera Epeorus and Maccaffertium; and the Isonychiidae genus Isonychia are especially well represented in the park.

Now, if the charts (beginning on page 69) of the high points of the more abundant species does not satisfy most appetites, after it is a listing of them all. I am not Preston Jennings, who coded fly hatches with the precision of the stops made by the Pennsylvania Railroad, so believe me when I tell you the days, times of day, hook sizes, and patterns are pretty fluid. Generally speaking, hook sizes are skewed more to dries, so when you go subsurface, knock it up a size or two, especially with the stone flies.

Non-Aquatic Insect Fly Pattern/ Time Recommendations

THE FOLLOWING TERRESTRIAL patterns are recommended for use on all streams in the Great Smoky Mountains National Park from mid-June through late October: Little River Ant (sizes No.10 to No.18), Joe's Hopper (sizes No.4 to No.10), and Japanese Beetle (No.12).

The following streamer patterns are recommended for use on all streams in the Great Smoky Mountains National Park year-round: Black Nose Dace (sizes No.6 to No.12), Muddler Minnow (sizes No.4 to No.8), Olive Wooly Booger (sizes No.6 to No.8), Gray Ghost (sizes No.6 to No.10), Little Rainbow Trout (sizes No.8 to No.10), and Spuddler (sizes No.6 to No.8).

(continued on page 78)

Hatches and Matches for Aquatic Insects

Late Winter Hatches & Matches for Aquatic Insects   (January/February)

COMMON & LATIN NAMES	EMERGENCE DAYS	TIME	HOOK SIZE	MATCHING DRY PATTERNS	MATCHING NYMPH/WET PATTERNS
Blue Winged Olive *Baetis vagans*	late January thru February	mid-day	14-18	Male Adams Royal Wulff Adams Parachute	My Pet Bead-Head Hare's Ear
Blue Quill *Paraleptophebia adoptive*	late February	late morning/ mid-afternoon	16	Adams Variant Thunderhead Blue Quill Dark Brown Spinner	Yallarhammar Solomon's Black Pupa Bead-Head Zug Bug George's Nymph
Little Black Caddis *Chimarra atterima*	January and February	late morning/ afternoon	14-18	Elk Wing Caddis Bucktail Caddis Adam Caddis	Little Black Caddis Pupa Bead-Head Nymph
Little Black Stone Fly *Allocapnia aurora*	January thru February	all day	16-18	Little Black Stone Black Caddis	Wooly Bugger Black Stone Fly Nymph Bitch Creek
Winter Black Stone Fly *Capnia vernalis*	January thru February	all day *(see Nymphs)*	18-20	Little Black Stone Black Caddis	Black Stone Fly Nymph Montana Stone Fly
Early Brown Stone Fly (or Dark Stone Fly) *Strophopteryx fasciata*	mid-to late February	mid-day	14-16	Deer Hair Caddis Pickett Fence Little Brown Stone Dark Elkwing Caddis	Yallarhammar Brown Stone Fly Bitch Creek
Olive Midge *Dixella*	January thru February	mid-day	18-20	Adams Variant Griffiths Gnat	Hare's Eare
Blue Winged Olive *Baetis vagans*	March thru May	mid-day	14-18	Male Adams Thunderhead Grey Hackle Blue Dun	Bead-Head My Pet Pheasant Tail

(charts continued on next page)

Hatches and Matches for Aquatic Insects (cont'd.)

Early Spring Hatches & Matches for Aquatic Insects   (March/April)

COMMON & LATIN NAMES	EMERGENCE DAYS	TIME	HOOK SIZE	MATCHING DRY PATTERNS	MATCHING NYMPH/WET PATTERNS
Blue Quill *Paraleptophebia adoptive*	late February	late morning/ mid-afternoon	16	Adams Variant Thunderhead Blue Quill Dark Brown Spinner	Blue Quill Nymph Muskrat Bead-Head Zug Bug
Red Quill *Ephemerella subvaria*	late March thru mid-April	late afternoon	12-16	Red Quill Hendrickson Male Adams	Hendrickson Nymph Bead-Head Muskrat
Quill Gordon *Epeorus pleuralis*	early March thru early April *(later at higher elevations)*	mid-day	12-16	Male Adams Quill Gordon Royal Wulff Tennessee Wulff	Bead-Head Hare's Ear Gordon Nymph Flashback Hare's Ear
March Brown *Maccaffertium vicarium* *(Stenonema vicarium)*	mid-March thru April	mid-day	12-16	March Brown Royal Wulff	Hare's Ear March Brown Nymph
Gray Fox *Stenonema fuscum*	mid-April to late April	mid- to late afternoon	14	Grey Fox Ginger Quill Gray Fox variant	Bead-Head Hare's Ear My Pet Secret Weapon
Green Drake *Ephemera guttulata*	last week of April	late afternoon to evening	8-12	Green Drake Paradrake White Wulff Coffin Fly	Green Drake Nymph Bead-Head My Pet My Pet Green Nymph Eastern Green Drake Nymph
Light Cahill *Stenonema ithaca*	late April	afternoon to late evening	12-16	Light Cahill Hazel Creek Jim Charlie	CottonTop Nymph George Nymph Cahill Nymph
Sulphur Mayfly *Ephemerella dorothea*	early May	late afternoon to evening	16-18	Sulphur Light Cahill Hazel Creek Jim Charlie	Dark Sulphur Nymph Tellico Nymph Yallarhammar
Dark Dun/Black Caddis *Brachycentrus americanus*	mid-April	mid-morning	14-16	Black Soft Hackle Tan Caddis Henryville Dark Elk Hair Caddis Yellow Palmer (green-tied)	Streaker (Stickbait) Yallarhammar Bead-Head Hare's Ear Secret Weapon
Green/Apple Green Caddis *Rhyacophila lobifera*	late April	mid-to late	14-18	Greenbrier Special Olive Caddis	Bead-Head Zug Bug Green Tellico Nymph Secret Weapon Rockworm Caddis

Early Spring Hatches & Matches for Aquatic Insects   (March/April continued)

COMMON & LATIN NAMES	EMERGENCE DAYS	TIME	HOOK SIZE	MATCHING DRY PATTERNS	MATCHING NYMPH/WET PATTERNS
Little Black Caddis *Chimarra atterima*	April thru March	late morning/ afternoon	14-18	Elk Wing Caddis Adam Caddis Bucktail Caddis	Yallarhammar Bead-Head Pupa MyPet
Brown Stone Fly (or, Dark Stone Fly) *Strophopteryx fasciata*	early mid-to-late February	mid-day	14-16	Deer Hair Caddis Pickett Fence Little Brown Stone Dark Elkwing Caddis	Olive Stone Fly Dark Stone Fly Forkytail Crow Nymph Brown Stone Soft Hackles
Little Yellow Stone Fly (or, Tawny Stone Fly) *Isoperla bilineata*	late March thru April	mid-day	12-16	Buck Tail Caddis Yellow Palmer Jim Charlie Elk Wing Caddis Greenbrier Special Lil Yellow Stone	Yallarhammar George Nymph Bead-Head Cotton Top Brooks Golden Stone Little Stone Fly Nymph Brassie
Giant Black Stone Fly *Pternarys scotti*	late March thru April	early morning	12-14	Giant Black Stone Crow Nymph Montana Nymph Black Stone Fly Nymph Bitch Creek	Dark Stone Fly
Olive Midge *Dixella*	March thru April	mid-day	18-20	Adams Variant Griffiths Gnat	Bead-Head Hare's Ear George Nymph
Cream Midge *Dixella*	March thru April	mid-day	20-24	Light Cahill	Light Cahill Nymph
Gray Fox *Stenonema fuscum*	May/June	mid-to late afternoon	14-16	Grey Fox Ginger Quill Gray Fox Variant	Muskrat Bead-Head Hare's Ear
Green Drake *Ephemera guttulata*	May	late afternoon to evening *(sporadic)*	8-12	Green Drake Paradrake White Wulff Coffin Fly	Green Drake Nymph My Pet Bead-Head Green Nymph Eastern Green Drake Nymph
March Brown *Maccaffertium vicarium* *(Stenonema vicarium)*	early May	mid-day	12-16	March Brown Royal Wulff Ausable Wulff	Bead-Head Hare's Ear March Brown Nymph Bead-Head Pheasant Yallarhammar

(charts continued on next page)

Hatches and Matches for Aquatic Insects (cont'd.)

Late Spring Hatches & Matches for Aquatic Insects   (May/June)

COMMON & LATIN NAMES	EMERGENCE DAYS	TIME	HOOK SIZE	MATCHING DRY PATTERNS	MATCHING NYMPH/WET PATTERNS
Light Cahill *Stenonema ithaca*	May/June	afternoon to late evening	14-16	Light Cahill Hazel Creek Jim Charlie	Light Cahill Nymph Yallarhammar
Sulphur Mayfly *Ephemerella dorothea*	May/June	late afternoon to evening	16-18	Sulphur Light Cahill Hazel Creek Jim Charlie	Yallarhammar Dark Sulphur Nymph Tellico Nymph
Maroon Drake *Isonychia sadleri*	May	late afternoon (sporadic)	8-10	Red Quill My Pet	Yallarhammar
Mahogany Dun (or Leadwing Coachman and Slate Drake) *Isonychia bicolor*	June	all day (sporadic)	12	Adams Royal Coachman	My Pet Hare's Ear
Rusty Spinners *Baetis tricaudatus*	May/June	afternoon and evening	14-16	Rusty Wulff Orange Palmer Humpie	Yallarhammar Tellico Nymph Secret Weapon
Tiny Blue-Wing Olives *Attenella attenuate*	late May thru June	early morning and late afternoon	18-22	BWO Standard BWO Parachute	Bead-Head My Pet Bead-Head Pheasant
Gray Drake *Siphlonurus occidentalis*	June	late afternoon thru evening	12-16	Gray Wulff Adams	Bead-Head My Pet
Green/Apple Green Caddis *Rhyacophila lobifera*	May	mid-to late morning	14-18	Greenbrier Special Olive Caddis Green Tied Tellico	Yallarhammar Chartreuse Caddis Secret Weapon
Mottled Green Caddis *Rhyacophila atrata*	late May thru June	mid-to late morning	14-18	Greenbrier Special Olive Caddis Female Caddis	Green Streaker Yallarhammar Goddard Nymph
Yellow Caddis *Hydropsyche Carolina*	late June	mid-to-late morning	14-18	Yellow Caddis Goddard Caddis Tellico Nymph	Bead-Head Prince Sparse Yallarhammar
Black Caddis *Chimarra aterrima*	May thru early June (at higher elevations)	mid-day to late evening	14-16	Dark Elk Wing Humpie	Forky Tail Crow Bead-Head George Nymph
Short-Horned Sedge Caddis *Glossosoma intermedium*	May/June	morning and evening	18-22	Goddard Caddis Tan Pale Green Caddis	Bead-Head My Pet

Late Spring Hatches & Matches for Aquatic Insects   (May/June continued)

COMMON & LATIN NAMES	EMERGENCE DAYS	TIME	HOOK SIZE	MATCHING DRY PATTERNS	MATCHING NYMPH/WET PATTERNS
Cinnamon Caddis *Ceratopsyche slossonae (mainly Abrams)*	June	mid-to-late morning	16-18	Dark Br. Elk Wing Cinnamon Caddis Adult	Yallarhammar
Little Sister Caddis (Little Olive Sledge) *Cheumatopsyche (mainly Abrams)*	June	early morning late afternoon	18	Elk Hair Caddis Pickett Fence Deer Hair Caddis	Bead-Head Solomon's Goddard Pupa Tellico Nymph
Little Yellow Stone Fly (or, Tawny Stone Fly) *Isoperla bilineata*	May thru June	mid-day	12-16	Buck Tail Caddis Yellow Palmer Yellow Sally Stimulator Elk Wing Caddis Greenbrier Special Lil Yellow Stone	Yallarhammar Yellow Stone Fly Nymph
Giant Black Stone Fly *Pternarys scotti*	May thru June	early morning	12-14	Giant Black Stone	Montana Nymph George Nymph Crow Nymph Montana Nymph Black Stone Fly Nymph
Brown Stone Fly *Isoperla bilineata*	May thru June	mid-day	14-16	Deer Hair Caddis Pickett Fence Little Brown Stone Dark Elkwing Caddis	Forky Tail Crow Dark Stone Brown Stone Soft Hackles
Golden Stone Fly *Acroneuria carolinensis*	late May thru June	mid-day	14-16	Yellow Palmer Chuck Caddis	Golden Nugget Golden Stone Fly Nymph
Olive Midge *Dixella*	May	mid-day	18-20	Adams Variant Griffiths Gnat	Hare's Ear
Cream Midge *Dixella*	May/June	mid-day	20-24	Light Cahill	Light Cahill Nymph

(charts continued on next page)

Hatches and Matches for Aquatic Insects (cont'd.)

Summer Hatches & Matches for Aquatic Insects   (July/August)

COMMON & LATIN NAMES	EMERGENCE DAYS	TIME	HOOK SIZE	MATCHING DRY PATTERNS	MATCHING NYMPH/WET PATTERNS
Gray Fox EarNymph *Stenonema fuscum*	early July *(higher elevations)*	mid-to late afternoon	16	Grey Fox Ginger Quill	Bead-Head Hare's Muskrat Gray Fox Variant
Light Cahill *Stenonema ithaca*	early July *(higher elevations)*	afternoon to late evening	16	Light Cahill Hazel Creek	Light Cahill Nymph Jim Charlie
Sulphur MayFly *Ephemerella dorothea*	early July *(higher elevations)*	late afternoon to evening	16-18	Sulphur Light Cahill Hazel Creek	Yallarhammar Dark Sulphur Nymph Jim Charlie
Mahogany Dun (or, Slate Drake or, Leadwing Coachman) *Isonychia bicolor*	August *(sporadic)*	all day	12	Adams Thunderhead	Bead-Head Hare's Ear Leadwing Coachman
Black Quill *Leptophlebia johnsoni*	July thru early August *(higher elevations)*	late evening	14	Gray Fox Secret Weapon	Forky Tail Crow
Rusty Spinners *Baetis tricaudatus*	July and evening	afternoon	14-16	Rusty Wulff Orange Palmer	Yallarhammar Tellico Nymph
Tiny Blue-Wing Olives *Attenella attenuate*	July thru August	early & late afternoon	18-22	BWO Standard BWO Parachute	Bead-Head Pheasant Bead-Head Hare's Ear
Gray Drake *Siphlonurus occidentalis*	July	late afternoon thru evening	12-16	Gray Wulff	Bead-Head My Pet Adams
Yellow Quill *Heptagenia julia*	August	late evening	14-16	Quill Paradun Gray Winged Yellow Quill	Yallarhammar
Grey Brown Caddie *Brachycentrus americanus*	July thru August	late afternoon until dark	14-18	Dark Elk Wing Chuck Caddis	Grey Brown Pupa Brown Caddis Pupa
Mottled Green Caddis *Rhyacophila atrata*	July thru August	mid-morning to late afternoon	14-18	Greenbrier Special Olive Caddis Goddard Nymph	Green Streaker Yallarhammar
Yellow Caddis *Hydropsyche carolina*	July thru early August	mid-morning to late afternoon	14-18	Yellow Caddis Sparse Yallarhammar Tellico Nymph	Bead-Head Prince
Tan Caddis *Heteroplectron americanus*	July thru August	mid-morning to late afternoon	14-18	Tan Caddis Caribou Caddis	Stickbait Tan Caddis Pupa
Black Caddis *Chimarra aterrima*	July thru August *(at higher elevations)*	mid-day to late evening	14-16	Dark Elk Wing	Black Tellico Nymph

Summer Hatches & Matches for Aquatic Insects   (July/August continued)

COMMON & LATIN NAMES	EMERGENCE DAYS	TIME	HOOK SIZE	MATCHING DRY PATTERNS	MATCHING NYMPH/WET PATTERNS
Short-Horned Sedge (or, Short-Horned Caddis) *Glossosoma intermedium*	July thru early August	morning & evening	18-22	Goddard Caddis Tan Pale Green Caddis	Bead-Head My Pet
Cinnamon Caddis *Ceratopsyche slossonae*	to mid July *(mainly Abrams)*	mid-to-late morning	16-18	Dark Brown Elk Wing Cinnamon Caddis Adult	Yallarhammar
Little Sister Caddis (Little Olive Sledge) *Cheumatopsyche*	early July *(mainly Abrams)*	early morning late afternoon	18	Elk Hair Caddis Pickett Fence Deer Hair Caddis	Bead-Head Solomon's Yallarhammar Goddard's Pupa
Little Green Stone Fly *Chloroperlidae Suwallia marginata*	July thru early August	early morning	16	Clark's Stone Fly Green Stimulator Little Green Stone Fly Madame X Greer	Madame X Sofa Pillow Stimulator Kaufmann's Stone Fly
Little Yellow Stone Fly (or, Tawny Stone Fly) *Isoperla bilineata*	July thru August	mid-day	12-16	Buck Tail Caddis Yellow Palmer Pickett Fence Elk Wing Caddis Greenbrier Special Lil Yellow Stone Yellow Sally Jim Charlie	Yallarhammar Yellow Stone Fly Nymph
Brown Stone Fly *Isoperla bilineata*	July	mid-day	14-16	Deer Hair Caddis Pickett Fence Little Brown Stone Dark Elkwing Caddis	Forky Tail Crow Dark Stone Brown Stone
Golden Stone Fly *Acroneuria carolinensis*	July thru August	mid-day	14-16	Yellow Palmer Chuck Caddis	Golden Nugget Golden Stone Fly Nymph Bitch Creek
Little Yellow Summer Stone (or, Roach Flies) *Peltoperlidae Acroneuria carolinensis*	July thru August	mid-day	14-16	Little Yellow Sally Madam X Edwards Yellow Stone Fly Jim Charlie	Yallarhammar Lil Sally Nymph Secret Weapon
Little Brown Needle Stone Fly *Paraleuctra sara*	late August	all day	18	Dark Elk Wing Caddis Little Brown Needle Stone Fly	Bead-Head My Pet
Cream Midge *Dixella*	July thru August	mid-day	20-24	Light Cahill	Light Cahill Nymph

(charts continued on next page)

Hatches and Matches for Aquatic Insects (cont'd.)

Autumn Hatches & Matches for Aquatic Insects   (September/October)

COMMON & LATIN NAMES	EMERGENCE DAYS	TIME	HOOK SIZE	MATCHING DRY PATTERNS	MATCHING NYMPH/WET PATTERNS
Light Cahill *Stenonema ithaca*	early September (higher elevations)	afternoon to late evening	16	Light Cahill Hazel Creek Jim Charlie	Light Cahill Nymph
Mahogany Dun (or, Slate Drake or, Leadwing Coachman) *Isonychia bicolor*	September	all day (sporadic)	12	Adams Thunderhead	Bead-Head Hare's Ear Leadwing Coachman
Little Yellow Quill *Leucrocuta hebe*	September thru October	late evening	14-16	Quill Paradun Gray Winged Yellow Quill	Yallarhammar
Rusty Spinners *Baetis tricaudatus*	early September (higher elevations)	afternoon and evening	14-16	Rusty Wulff Orange Palme	Yallarhammar Tellico Nymph
Tiny Blue-Wing Olives *Attenella attenuate*	September thru October	early & late morning	18-22	BWO Standard BWO Parachute	Bead-Head Pheasant Bead-Head Hare's Ear
Gray Drake *Siphlonurus occidentalis*	September thru October	late afternoon thru evening	12-16	Gray Wulff Adams	Bead-Head My Pet
Grey Brown Caddis *Brachycentrus americanus*	September	late afternoon until dark	14-18	Dark Elk Wing Chuck Caddis Copper Caddis Pupa Brown	Gray Caddis Pupa Dark Caddis Pupa
Yellow Caddis *Hydropsyche carolina*	September thru October	mid-to-late morning	14-18	Yellow Caddis	Bead-Head Prince Sparse Yallarhammar Tellico Nymph
Tan Caddis *Heteroplectron americanus*	September thru October	mid-to-late	14-18	Tan Caddis Caribou Caddis	Stickbait Tan Caddis Pupa
Black Caddis *Chimarra aterrima*	September	mid-day to late evening (at higher elevations)	14-16	Dark Elk Wing	Black Tellico Nymph
Great Brown Autumn Sledge *Limnephilidae*	September thru October	all day	14	Dark Elk Wing Copper Caddis Pupa Brown	Dark Caddis Pupa
Short-Horned Sedge (or, Short-Horned Caddis) *Glossosoma intermedium*	September thru October	morning & evening	18-22	Goddard Caddis Tan Pale Green Caddis	Bead-Head My Pet
Little Yellow Stone Fly (or, Tawny Stone Fly) *Isoperla bilineata*	September thru October	mid-day	12-16	Buck Tail Caddis Yellow Palmer Jim Charlie Elk Wing Caddis Greenbrier Special Lil Yellow Stone Yellow Sally	Yallarhammar Yellow Stone Fly Nymph

Autumn Hatches & Matches for Aquatic Insects   (September/October continued)

COMMON & LATIN NAMES	EMERGENCE DAYS	TIME	HOOK SIZE	MATCHING DRY PATTERNS	MATCHING NYMPH/WET PATTERNS
Little Yellow Summer Stone (or, Roach Flies) *Peltoperlidae Acroneuria carolinensis*	September thru October	mid-day	14-16	Little Yellow Sally Madam X	Yallarhammar Lil Sally Nymph Edwards Yellow Stone Fly
Little Brown Needle Stone Fly *Paraleuctra sara* Stone Fly	September	all day	18	Dark Elk Wing Caddis	Bead-Head My Pet Little Brown Needle
Cream Midge *Dixella*	September thru October	mid-day	20-24	Light Cahill	Light Cahill Nymph

Early Winter Hatches & Matches for Aquatic Insects   (November/December)

COMMON & LATIN NAMES	EMERGENCE DAYS	TIME	HOOK SIZE	MATCHING DRY PATTERNS	MATCHING NYMPH/WET PATTERNS
Mahogany Dun (or, Slate Drake or, Leadwing Coachman) *Isonychia bicolor*	to mid-November	all day *(sporadic)*	12	Adams Thunderhead	Bead-Head Hare's Ear Leadwing Coachman
Little Yellow Quill *Leucrocuta hebe*	to mid-December	afternoon	14-16	Quill Paradun Gray Winged Yellow Quill	Yallarhammar
Tiny Blue-Wing Olives *Attenella attenuate*	November thru December	early & late morning	18-22	BWO Standard BWO Parachute	Bead-Head Pheasant Bead-Head Hare's Ear
Yellow Caddis *Hydropsyche carolina*	November thru December	mid-to-late morning	14-18	Yellow Caddis	Bead-Head Prince Sparse Yallarhammar Tellico Nymph
Little Brown Needle Stone Fly *Paraleuctra sara*	November thru December	all day	18	Dark Elk Wing Caddis Little Brown Needle Stone Fly	Bead-Head My Pet
Olive Midge *Dixella*	November thru December	mid-day	18-20	Adams Variant Griffiths Gnat	Hare's Ear

(continued from page 69)

There are several old patterns that are well known to many local fly-fishermen, most notably the Tellico Nymph and the notorious Yallarhammar. (A word of caution: only carry Yallarhammar flies made with feathers dyed to match the amber-hued wing feathers of the yellow-shafted flicker, or yellow-hammer woodpecker. Rangers who catch anglers using flies with real yellow-hammer feathers are not happy people.)

Other local patterns noted earlier in the fly emergence/fly pattern chart, as well as those noted in my first book, include the Stickbait, Streaker Nymph, George Nymph, My Pet, Forky Tail, Cotton Top, Squash Bug, Thunderhead, Ellison's Greenbriar Special, Ugly Devil, Ramsey Brown Hackle, Little River Ant, Copperhead, Jim Charley, Wood Bee, Tennessee Wulff, Secret Weapon, Red Fox Squirrel Nymph, Smoky Mountain caddis, Yellow Palmer, and Gray Hackle Yellow. These are only a few of the many patterns old and modern fly-tiers have created in this region. Each of the patterns and the men who created them could be made into additional chapters in this fly-fishing guide book to the greatest angling destination in the eastern United States.

I, and a large number of other Smoky Mountains fly-fishermen, find the above tables to be somewhat cumbersome, which is largely why I chose not to include such a list in my previous fishing guidebooks to park waters. (It was at the request of many other anglers that it is now offered.) My theory on fishing is to keep it as simple as possible. My friend Greg Ward, owner of Rocky Top Outfitters located in Pigeon Forge, Tennessee, who is also a master fly-fisherman, has developed what I believe is the best, most down-to-earth approach to understanding aquatic fly hatches in the streams of the Great Smoky Mountains National Park. Like me, he doesn't give a hoot in Hell about most of the information that can be garnered by studying fly identification or hatch charts. He carries no more than a dozen different flies in his fly boxes. Chapter 10 contains Ward's advice.

Aquatic Insects Found In the GSMNP

- *Ameletidae*
- *Ameletus cryptostimulus*
- *A. lineatus*
- *A. tertius*
- *Baetidae*
- *Acentrella* (new species)
- *A. parvula*
- *A. turbida*
- *Acerpenna macdunnoughi*
- *A. pygmaea*
- *Baetis brunneicolor*
- *B. fl avistriga*
- *B. intercalaris*
- *B. pluto*
- *B. tricaudatus*
- *C entroptilum* (new species)
- *C. triangulifer*
- *Diphetor hageni*
- *Heterocloeon curiosum*
- *H. davidi*
- *H. frivolum*
- *Paracloeodes minutus*
- *Plauditus dubius*
- *P. punctiventris*
- *P. virilis*

- *Procloeon* (new species)
- *P. rivulare*
- *P. viridoculare*
- *Pseudocentroptiloides usa*
- *Pseudocloeon frondale*
- *P. propinquum*
- *Baetiscidae*
- *Baetisca carolina*
- *B. gibbera*
- *Caenidae*
- *Brachycercus nitidus*
- *Caenis anceps*
- *C. hilaris*
- *C. latipennis*
- *C.macafferti*
- *Ephemerellidae*
- *Attenella attenuate*
- *A. margarita*
- *Dannella lita*
- *D. simplex*
- *D. provonshai*
- *Drunella allegheniensis*
- *V D. lata*
- *D. tuberculata*
- *D. walkeri*
- *Ephemerella catawba*

- *E. dorothea dorothea*
- *E. excrucians*
- *E. hispida*
- *E. invaria*
- *E. septentrionalis*
- *E. subvaria*
- *Eurylophella aestiva*
- *E. funeralis*
- *E. minimella*
- *E. verisimilis*
- *Serratella defi ciens*
- *S. molita*
- *S. serrata*
- *Ephemeridae*
- *Ephemera blanda*
- *E. guttulata*
- *E. varia*
- *Hexagenia limbata*
- *Heptageniidae*
- *Cinygmula subaequalis*
- *Epeorus dispar*
- *E. fragilis*
- *E. pleuralis*
- *V E. subpallidus*
- *E. vitreus*
- *Heptagenia julia*
- *H. marginalis*
- *Leucrocuta aphrodite*

Aquatic Insects Found In the GSMNP (continued)

• *L. hebe*	• *Rhithrogena amica*	*americana*
• *L. juno*	• *R. exilis*	• *Leptophlebia johnsoni*
• *L. maculipennis*	• *R. fasciata*	
• *L. thetis*	• *R. fuscifrons*	• *Paraleptophlebia adoptiva*
• *V Maccaffertium carlsoni*	• *R. uhari*	
	• *Stenacron carolina*	• *P. assimilis*
• *M. exiguum*	• *S. interpunctatum*	• *P. guttata*
• *M. ithaca*	• *S. pallidum*	• *P. moerens*
• *M. mediopunctatum mediopunctatum*	• *Isonychiidae*	• *P. mollis*
• *M. meririvulanum*	• *Isonychia bicolor*	• *P. swannanoa*
• *M. modestum*	• *V I. georgiae*	• *P. volitans*
• *M. mexicanum integrum*	• *I. hoffmani*	• *Neoephemeridae*
	• *I. obscura*	• *Neoephemera purpurea*
• *M. pudicum*	• *I. rufa*	
• *M. pulchellum*	• *I. sayi*	• *Potamanthidae*
• *M. sinclairi*	• *I. similis*	• *Anthopotamus distinctus*
• *M. terminatum terminatum*	• *I. tusculanensis*	
	• *Leptophlebiidae*	• *Siphlonuridae*
• *M. vicarium*	• *Habrophlebia vibrans*	• *Siphlonurus mirus*
• *Nixe perfida*		
• *N. spinosa*	• *Habrophlebiodes*	• *S. typicus*

Plecoptera of Great Smoky Mountains National Park

• *Capniidae*	• *A. rickeri*	• *A. nanina*
• *Allocapnia aurora*	• *A. stannardi*	• *A. neglecta*
• *A. frisoni*	• *Paracapnia angulata*	• *A. petasata*
• *V A. fumosa*	• *Chloroperlidae*	• *A. usa*
• *A. granulata*	• *Alloperla atlantica*	• *Haploperla brevis*
• *A. recta*	• *A. chloris*	• *H. parkeri*

- *Rasvena terna*
- *Suwallia marginata*
- *Sweltsa lateralis*
- *S. mediana*
- *S. urticae*
- *Leuctridae*
- *Leuctra alexanderi*
- *L. biloba*
- *L. carolinensis*
- *L. ferruginea*
- *L. grandis*
- *L. maria*
- *L. mitchellensis*
- *L. monticola*
- *L. nephophila*
- *L. sibleyi*
- *L. tenella*
- *L. tenuis*
- *L. triloba*
- *L. truncata*
- *L. variabilis*
- *Megaleuctra williamsae*
- *Paraleuctra sara*
- *Nemouridae*
- *Amphinemura appalachia*
- *A. delosa*
- *A. nigritta*
- *A. wui*
- *Prostoia completa*
- *P. similis*

- *Soyedina carolinensis*
- *S. kondratieffi*
- *Zapada chila*
- *Peltoperlidae*
- *Tallaperla anna*
- *T. cornelia*
- *V T. elisa*
- *T. laurie*
- *T. maria*
- *Viehoperla ada*
- *Perlidae*
- *Acroneuria abnormis*
- *A. arenosa*
- *V A. arida*
- *A. carolinensis*
- *A. fi licis*
- *A. frisoni*
- *A. internata*
- *A. perplexa*
- *V A. petersi*
- *Attaneuria ruralis*
- *Agnetina capitata*
- *V Beloneuria georgiana*
- *V B. stewarti*
- *Eccoptura xanthenes*
- *Hansonoperla appalachia*
- *Neoperla clymene*
- *N. coosa*
- *N. occipitalis*

- *Paragnetina ichusa*
- *P. immarginata*
- *P. media*
- *Perlesta decipiens*
- *P. frisoni*
- *P. nelsoni*
- *P. placida*
- *Perlinella drymo*
- *P. ephyre*
- *Perlodidae*
- *Clioperla clio*
- *Cultus decisus isolatus*
- *C. verticalis*
- *Diploperla duplicata*
- *D. robusta*
- *Helopicus subvarians*
- *Isogenoides hansoni*
- *V Isoperla bellona*
- *I. bilineata*
- *I. dicala*
- *V I. distincta*
- *I. frisoni*
- *I. holochlora*
- *I. lata*
- *I. orata*
- *I. similis*
- *Malirekus hastatus*
- *Oconoperla innubila*
- *Remenus bilobatus*
- *Yugus arinus*

Plecoptera of Great Smoky Mountains National Park (continued)

• Y. bulbosus	• Bolotoperla rossi	• S. limata
• Pteronarcyidae	• Oemopteryx contorta	• Taenionema atlanticum
• Pteronarcys dorsata		
• P. scotti	• Strophopteryx fasciata	• Taeniopteryx burksi
• Taeniopterygidae		• T. maura

Megaloptera of Great Smoky Mountains National Park

• Corydalidae	• Corydalus cornutus	• Sialis joppa
• Chauliodes pectinicornis	• Nigronia fasciatus	• S. velata
	• N. serricornis	
• C. rastricornis	Sialidae	

Trichoptera of Great Smoky Mountains National Park

• Apatania praevolans	• Calamoceratidae	• A. tomus
• A. rossi	• Anisocentropus pyraloides	• Glossosoma nigrior
• Beraeidae		• Matrioptila jeanae
• Beraea species	• Heteroplectron americanum	• Goeridae
• Brachycentridae	• Dipseudopsidae	• Goera calcarata
• Brachycentrus appalachia	• Phylocentropus auriceps	• G. fuscula
• B. lateralis	• P. carolinus	• Goerita betteni
• B. nigrosoma	• P. lucidus	• G. fl inti
• B. spinae	• Glossosomatidae	• Helicopsychidae
• Micrasema bennetti	• Agapetus crasmus	• Helicopsyche borealis
• M. burksi	• A. hessi	• Hydropsychidae
• M. charonis	• A. iridis	• Arctopsyche irrorata
• M. rickeri	• V A. jocassee	• Cheumatopsyche analis
• M. rusticum	• A. minutus	
• M. scotti	• A. pinatus	• C. campyla
• M. wataga	• A. rossi	• C. ela

- *C. enigma*
- *C. geora*
- *C. gyra*
- *C. halima*
- *C. harwoodi*
- *C. helma*
- *C. oxa*
- *C. pasella*
- *C. speciosa*
- *Diplectrona metaqui*
- *D. modesta*
- *Homoplectra doringa*
- *Hydropsyche (Ceratopsyche) alhedra*
- *H. (Ceratopsyche) bronta*
- *H. (Ceratopsyche) cheilonis*
- *H. (Ceratopsyche) macleodi*
- *H. (Ceratopsyche) morosa*
- *H. (Ceratopsyche) slossonae*
- *H. (Ceratopsyche) sparna*
- *H. (Hydropsyche) betteni*
- *H. (Hydropsyche) carolina*
- *H. (Hydropsyche) depravata*
- *H. (Hydropsyche) franclemonti*
- *Hydropsyche*

- *(Hydropsyche) rossi*
- *H. (Hydropsyche) scalaris*
- *H. (Hydropsyche) simulans*
- *H. (Hydropsyche) venularis*
- *Parapsyche apicalis*
- *P. cardis*
- *Hydroptilidae*
- *Dibusa angata*
- *Hydroptila amoena*
- *H. armata*
- *H. callia*
- *H. chattanooga*
- *H. delineata*
- *H. fi skei*
- *H. grandiosa*
- *H. hamata*
- *H. oneili*
- *H. remita*
- *H. scolops*
- *H. talladega s*
- *H. valhalla*
- *H. waubesiana*
- *Leucotrichia pictipes*
- *Mayatrichia ayama*
- *Oxyethira michiganensis*
- *O. novasota*
- *O. pallida*
- *Palaeagapetus celsus*
- *Stactobiella delira*

- *S. martynovi*
- *S. palmata*
- *Lepidostomatidae*
- *Lepidostoma americanum*
- *L. bryanti*
- *L. carrolli*
- V *L. compressum*
- *L. excavatum*
- V *L. fl inti*
- *L. frosti*
- *L. griseum*
- *L. latipenne*
- V *L. lobatum*
- *L. lydia*
- *L. mitchelli*
- *L. modestum*
- *L. ontario*
- *L. pictile*
- *L. sackeni*
- *L. styliferum*
- *L. tibiale*
- *L. togatum*
- *Theliopsyche corona*
- *T. epilonis*
- *T. grisea*
- *Leptoceridae*
- *Ceraclea ancylus*
- *C. cancellata*
- *C. diluta*
- *C. fl ava*
- *C. maculata*

Trichoptera of Great Smoky Mountains National Park (continued)

• *C. nepha*	• *Pycnopsyche antica*	• *Wormaldia moesta*
• *C. tarsipunctata*	• *P. conspersa*	• *W. mohri*
• *C. transversa*	• *P. divergens*	• *W. shawnee*
• *Leptocerus americanus*	• *P. fl avata*	• *Phryganeidae*
	• *P. gentilis*	• *Agrypnia vestita*
• *Mystacides sepulchralis*	• *P. guttifer*	• *Ptilostomis ocellifera*
• *Nectopsyche candida*	• *P. lepida*	• *P. postica*
• *N. exquisita*	• *P. luculenta*	• *Polycentropodidae*
• *Oecetis avara*	• *P. sonso*	• *Cyrnellus fraternus*
• *O. inconspicua*	• *P. subfasciata*	• *Neureclipsis crepuscularis*
• *O. nocturna*	• *Molannidae*	
• *O. persimilis*	• *Molanna blenda*	• *Nyctiophylax affi nis*
• *Setodes stehri*	• *M. ulmerina*	• *N. moestus*
• *Triaenodes ignitus*	• *Odontoceridae*	• *N. nephophilus*
• *T. injustus*	• *Pseudogoera singularis*	• *N. uncus*
• *T. marginatus*	• *Psilotreta amera*	• *N. banksi*
• *T. perna*	• *P. frontalis*	• *N. celta*
• *T. taenius*	• *P. labida*	• *N. denningi*
• *T. tardus e*	• *P. rossi*	• *Polycentropus blicklei*
• *Limnephilidae*	• *P. rufa*	
• *Frenesia diffi cilis*	• *Philopotamidae*	• *V P. carlsoni*
• *F. missa*	• *Chimarra aterrima*	• *P. carolinensis*
• *Hydatophylax argus*	• *C. augusta*	• *P. cinereus*
• *Ironoquia punctatissima*	• *C. obscura*	• *P. colei*
	• *C. socia*	• *P. confusus*
• *Platycentropus radiatus*	• *Dolophilodes distinctus*	• *P. crassicornis*
• *Pseudostenophylax sparsus*		• *P. maculatus*
	• *D. major*	• *P. rickeri*
• *P. uniformis*	• *D. sisko*	• *Psychomyiidae*
		• *Lype diversa*

- *Psychomyia fl avida*
- *P. nomada*
- *Rhyacophilidae*
- *V Rhyacophila accola*
- *R. acutiloba*
- *V R. amicis*
- *R. appalachia*
- *R. atrata*
- *R. banksi*
- *R. carolina*
- *R. carpenteri*
- *R. celadon*

- *R. formosa*
- *R. fuscula*
- *R. minor*
- *R. montana*
- *R. mycta Ross*
- *R. nigrita*
- *R. glaberrima*
- *R. ledra*
- *R. mainensis*
- *R. teddyi*
- *R. torva*
- *R. vibox*
- *Sericostomatidae*

- *Agarodes tetron*
- *Fattigia pele*
- *Uenoidae*
- *Neophylax aniqua*
- *N. concinnus*
- *N. consimilis*
- *N. fuscus*
- *N. kolodskii*
- *N. mitchelli*
- *N. oligius*
- *N. ornatus*

Adult mayfly

chapter 8

Pondering Caddis Flies

REMEMBERING THE FIRST TIME I encountered a big hatch of caddis flies on a trout stream in the Great Smoky Mountains National Park is easy. From a young age, I spent as much time with my dad as possible, splashing about in the trout streams of these mountains. How I managed to ignore so much of what occurred around me in those days is still a mystery. That changed some 30 years ago during a Memorial Day weekend. Rising well in advance of dawn, as was our custom, we made the 80-mile trek to the south end of Cades Cove.

This is where Abrams Creek emerges from the ground after traveling almost three miles through a limestone depression. Whereas all of the other 700 or so miles of trout streams in the national park have a pH of 5.6 to 6.5, the short subterranean trip through limestone jolts Abrams Creek's pH to 7.8 to 8.5. Coupled with the fecal bacteria and other nutrients contributed by the many cattle grazing in the open fields of the cove, this particular stream is blessed with a rich aquatic culture unique to the freestone streams of the Appalachian Mountains.

All of this was unknown to us at the time, and had we known, it really would have made little impression on us. What we did know by the end of that Sunday afternoon was that we had stumbled upon something that was nothing short of marvelous. Sometime around eight o'clock that morning the behavior of the trout changed. Trout that were otherwise spooky and reticent became bold, if not hell-bent on gorging themselves. Even in our uneducated state, we knew something we had never seen before was unfolding before us. It was a caddis fly hatch of the highest order.

We had read about air-filling flights of emerging mayflies, and were aware of caddis flies. We knew the trout were darting about under the water snatching morsels. However, the two telltale signs of a grand hatch—duns riding on the surface to take flight, and trout methodically dimpling the surface while feeding on the emerging flies—were missing. What was not missing was torrid feeding by the rainbow trout crowding this medium-size trout stream.

On an average, we hooked and landed a trout every four or five casts, and missed strikes at least two out of three casts. Using tandem rigged nymphs, a Tellico Nymph and a Yallarhammar, on at least a dozen occasions I caught two trout at a time. On numerous other instances, I would be working a trout to my net only to see one and sometimes two other trout charge up to attempt taking the fly hooked in the jaw of the first trout. During the course of that day I had over a dozen flies shredded to the point they had to be retired—a fitting end for any feather-shrouded offering. I do not remember how many rainbows Dad and I landed and released, but I recall losing count around noon at more than 100 fish. This madness went on unabated until dark, when I finally stumbled out of the creek.

Looking back, that day changed my perception of trout fishing on the streams of the Great Smoky Mountains National Park. Only on a few other occasions have I encountered trout fishing of that caliber, even on virgin waters in the Arctic, or at north woods beaver ponds where brook trout are packed in and nearly starving. A creek in the park that normally gave up 40 to 50 trout on a typical day, rewarded our efforts with several times its usual limit. Frankly, had someone told me so many trout were crowded into the pocket water of Abrams Creek that day, I would not have believed them.

Literature regarding fly-fishing for trout is so heavily loaded in the direction of mayflies, it is easy for unknowing anglers to overlook the importance of caddis flies. However, in the waters of the Smokies, the caddis fly does not take a backseat to the more highly touted mayfly clans in the local food chain. In many ways mayflies and caddis flies are very similar. Each breeds as a winged adult and lays its eggs in water. Upon hatching, the differences in these two aquatic insects are at their most evident.

Mayfly offspring begin life as a nymph, residing beneath the surface, clinging to rocks and debris located along the bottom, or burrowed in the sand.

With limited swimming ability, mayfly nymphs live underwater for six to twelve months and sometimes longer. During that time, they may shed their nymphal outer shell more than one time to accommodate growth. Upon reaching maturity, mayflies emerge to the surface as winged duns. Once airborne, the duns undergo a second metamorphosis to become breeding adults. Adults return to the streams in great swarms to perform their famous mating dance. Unable to feed because they have no mouth, adult mayflies mate, and they fall spent on the surface of the water, where waiting trout seize these protein-rich morsels thus completing their life cycle.

Understanding the importance of caddis flies to Smoky Mountains trout can help make this happen for you.

Caddis flies also begin life as waterborne sub-adults. The caddis fly off-spring are what biologists refer to as a pupa. Whereas a mayfly nymph is a well-armored creature complete with legs and most other visible attributes of an insect, a caddis fly pupa usually looks like a plump, soft, little worm resembling a common grub. In His infinite wisdom though, the Creator endowed the caddis fly pupa with all of the tools needed not only to survive in the hostile surroundings of a trout stream, but also to prosper. Caddis fly pupae construct "houses" for themselves that protect them from most predators.

In park waters some caddis flies construct houses of sticks and leaves, while others rely on tiny pebbles and even sand as home-building materials. Sticks, leaves, pebbles, and sand are held together by secretions produced by the caddis fly pupa. One large group of caddis flies in the park constructs seines, which they use to capture their food.

Usually measuring around an inch long, "stickbait," as old-timers refer to the caddis fly pupae, can be found still occupying their abodes when you turn over boulders and pick up the submerged sticks used by these creatures to secure their homes.

Mayflies and caddis flies emerge in a similar manner. Maximum reproduction is facilitated by peak emergences of ready-to-breed adult flies. Sledges, as adult caddis flies are called, rarely ride the surface as long as a mayfly dun. Emerging sledges skitter upstream along the surface in a rapid, erratic fashion. This makes them far more difficult for trout to nab than a stodgy dun that rides along the moving surface waiting for its waxy wings to dry sufficiently for it to become airborne. Many times, peak emergences of caddis flies are difficult to see, while peak emergences of mayflies are often more visible.

Trout in the Smokies tend to prey on caddis fly pupae just under the surface where these small aquatic insects struggle to shuck their pupal husk. These efforts to emerge as a winged adult often result in the caddis fly pupa being highly vulnerable for several minutes, providing trout with easy pickings. However, except for an occasional dorsal or tail fin breaking the surface, spotting the darting movement of a trout helping itself to a mass emergence of the caddis fly pupae is the only other visible hint we are given.

Many angling scribes have long penned prose expounding how trout relish mayfly adults and nymphs. While I am not contending these fish are not extremely fond of these aquatic insects, experience has taught me the trout will ignore hatches of mayflies to pick off the subsurface struggling caddis fly pupae instead. Insofar as trout are classic predators, that is, they prey on that which is most readily available to them, it appears that the abundance of emerging caddis flies is an important occurrence that trout fishermen need to understand.

Unlike the mayfly and stone fly, the caddis fly undergoes a complete metamorphoses, starting as an egg, then becoming a larva, and then morphing into a pupa before the final transition to an adult ready to emerge. Caddis fly larvae are either cased or uncased, and can be split into five groups: free-living caddis flies, net spinners, saddle case builders, purse case builders, and tube case builders. Actually, there are nine groups, but let's keep this as simple as we can. With or without shielding, they resemble a quasi-maggot-looking worm.

Larvae mature to the pupa stage, but only for a comparatively short time. Cased caddis are then outside of their protective homes, while as pupae, free-living larvae find a protective nook where they remain ready to emerge. Ready-to-emerge pupae, or pharate, are fully formed, save for a thin membrane that compressed, as in plastic wrap, which is discarded so the wing can be free to dry and fly. This is when aquatic insects are of keen interest to fly fishermen, as this is when caddis are most vulnerable to hungry trout.

The lucky ones make it to the surface where their wings sprout for the terrestrial portion of their lives. Most of them wiggle their way to the surface to go airborne, but several species of caddis flies head to the edge of the water to climb free from the killing zone. Mating quickly ensues in streamside greenery, on rocks, and other structures near the water.

Once fertilized, the female returns to her native waters to deposit her eggs. Some species simply drop their eggs, while others skip the surface before diving back into the water to deposit their eggs. As with mayflies, successful mating is the final act for these insects.

Ironically, surface-riding caddis fly patterns, such as the Picket Fence, Elkwing Caddis, Orange Palmer, Royal Trude, Chuck Caddis, or Greenbriar Special series, often produce more strikes when surface caddis fly activity is not especially brisk. Admittedly, these dry fly patterns do produce best at streams and rivers where caddis flies occupy a prominent position in the food chain, which accurately describes most of the waters of the Great Smoky Mountains National Park. However, in my opinion, many times current-riding caddis fly patterns serve as well as prospecting flies such as a Royal Coachman, as they do as a traditional hatch-matching imitator.

When it comes to fooling these trout during peak caddis fly emergence activity, wet flies and nymphs are without peer. Remarkably simple patterns such as the Tellico Nymph and Solomon's Pupa in sizes No.18 to No.10 can be used to effectively imitate most of the vast numbers of caddis fly emergers common to these waters. Most caddis fly emergers are either dark brown to blackish in late winter to very early spring, to pale cream, yellow, tan, or bright apple green—the latter being dominant a mid- to late-summer color.

Caddis fly emergence imitators can usually be fished up or downstream, depending mostly on stream clarity and size. When fly-fishing smallish-to-medium-size, gin-clear mountain rivulets, cast upstream and allow the current to deliver your offering. This technique requires mending your line to ensure a natural drift as well as the ability to efficiently set the hook when a strike occurs. Casting upstream is essential at small, clear streams where your presence upstream from trout facing into the current would foil your efforts.

When water is murky, or when on larger waters where more than 20 feet of line can be played out, fly-fishing downstream is not only equally effective, but far easier and more relaxed. Trolling is a fly-fishing technique wherein you simply stand upstream from a potentially productive run where a fly is either still-fished in the current, retrieved very slowly, or methodically jerked back and forth. Casting upstream to a ten o'clock position and quartering your fly across the current to a two o'clock position is another time-honored medium- to large-water caddis fly pupa imitator fly-fishing ploy.

Old-time trout fishermen of the Smoky Mountains streams are quick to point out you do not need to wait for subsurface activity among caddis fly pupae to catch lots of trout. In fact, as these fellows are fond of saying, you don't even need a fly rod. Fishing with stickbait provides an angler with what is perhaps the single most deadly trout bait, as a few unhappy anglers who have been caught plucking them from the back sides of stream boulders in these "artificial only" waters have explained. In fact, it is not inaccurate to say that collecting a dozen stickbaits and freeing them from their houses can take longer than wrestling as many trout from a stream, but can give you remarkable fishing. However, resist the temptation. To be spotted just turning over rocks to "look at stickbait" can land you in hot water in the national park.

If you are unfamiliar with these streams, you may not realize that the caddis fly, even though it is overlooked by many, is a key element in your favorite trout stream. Understanding these interesting members of the aquatic insect community will improve your odds of catching more and bigger trout.

chapter 9
Terrestrials:
Too Important to Overlook

A TREMENDOUS DEPENDENCE by trout and bass on terrestrial insects for food is one of the most interesting tidbits about fly-fishing in the Great Smoky Mountains National Park. Beginning with the spring and continuing through the summer months, and especially during autumn, land-dwelling insects are vitally important sources of food for these fish.

When the feeding attention of trout and bass is keyed on terrestrial insects, it is a magical time for fly-fishermen. Rarely are these streams more productive than when these fish are taking grasshoppers, ants, and other terrestrial insects during the days of summer. Granted, most of the time these waters are low and clear, which does little to help the efforts of the average angler. However, early morning, late evening, rainy days, or days when it rained the day before, typically provide great fishing. Understanding what foods are most available to stream trout during this time is the secret to catching these fish during the hot-weather months as well as most of autumn.

Between mid-summer and late autumn the trout in these streams rely less on their usual sources of nutrition, such as aquatic insects, than at any other time of year. This happens for two reasons. One is the cyclic availability of aquatic insects. Beginning in early spring, hatches of mayflies, stone flies, and caddis flies dominate trout feeding efforts. Members of these orders deposit most of their eggs in the streams between March and June to replenish their populations. It is not until late autumn that many of these hatch and become significant sources of food for what anglers refer to as "catchable-size trout." This gap corresponds with the abundance of land, or terrestrial, insects during the summer.

Terrestrials become available to stream trout in a variety of ways, from simply jumping into water, as is often the case of a grasshopper, to falling from limbs and other greenery hanging over the water, as is the case with caterpillars and jassids. Other terrestrial insects that can fly, such as bees, Japanese beetles, and locusts, often find their way onto the surface of a stream. Generally, frequent late-summer and early-autumn rains wash a bounty of terrestrial insects into the water. At this time buggy, nondescript terrestrial fly patterns, such as the Wooly Worm, are deadly on these trout and bass.

Terrestrial insects provide easily sized, high-quality food at a time when the fish might otherwise have to expend considerable effort chasing minnows or crayfish. There are few terrestrial insects stream trout will not gulp down with gusto, especially on medium-size to small streams where land critters play a key role in the daily diets of trout.

One of the most interesting things about terrestrial insects fly-fishermen should understand is that even when dead these insects always float. This was first pointed out to me in the 1970s by Gerald Almy, then a staff writer for *Sports Afield*. Gerry wrote the well-known book, *Tying and Fishing Terrestrials* (Stackpole Books, 1978). I took him on his first fishing trip to the Smokies, a bright early-morning jaunt to the falls at Abrams. He keeps telling me that he will eventually forgive me for that little outing.

According to Gerry, nature protects terrestrials from soaking up water when they are alive by providing them with a nonporous body that is overlaid with wax. Terrestrials are essentially waterproof. That is not to say a trout will not nab a grasshopper you offer on a line weighted down with a split shot sinker. However, it is a fact that a trout is more accustomed to taking a grasshopper from the surface than from beneath it.

Grasshoppers are to Smoky Mountain trout what a rib-eye steak is to you or me. It is a tasty, substantial mouthful that does not come around frequently enough to pass up. Grasshoppers certainly are not the only major terrestrial that stream trout feed upon, but in many instances they are of primary concern to anglers. When grasshoppers are available in large quantities, trout watch for these rib eyes on the surface. Anyone who has ever found themselves on a quality trout stream armed with a few good grasshopper imitations at a time when these terrestrials are numerous knows what it is like to experience a little bit of heaven on earth.

Another terrestrial insect these trout often key in on is the jassid, or leaf-hopper. Related to the grasshopper, but much smaller, jassids commonly live in streamside grasses and other greenery. When fishing streams where you see trout dimpling the surface along the extreme edge of the water, odds are these fish are munching down jassids, although occasionally this will happen when wood ants are working near the water.

At this time of the season, stream trout must keep a sharp eye out for any possible source of food. Several summers ago, while fishing Panther Creek, I came upon a pool where a basketball-size hornet's nest hung over the tail of a pool. Apparently the hornets were cleaning house, as enough debris was hitting the water to attract three foot-long trout. Tying on a bee pattern dry fly, I caught two of the trout before the third wised up and left.

Late-summer and early-autumn trout depend on terrestrial insects to varying degrees. At food-rich streams such as Abrams Creek, where stream-borne food is always available in large quantities, terrestrial patterns are often out-produced by patterns such as the Adams. However, in the most classic free-stone streams of the park, terrestrials are vital sources of nutrition.

And there are many seasonal terrestrials that are easy to overlook. For example, when the sourwood worms are available in early summer, these whitish-colored morsels are relished by trout. The thin, bright green inchworms we often see suspended from trees are another often overlooked, but highly sought-after, tidbit. When they are common, Japanese beetles can be imitated with great success by fly-fishermen. During summer and autumn, it is usually a big mistake not to have a supply of terrestrial fly patterns with you.

Fly-fishermen who have not discovered the effectiveness of late summer and early autumn terrestrial patterns will be astounded when trying these offerings. Fly catalogs boast many patterns designed to mimic grasshoppers, jassids, ants, beetles, grubs, and more. Grasshopper patterns are my personal favorite, with the old reliable Joe's Hopper being tough to top. Should you find yourself at the stream without a hopper pattern when you need one, you can push a Muddler Minnow into service. Dressed with a floatant, a Muddler Minnow is a pretty good grasshopper imitation. Frankly there are a couple dozen hopper patterns that will work, and one is about as good as another.

When fly-fishing for trout in late summer and early autumn, ant patterns are also worth trying—they are the unsung heroes of this time of the year. Now is the time to periodically examine the contents of the stomachs of trout you catch. If they are feeding heavily on grasshoppers, the stiff legs of these creatures will be easily seen when the stomach is split. Ants, on the other hand, are not so easily discerned. Sometimes you will find complete or partial bodies of ants, but most of the time you'll see only a blackish, or sometimes reddish, blob in the stomach.

At this time of year ants are extremely common along trout streams. Although an ant is small, trout will always seize one when it becomes available. Ant patterns in black and red, in sizes No.10 to No.18, should always be carried when fly-fishing for trout during late summer and early autumn. My best results have occurred when concentrating only on the edges of streams, but trout will take ant patterns just about anywhere they are offered during this time of year.

Ant patterns and just about all other terrestrial insect patterns are fished in much the same way dry fly patterns are presented. Exceptions are when fly-fishing along grassy edges, where many terrestrial insects typically fall into streams. Fantastic fly-fishing is often available along shallow runs by offering terrestrial fly patterns such as a leafhopper or Japanese beetle within a foot or less of the stream's bank.

One of the best things about fly-fishing using terrestrial patterns at this time of year is you do not have to be there when a hatch comes off. You don't even have to get up early to get in on prime fishing. The warmer it gets, the more active many species of terrestrial insects become. High noon fishing can often be high octane fishing, if stream flow levels are in your favor.

If you have not discovered how using the abundance of terrestrial insects can increase your catches of stream trout during late summer and early autumn, you'll be pleasantly surprised. Trout that have grown large since spring are there for the taking.

Late-summer and autumn fly boxes should have at least half of the following:

Green tied Hopper (No. 10-14)		Brown/Amber tied Hopper (No. 8-12)	
Little River Ant	(No. 12-18)	Cinnamon Ant	(No. 12-18)
Green Inchworm	(No. 10-14)	Japanese Beetle	(No. 12-14)
Wood Bee	(No. 10-14)	Yellowjacket	(No. 8-12)
Black Beetle	(No. 12-16)	Loco Beetle	(No. 12-16)
HiVis Ant	(size 14-18)		

chapter 10

Greg's Deadly Dozen and How to Use Them

by Greg Ward

*F*LIES, FLIES, AND MORE FLIES. I've had clients show up for trips accompanied by six to ten boxes full of thousands of dollars worth of flies. I have watched grown men stumble around the streams of the Smokies with a small net trying to catch aquatic insects. They catch one, then rush to their trucks, put the specimen in a vial and thumb through the pages of a hatch chart or identification book to be sure they can accurately name the little critter, open a fly-tying kit, and whip up a perfect imitation of the hatch-of-the-day. Then they return to the stream and log the water temperature and time of day as well as other meteorological data.

I, however, prefer a different approach to fly-fishing the Smokies. I don't have dozens of boxes of flies sitting around the house waiting to be called to duty depending on the latest hatch. Instead, I focus on a few tried-and-true flies that will always work in a free-flowing stream. Over the years, I've read many articles and books that claim that fly hatches in the Smokies are sparse at best—I beg to differ. If you race to the streams at daylight and fish until noon or so like your granddad or father told you to do, the hatches will be sparse. If you fish the Smokies like I do, however, you'll see some phenomenal hatches. Stream temperatures fluctuate seven to eight degrees daily. Hatches, therefore, are much better in the afternoon. In fact, the most prolific yellow stone fly hatches I have ever witnessed began two hours before dark. I've seen such hatches on Little River, the West Prong and Middle Prong of the Little Pigeon River, and Roaring

Fork. Most anglers are having dinner with their wives in Gatlinburg while the trout are feeding like piranhas in the Smokies.

Don't get me wrong though. I do believe in matching the hatch to some extent, but I also know that a properly presented large fly will catch larger fish on average. When the white midges hatch in the fall, they literally look like snow; so I like to cast a No. 10 Adams right in the middle of the hatch. Nine times out of ten the largest trout in the riffle will engulf the Adams. I call this method Meat and Potatoes. While all the small fish are having rabbit food, I offer the big boys meat and potatoes. It works for me. I don't own a fly smaller than a No. 18 for fishing the Smokies; in fact, most of my flies are No. 14, 12, and 10. I do have some small Black Caddis, Parachute Adams, Blue-wing Olives, and Cahills in 18 and 16. Descending, free-flowing streams like we have in the Smokies are a lot alike. I noticed some years ago that aquatic insect color patterns correspond to the scenery. For example, dull black or brown flies dominate the cooler months whereas more colorful hatches dominate warmer months. Bright yellow and chartreuse green hatches prevail during the summer months. Flies literally resemble the plants and leaves of their environment, providing an easy way for anglers to match their flies to the current hatch. Anglers also need to keep in mind that the warmer the water, the larger the flies. One exception is the massive March browns that dance among the tiny black caddis and stones in early spring. The big orange caddis of the fall matches the orange foliage of the maple and oak trees that so many tourists flock to the Smokies to see every October.

A Guide's Secrets

KNOWING WHICH FLIES TO FISH and how to fish them should increase your catch and lighten your load a lot. First, you need to learn how to fly-fish for shear numbers, and your clothing choices can have a huge impact on how many fish you catch. Basically, dress in dull colors: browns, tans, greens, and blues are all good earth-tone colors. Bright colors will not only spook the fish but also attract biting insects. A hat and polarized sunglasses should be in every fly-fisherman's kit along with a good pair of wading shoes. All I carry is a small, belted bag that can hold one, yes, just one, fly box with a couple of extra leaders, 6x5x4x tippet, a Tie-Fast Knot-Tying Tool, nippers, Loon Aquel Floatant, hemostats, and some lead. I have not worn a vest since 1991. A vest gets in my way and tempts me to bring things I don't really need. I also don't wear waders; they leak. If they don't leak today, they'll leak tomorrow. Plus, waders burn me up. I wet wade and position myself to fish even when water temperatures are cooler. Mid-April through October the water actually feels great. I rarely fish the Smokies in the winter. Leaves choke the streams in November; I guide bear hunts throughout much of December; and by January and February the fish are dormant, and I'd much rather be hunting deer in the woods of LA (lower Alabama), or fishing below Douglas Dam in Tennessee for sauger and walleye. However, I do fish Gatlinburg's stock trout waters during the winter. Their delayed harvest program, implemented in 1997, offers some of the finest fishing in the Southeast during cold weather.

High-sticking is one of the best ways to catch numbers of fish on the smaller streams of the Smokies. A cane pole will work just as well as my $700 fly rod. This nonsense about short fly rods in small streams is simply that— nonsense. An 8-foot to 9-foot rod will help you manipulate your fly line as well as your fly. When high-sticking, simply let out about 4 feet of fly line past your tip and a 7½ foot leader. Hide behind boulders and lay your dry fly or nymph in the pool upstream. Hold the rod high and only let the leader touch the water. Pay close attention because wild trout hit like lightening. This method works great up high in the smaller, boulder-strewn streams. You can cast in the lower sections where streams widen, slow down, and meander down the mountain. I fish upstream 90 percent of the time. I am no purist, but you will find me fishing dries most of the time. Watching a trout come up and engulf a dry is why I fly-fish.

The Deadly Dozen

TROUT IN THE SMOKIES BEGIN to feed more aggressively as water temperatures start to rise in early spring. Mid-March is a good rule of thumb, but three- to four-day periods of warm weather or rain can jump-start a feeding frenzy just as dropping water temperatures from a snowmelt will stop it. A good 60-to-65- -degree spring flood will get things rolling quicker than anything. Little Black Caddis, the first of my deadly dozen, No. 18 and 16, tied with blond elk hair are hard to beat this time of the year. They ride well on the water and imitate all small black flies hatching including stones, alder flies, and ants. The trout couldn't care less about the wings—wings are for fishermen to see! All the fish see is the bottom of the fly. I know this because I've been known to lie on the bottom of a stream with a mask and snorkel—trust me, size and color are all that matter! A No. 16 Blond Elk Hair Black Caddis looks the same as a 16 Black

Stone, 16 Black Gnat, and a 16 Black Ant. This is why I fish so many parachute patterns. I can see the fly, and the trout sees the bottom of the fly. There is no difference as long as the size and color are the same in any dry fly. You could literally fish all Blond Elk Hair Caddis as long as the body is tied in different colors and sizes. Tan, yellow, chartreuse, olive, black, brown, and orange Caddis would match most hatches I care about. My 47-year-old eyes do not see an Adams as well as they used to, so I fish a Parachute Adams or a Wulff No. 12 and 10. March Browns are awesome as well as Blue-wing Olives No. 18, 16, and 14, from March through April. Nymphs of choice would be Bead Head Pheasant Tails followed by Gold-ribbed Hare's Ears in No. 18, 16, and 14. Parachute Adams will work in any stream in the world. I think there is always a fly hatching that resembles an Adams; it's an excellent neutral color to use when temperatures are transitioning from cool to warm in the spring, then back to cool in the fall.

The advent of May brings on yellow. Start with pale yellows and progressively get brighter and brighter and peak with chartreuse in late June, July, and August. Start out with Parachute Light Cahills, No. 16, 14, and 12, then switch to bright Yellow Stimulators, sizes 14, 12, and 10, and Chartreuse Blond Elk-haired Caddis, sizes 14 and 12, in the heat of the summer. Drowning a Bead Head Chartreuse Inchworm Nymph, size 16, 14, and 12, will increase your catch considerably.

In September and October, things start calming down as far as color is concerned. Big Orange (go Vols!) Elk-hair Caddis usher in football season. Try sizes 12 and 10. The neutral color of a size 12 or 10 Parachute Adams tricks spawning browns as well.

Number twelve of my deadly dozen is a Muddler Minnow, size 6. This streamer is by far the most productive if tied correctly. If the tail and tip of the wings coming down the side of the Muddler are white, it will catch 10 to 1 fish. Cast it across the current, give an upstream mend, then strip it back in 6-inch to 10-inch intervals. The trout will hammer it in the belly of the cast.

Honorable Mentions

There are a few more flies that also deserve mention in addition to my Deadly Dozen. I've arranged them by my fish-by-the-seasons rule.

Late March to Early April:　Red Quills (dry)—sizes 14 and 12

March to November:　Crème and Olive Caddis Pupae (nymph, bead head)—Sizes 16, 14, and 12

April to November:　Tellico Nymph—sizes 16, 14, and 12

Summer:　Tennessee Wulff (dry)—sizes 14 and 12

Late summer and fall:　Ausable Wulff (dry)—sizes 14 and 12

Fall:　Orange Stimulator (dry)—sizes 12 and 10

Late fall and winter to early spring:　Black Midge (nymph, bead head)—size 18, scud hook, tungsten bead and black thread only

Any season:　Prince Nymph (bead head)—size 16, 14, and 12;
Thunderhead (dry)—sizes 16, 14, 12, and 10—use this in place of an Adams
Black, Olive, and Brown Woolly Boogers (streamer)—size 8 and 6

It's important to remember that all nymphs and streamers should have lead tied to the hook prior to tying the fly so it will sink.

My Last Secret

To INCREASE YOUR CATCH, double your chances by fishing dries and nymphs in tandem. For example, during neutral periods (spring and fall) fish a size 16 Bead Head Pheasant Tail dropped 18 inches to 24 inches below a size 12 Parachute Adams. In early spring, drop a size 18 Black Midge beneath a size 14 Black Caddis. In the summer, try a size 14 Bead Head Inchworm dropped from a size 12 Yellow Stimulator—it's absolutely deadly! In the fall, drop a size 14 Pheasant Tail under a size 10 Orange Caddis or Stimulator, and hang on. I only use this method when I am after numbers of fish. The nymph catches most of the fish before the dry gets a chance. The nymph also alters the proper drift of a dry. The nymph must be at least 18 inches below the dry to be legal in the Smokies.

Once you've decided on the best fly, it's important to be observant. Sit back and watch the fish for a few minutes before entering the stream. The trout may tell you what they want if you'll only watch and let them.

chapter 11

Ben Craig:
Master Fly Tyer of the Smokies

THE REGION COLLECTIVELY KNOWN as the Great Smoky Mountain National Park has produced many of Dixie's best-known tyers of feathery trout flies. Nationally known patterns such as the Yallarhammar and Tellico Nymph have origins richly steeped in the fly-tying lore of these misty mountains. In fact, over the course of the last three decades, I have spoken with at least three fly tyers (all now dead) who told me they recall seeing the now-famous Wulff-style hair wing tied dry flies long before Lee Wulff is reported to have initiated this wise practice.

Life has been good, allowing me to meet such fly tying legends as Kirk Jenkins, Ernest Ramsey, Fred Hall, Eddie George, and dozens of other local old-time fly tyers. Since my first book came out, it spawned interest not only in additional research on the information that I first brought before the public, but also two generations of new fly tyers as well as a handful of books and Web sites devoted exclusively to southern Appalachian fly patterns.

While each of the old-time fly tyers has earned his own degree of greatness, none has reached the pinnacle of this craft like the late Ben Craig of Waynesville, North Carolina. At least a second-generation tyer, Craig was 64 years old and still working at his tying table when I met him. This trout-fishing expert and master fly tyer not only originated many of the fly patterns we use today, but also trained or influenced virtually everyone now tying flies in western

North Carolina. I first met him in the 1980s when Greg Ward took me to Craig's home to meet the master tyer of the mountains.

"I've been tying flies for over half a century," said Craig, as we chatted in his fly-tying parlor. Adorned with enough feathers, fur, thread, and yarn to keep a dozen fly tyers in business for years, the room also housed a portion of his collection of vintage bamboo fly rods. A mount of a native 13-inch speckled trout, a prized possession, hung beside the slightly built Craig as we conversed. His fly-tying parlor featured wildlife art in addition to his fly-tying paraphernalia.

One entire wall of shelves in Craig's fly-tying parlor stored his current inventory of flies, which was never very large, as a result of the high demand for his tying efforts. Craig sold his flies to anglers all across the country, including Quaker Boy of Pennsylvania.

"As a youngster, I learned to tie flies by watching my father, who was a lifelong trout fisherman fond of fly-fishing. He kept his fly-tying material in a cardboard box, buying only thread and hooks for creating his flies. I don't think there are many farms in a three-county area where he and I didn't chase down roosters to pick a few choice hackles from their necks.

"As a young fly tyer, my friends and I were exceptionally fond of floating Royal Coachman dries at the streams of the Great Smoky Mountains National Park. The most deadly addition we discovered for our home-tied Royal Coachman flies was the bright red plastic band used to seal packs of Lucky Strike cigarettes. Early on Saturday mornings, we would go to downtown Waynesville to patrol the streets for discarded plastic bands for making these flies."

Ben Craig shared much of the same fly-fishing and fly-selection philosophy as I and many others in and around the Great Smoky Mountains National Park do. Proper presentation of your fly and a general understanding of the region's aquatic insect community are far more important than knowing the Latin name for three dozen different species of mayfly. Craig's all-time favorite fly pattern was Adams. Of course, he carried these in a wide assortment of sizes and varieties, including the Adams Parachute and Adams Wulff, as well as the Black Adams and the Adams Variant. In addition to this, Craig also varied the body of the Adams he fished, using dark bodies in late winter and spring, and lighter bodies in summer. Similarly, he switched from a dark brown hackle in winter and spring, to a grizzly hackle in summer.

Craig was a treasure-trove of knowledge on fly-fishing for trout in the Great Smoky Mountains National Park. While he preferred to keep his fly pattern selection ultra simple, he had several recommendations he knew would consistently produce trout in these waters at certain times of the year, including the well-known Thunderhead and the Chocolate Thunderhead, which, in his opinion, differ little from an Adams Wulff. He believed the Chocolate Thunderhead is particularly effective during May and June.

Another fly pattern recommended by Craig is the Elk Wing Hopper, a high-riding imitation of the grasshoppers that are common to the region and relished by trout and bass in these streams. The secret to making a highly deadly Elk Wing Hopper is dressing its flanks with a speckled feather from a bronze-colored domestic turkey. Extremely rare, such matched speckled feathers were Craig's most prized fly-tying material.

The Orange Palmer is another fly pattern Craig recommended anglers carry when visiting the streams of the Great Smoky Mountains National Park. A highly efficient imitation of the orange-colored caddis flies common to these waters, the Orange Palmer is a simplistic pattern Craig said came about around 50 years ago. He was not certain, but he strongly believed the Orange Palmer pattern originated in the hollows of Haywood County, North Carolina.

Craig also liked the Tellico Nymph for mimicking emerging caddis pupae, but believed nothing tops the old-fashioned Stickbait Nymph for this chore. He tied his from a special latex material that perfectly matches the dingy, yellowish-white color of these highly sought after trout foods. Being a long-time angler here, Craig was quick to point out that nothing ever whipped onto a hook by a fly tyer as well as the real thing—soft, pulpy stickbait.

The Green Inchworm was another pattern highly recommended by Craig. This, along with a Sourwood Worm fly he created at the request of his son, Kevin, is deadly for taking trout during the late spring and summer months.

When asked about the older patterns used over the years in the Great Smoky Mountains National Park, Craig noted that while the Yallarhammar may be one of, if not the, oldest patterns here, its trout-catching magic is overrated.

A lot of the local fly-fishermen swear by the Yallarhammar, but I can name a dozen fly patterns that will out-produce this old-timey pattern. In fact, the best way to catch trout on a Yallarhammar is to put stickbait on it!

"Indeed, I have tied many of them, having split as many yellow flicker wings as anyone, I suppose. And because there is still considerable demand for Yallarhammar flies, I still tie them, but not with the traditional yellow flicker feathers. I have developed a dyed substitute that is just as effective as the real thing, and certainly less likely to get you in trouble with park rangers, who are always alert for Yallarhammar flies made from the feathers of the protected birds they are named for," said Craig.

Craig tyed what he called the traditional Yallarhammar fly, which is a full-length Palmer hackle. He said this is the original way the fly was tied, not the shortcut version found in Tennessee. The Tennessee Yallarhammar usually has a peacock herl body and two to three wraps of yellow flicker feather dressing. I have used many of the Palmer hackled versions referred to by Craig, tied by Ernest Ramsey of Muddy Creek, Tennessee.

"Another old fly rarely seen these days is the Wasp Nymph, which I believe was a caddis fly imitator. The Forked Tail (which may have been tied by Kirk Jenkins of Newport, Tennessee, for the Weber Company) was another favorite pattern, as was the Pale Watery Dun. The latter fly has large mallard wings and a large, forked tail that enables it to ride high in the water," said Craig.

Ben Craig was the quintessential Smoky Mountains fly tyer. An ordained deacon in his Southern Baptist Church, he probably spent less money to produce more flies than anyone else. Tucked away in his fly-tying parlor were remnants of the rabbit fur coats popular among women years ago. Rather than buy expensive fur dubbing, Craig placed chunks from these coats and other sources in a blender. In three seconds, he had a handful of fur dubbing equal to that sold in fly shops. Craig received all types of fur and feathers, from caribou and elk, to wild turkey and wood duck, from his many hunting friends.

Craig was asked to help write books on fly tying in the Great Smoky Mountains, as well as to help produce instructional videos on how to tie the many flies of the region. However, until my interview with him, he had never allowed a writer to publish this information.

"Trout fishing in the Great Smoky Mountains National Park is a very personal thing for me. In recent years it has become increasingly difficult to find a stretch of stream where tubers and tourists don't pester you to death," said Craig. "I have shared my tying knowledge with many local tyers, but my privacy is extremely important to me."

Such well-known modern tyers in western North Carolina as Kevin Howell and Roger Lowe are living proof that Benny Joe Craig passed along a heap of knowledge before going to that placid pool at the greatest of all Back of Beyonds.

chapter 12

Ray Ball:
The Last Mountain Man

by Greg Ward

I FIRST MET RAY BALL in 1993 when I opened a fly shop and fishing store in Pigeon Forge, Tennessee. A tall, lanky man wearing his trademark coveralls and an old floppy hat, Ray was looking for fly-tying thread, and I had the best. Gudebrod thread started a friendship that has lasted for years. I soon learned that Ray Ball has mastered the outdoors. He is the only person I know who does it all. I have never spoken with Ray and not learned something new.

Ray, who is 59 years old, is the son of a Baptist minister and has been married to his wife, Connie King, for 40 years. An accident with a blasting cap cost him most of his left hand when he was only 8 years old, but you would never know it. He runs heavy machinery, sings gospel music, farms, and owns several rental cabins in Sevier County, Tennessee. A couple of the cabins built by Ray have been featured in *Better Homes & Gardens* magazine. Whether he is building a cabin, tying a fly, or casting a fly rod, Ray is poetry in motion.

Ray took his first trip into the Smokies to fish in 1963, the year I was born. He fished Elkmont on that first trip and has steadfastly fly-fished the Smokies since I met him in 1993. He ties his own flies and, like me, prefers to dry fly-fish. Neither Ray nor I are purists by any stretch of the imagination. We both enjoy the thrill of tricking wild trout to feed from the surface.

Ray often begins a trip to the Smokies in his tack room gathering bridles, saddles, and packs to venture deep within the mountain on horseback. Once he has set up a base camp, he moves on to areas where few boot prints have ever

Ray Ball working pocket water at one of his secret high-country streams.

marred the soil. He sometimes spends up to two weeks in the rough, covering more ground than I can cover in a season. Ray only keeps enough fish to make a good evening supper.

A fresh mess of trout is the way to go, and a lot of Ray's day trips are purely catch and release. Thank God for that because Ray Ball could deplete an area of fish if he were not an ethical angler and woodsman. If you searched any of Ray's campsites, you would find only a boot print or a horse print. Many old-timers ask Ray to bring them a mess of wild trout. Reverend Melvin Carr did just that last fall. I received a phone call from Ray—

RAY: *Greg, do you think the good Lord helps us to catch fish?*

GREG: *Absolutely.*

RAY: *Do you know Dr. Charles Stanley?*

GREG: *I have a couple of his books and my mother goes and sees him when he is in town and watches him on TV.*

RAY: *Well, last fall Preacher Carr asked me if I could catch Dr. Stanley a mess of fish while he was in town. I was too busy the first afternoon but went the second. I went to Little River after work and caught four rainbows and a brown that was all of 14 to 16 inches. They was all fat as a tick on a coon dog and I had 'em clean and up to Melvin's house in less than an hour. I'll send you a picture on your phone.*

GREG: *OK.*

RAY: *See ya, bye.*

The picture I received a few minutes later shocked me. Five trout—four bows and a brown—that were all 14- to 16-inch fat fish. Ray's Case XX knife was on the rock he had laid the fish on to take the picture. I would have to fish for a month to catch five quality fish like those which he caught. Noteworthy too is the fact that Ray caught them on a dry in a mere 30 minutes. I can only hope that Melvin fed them to Dr. Stanley because a limit of fish like that is as rare as hen's teeth.

Ray fishes Sage and Orvis rods. If they ever wanted the USA to medal in the fly-fishing part of the Olympics, they need to send Ray Ball.

Here's another snippet of a conversation I had with Ray a few weeks ago.

GREG: *Hey, Ray. Where you been?*

RAY: *I told you I've been up a campin' in the mountains. I was wantin' a mess of brook trout!*

GREG: *Do you still have skillets hidden along the streams?*

RAY: *No, the bears have been diggin' 'em up. I used to just hang an iron skillet on a hemlock tree but the bears was gettin' 'em. So I started puttin' 'em in a plastic bag and buryin' 'em. The bears is diggin' 'em up though. I think they're after the curin' or they can smell the trout or taters and onions I fried in 'em. I take a stainless steel one in my backpack if I'm a goin' for a short trip and ain't got my horses or in a place you can't take horses.*

GREG: *How did you do?*

RAY: *I caught the hound out of 'em. I was a wantin' brook trout so I went where they ain't no trails but the creek. I was up close to the Appalachy Trail. They must of been a big flood or mudslide cuz the river changed.*

GREG: *What do you mean?*

RAY: *The river wasn't where it was supposed to be. It was gone for about a half a mile. They was a mudslide that made a dam about 30 feet high full of big trees, and the creek went off another holler and made a new 60-foot-high falls and come back around were it was suppose to be. They weren't no fish above that slide. I guess it warshed 'em over when it went. I figured I'm gonna have to get on up outta here.*

GREG: *How many did you catch?*

RAY: *A hundred and sixty.*

GREG: *In one day?*

RAY: *No, I stayed overnight in the mountains. They is an overhangin' rock you can get up in under if it starts to rain or you're a needin' a place to shelter up there. I got me one of those one burner stoves to carry in my back pack. The brook trout was everywhere. They had black backs like a rainbow does in a deep pool. I'll send you a picture when we hang up.*

GREG: *How many rainbows did you catch?*

RAY: *Five or six both days. It was mainly brook trout and they was nice ones. You reckon they got sun burnt with black backs?*

GREG: *I have caught largemouth in Florida that don't look anything like ours. They're black. I think it's got something to do with the acidity of the water.*

RAY: *Well, they was real good eatin'.*

GREG: *Anything is when you're up in the mountains like that.*

RAY: *See ya, bye.*

chapter 13

Bases of Operations, Guides, and Fly Shops

EIGHT TO 10 MILLION PEOPLE annually visit the Great Smoky Mountains National Park, making it the most visited national park. The second most heavily visited national park is Grand Canyon with 4.4 million visitors; third is Yosemite with 3.4 million; and fourth is Olympic with 3.1 million. Approximately 60 percent enter the Great Smoky Mountains National Park by way of Gatlinburg; approximately 23 percent enter by way of Cherokee; and approximately 10 percent enter by way of Townsend. Most stay in or near these locales or at Fontana Village Resort on the south shore of Fontana Lake. There are streams within minutes of each of these four major tourist stops.

GATLINBURG: The West Prong of the Little Pigeon River flows through the heart of the busy resort area. It offers excellent rainbow and brown trout fishing. Greenbrier River (the Middle Prong of the Little Pigeon River) is located 6 miles east of Gatlinburg off TN 73. This beautiful rivulet offers mediocre fishing for rainbow and brown trout. Little River, located 6 miles from Gatlinburg by way of the Little River Road (formerly TN 73), offers good rainbow and brown trout fishing. Abrams Creek, one of the better streams in the park, is easily accessible from the Cades Cove area, located 30 miles from Gatlinburg.

CHEROKEE: The Oconaluftee River and Raven Fork flow together just upstream from this picturesque town. Both of these fine streams offer very good

110

fishing. The Transmountain Highway (formerly US 441) follows alongside the Oconaluftee, offering excellent access. Raven Fork is accessible upstream from the park boundary by trail only. Deep Creek, which flows out of the park near Bryson City, is also a sound bet for a day of good fishing.

FONTANA: Anglers wishing to sample the streams that flow into beautiful Fontana Lake can find no better base of operations than the Fontana Village Resort. Eagle, Hazel, Forney, and Chambers Creeks all flow into Fontana Lake. The resort's marina will rent boats to cross the lake, or will caddy anglers across to these streams and pick them up later for a modest fee. The lake offers superb smallmouth, walleye, and musky fishing. More information is available from the Fontana Village Resort, Fontana Dam, NC 28733.

THE GATLINBURG, CHEROKEE, AND TOWNSEND entrances to the Great Smoky Mountains National Park account for anywhere from 80 to 90 percent of the annual traffic. There are other areas which, though less well known, can be equally sound choices.

COSBY: This entrance is popular, particularly among campers. From here you have excellent fishing opportunities at the nearby Greenbrier River (Middle Prong of the Little Pigeon River), the West Prong of the Little Pigeon (near Gatlinburg), Big Creek (off I-40 in North Carolina), and, of course, Little Cosby Creek at the campground.

BIG CREEK CAMPGROUND: Anglers staying here are among the most isolated, since waters outside the Big Creek drainage are a considerable distance away. The nearest are the Greenbrier River (the Middle Prong of the Little Pigeon River in Tennessee) and the Cataloochee Creek in North Carolina.

CATALOOCHEE CREEK: Campers/anglers here are in much the same shape as those staying at the primitive campground at Big Creek. Big Creek is the only other trout stream within a reasonable driving distance of Cataloochee Creek.

BRYSON CITY: This town makes one of the finest trout fishing bases on the North Carolina side of the park. Deep Creek is only minutes from the Bryson City limits, and Noland Creek is only a short drive away on the unfinished North Shore Road. The Oconaluftee River is also nearby.

ABRAMS CREEK CAMPGROUND: This primitive campground makes an excellent base of operations for fishing not only the lower portion of Abrams and its tributary, Panther Creek, but also nearby Twenty Mile Creek and Eagle Creek, plus a number of smaller streams such as Tabcat Creek in North Carolina.

Fly Shop Information

WHEN MY *Smoky Mountains Trout Fishing Guide* first went to press in the early 1980s there was not a decent fishing tackle shop that concentrated exclusively on the Smokies, or any guide services of note in the area. Today there are several. My personal favorite is the coauthor of this book, Greg Ward of Rocky Top Outfitters. He has a no-nonsense, hard-core, catch-em-while-they're-hot approach that fits my personality. Greg is one of the Smokies' top fly-fishing experts, and his guides are outstanding.

TENNESSEE

Adam's Fly Shop
Route 2, Box 122
Reliance, TN 37369
(423) 338-2162

Choo-Choo Fly & Tackle
319 Cherokee Boulevard
Chattanooga, TN 37405
(423) 267-0024

Clinch River House Guides
526 New Clear Branch Road
Lake City, TN 37769
(865) 426-2715

The Creel
6907 Kingston Pike
Knoxville, TN 37919
(865) 588-6159

Dry Fly Outfitters
Highway 411 & Highway 30
Benton, TN
(423) 338-6263

East Tennessee Fly Fishing
111 Infinity Drive
Elizabethton, TN 37643
(423) 474-4388
www.tnflyfishing.com

Fair Game Ltd.
5703 Old Harding Pike
Nashville, TN. 37205
(615) 353-0602

Fightmaster Fly Fisher
PO Box 4146
Maryville, TN 37802
(865) 233-0914

Feather & Fly
2401 South Broad Street
Chattanooga, TN 37408
(423) 265-0306

Fly Fish Tennessee
Guide Service
www.flyfishtennessee.com

Fly Shop of Tennessee
102 Willmary Road
Johnson City, TN 37601
(423) 928-2007

High Country Angler Fly Fishing
Gray, TN
(704) 641-6815

Hiwassee Angler
179 Tellico Reliance Road
Reliance, TN 37369
(423) 338-8500
www.hiwasseeangler.com

The Holston Angler
110 Poplar Ridge Road
Piney Flats, TN 37686
(423) 538-7412

Little River Outfitters
7807 E. Lamar Alexander
Parkway
Townsend, TN 37882
(865) 448-9459
www.littleriveroutfitters.com

Mahoney's
830 Sunset Drive
Johnson City, TN 37604
(423) 282-5413

Old Smoky Outfitters
511 Parkway
Gatlinburg, TN 37738
(865) 430-1936
 www.oldsmokyoutfitters.com

Orvis Retail Store
136 Apple Valley Road
Sevierville, TN 37862
(865) 774-4162

Rocky Top Outfitters
2611 Ruth Hall Road
Pigeon Forge, TN 37863
(865) 661-3474

Outdoor Adventures
2501 North Ocoee Street
Cleveland, TN
(423) 472-4772

R & R Fly Fishing
PO Box 60
Townsend, TN 37882
(865) 766-5935

Smoky Mountain Anglers
Brookside Village,
Highway 321 North
Gatlinburg, TN 37738
(865) 436-8746

Smoky Mountain Gillies
4524 Martin Mill Pike
Knoxville, TN 37920
(865) 577-4289

Smoky Mountain Troutfitters
(865) 567-2441
www.smokymountain
 troutfitters.com

Telliqua Outfitters
1650 Cherohala Skyway
Tellico Plains, TN 37385
(423) 536-8143
www.telliquahoutfitters.com

Wynn's Sporting Goods
541 Wynnfield Dunn Parkway
Sevierville, TN 37864
(865) 453-4877

Xtreme Trout
(615) 438-2119
www.xtremetrout.com

NORTH CAROLINA

Altamont Anglers
Fly Fishing Guides
30 Caledonia Road
Asheville, NC 28803
(828) 252-9266 or
(828) 775-0714

Appalachian Angler Fly Shop
174 Old Shulls Mill Road
Boone NC 28607
(828) 963-8383

Asheville Drifters Fly Fishing
Guides
48 Westall Avenue
Asheville, NC 28804
(828) 215-7379

Brookings Fly Shop
Chestnut Square Highway 64
Cashiers, NC 28717
(828) 743-3768

Brown Trout Fly Fishing Guides
Asheville, NC
Brown Hobson
(803) 431-9437

Casters Fly Shop & Guide
 Service
3034-A North Center Street
Hickory, NC 28601
(828) 304-2400

Curtis Wright Outfitters
 Fly Shop
24 North Main Street
Weaverville, NC 28787-9427
(828) 645-8700

Curtis Wright Outfitters
 Fly Shop
111 East Main Street
Saluda, NC 28773
(828) 749-3444

Curtis Wright Outfitters
 Fly Shop
5 All Souls Crescent
Asheville, NC 28803
(828) 274-3471

Davidson Outfitters Fly Shop
4 Pisgah Highway
Pisgah Forest, NC 28768
(828) 877-4181

Foscoe Fishing Fly Shop
9378-1 Highway 105 South
Banner Elk, NC 28604
(828) 963-6556

Headwaters Outfitters Fly Shop
25 Parkway Road
Rosman, NC 28772
(828) 877-3106

Hunter Banks Fly Shop
29 Montford Avenue
Asheville, NC 28801
(800) 227-6732

NORTH CAROLINA

Jeffrey Wilkins Fly Fishing
3703 Windspray Court
Summerfield, NC 27358
(336) 644-7775
www.jeffreywilkins
    flyfishing.com

Lowe Guide Service
(828) 452-0039
Waynesville, NC

One Fly Outfitters, LTD
112 Cherry Street
Black Mountain, NC 28711
(828) 669-6939
www.oneflyoutfitters.com

Rivers Edge Outfitters
280 Oak Avenue
Spruce Pine, NC 28777
(828) 765-3474
www.riversedge
    outfittersnc.com

Smoky Mountain Adventure
PO Box 995
Bryson City, North Carolina
28713
(828) 736-7501
www.steveclaxton.com

Smoky Mountain Flyfishing
PO Box 1169
Cherokee, NC 28719
(828) 497-1555
www.smokymountain
    flyfishing.net

Smoky Mountains On The Fly
(828) 586-4748
www.smokyonthefly.com

Smoky Mountain Outdoors
    Unlimited
1012 East Alaska Road
Bryson City, NC 28713
(828) 488-9711
www.smokymountains
    outdoorsunlimited.com

Waynesville Fly Shop
168 South Main Street
Waynesville, NC 28786
(828) 246-0306
www.waynesvilleflyshop.com

License Requirements and Park Fishing Regulations

EITHER A NORTH CAROLINA OR TENNESSEE license entitles the angler to fish anywhere within the park boundaries. Fishing regulations change. Currently, regulations allow artificial-only lures/flies; four trout/bass (minimum 7 inches long); daytime only, year-round fishing. The devil is in the details. Some creeks have been closed since 1975, while others are open. We strongly recommend that you obtain a copy of the current fishing regulations and peruse them carefully. Fines for infractions can be substantial; however, threats of summary execution for possessing live grasshoppers are just some rangers' way of having a little fun in the great outdoors. Copies of current fishing regulations may be obtained at the Sugarlands Visitors Center, located 2 miles south of Gatlinburg in the park, or by writing the Superintendent of the Great Smoky Mountains National Park, Gatlinburg, TN 37738.

chapter 14

Middle Prong of the Little Pigeon River System

Middle Prong of the Little Pigeon River

SIZE: Large at the park boundary, smaller upstream

FISHING PRESSURE: Heavy

FISHING QUALITY: Fair, at its best in early spring

ACCESS: Greenbrier Road; Ramsey Prong Road Trail

USGS QUADS: Mt. LeConte, NC–TN; Mt. Guyot, NC–TN

IF YOU ARE STAYING IN THE GATLINBURG/PIGEON FORGE AREA, this is the place to go if you want to beat the crowds. This streamshed gets less pressure these days than it did when my first trout fishing guidebook on park waters was published in 1979. That's remarkable, because angling success has improved on these waters.

The Middle Prong of the Little Pigeon River (locally referred to as the Middle Prong or Greenbrier Creek) is one of the more rugged watersheds. Prior to becoming part of a national park, Greenbrier Cove was a sparsely populated, primitive area. The terrain displays an ancient face. Wisely, the National Park Service chose not to develop this area, slowly phasing out camping and auto access. Partially logged in the very early 1900s, the area is well known for its virgin stands of huge trees, including giant cherry tree. The Greenbrier Creek watershed is located in the northwest section of the park upstream from Emert's

115

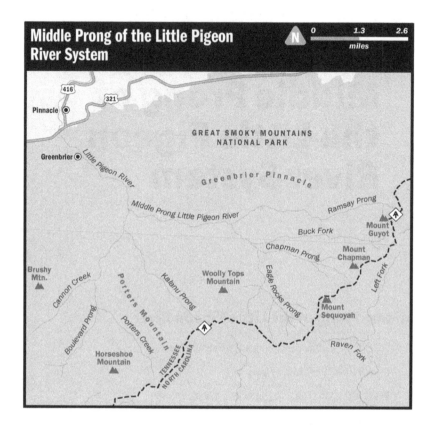

Cove. Mt. LeConte, one of the highest peaks in the eastern United States, forms the boundary of the watershed to the south, with Mt. Guyot to the east. The primary tributaries are Porters Creek, Ramsey Prong, Buck Fork, Eagle Rock Prong, and Chapman Prong.

The Greenbrier is a rough-and-tumble cascading creek, rushing over thousands of huge boulders, forming countless trout-holding pools. Getting to these trout requires a bit of work, due to the extreme ruggedness of the terrain. But a day of fishing here is a surefire cure for insomnia.

Greenbrier Creek sports all three species of trout. Rainbows are the most abundant. Brown trout have established a foothold in the lower reaches as a result of stockings outside the park. In recent years the state of Tennessee has dramatically curtailed its brown trout stocking efforts downstream from the park, resulting in fewer catches of these large fish in the park. Brook trout still flourish in the majority of the headwater streams.

Greenbrier Creek is not a premium trout stream, although if you hit it at the right time it can be very good fishing. This watershed has traditionally been prone to flash floods, which not only kill fish but have a scouring effect on the bottom fauna. This is a problem that hits all streams in the Smokies from time to time. Its effects are certainly evident, but these splashes of water have been here a long time. Back in the 1960s, Sue Lungsford of nearby Cosby taught me a method for catching trout on flies, which has long been quite popular with the local fishermen. Using pretty ho-hum fly tackle, rather than a traditional leader, 40 feet of 4-pound test monofilament line is spooled onto a fly reel (preferably an automatic South Bend if you are a traditionalist). Using heavily weighted Yallarhammers with plumb peacock herl bodies, these are cast into the run much the same as fly line is shot, but then they are fished much the same as the way Europeans pin. It takes a bit of practice, but because flies get down so fast on taut lines, it's a little tough not to set the hook when a strike occurs—and strikes will occur nearly every cast. This approach does not work well if you are like me and prefer to fish upstream to avoid spooking trout. However, it is awesome for "side flicking" if you are nimble enough to slither along the boulders on your belly.

The upper reaches of this streamshed are packed with native brookies.

Greenbrier Creek is at its best in early spring. There is a good population of stone flies in this watershed, so stone fly imitations (basically nymphs) are always trout-getters. Nice hatches of small, gray mayflies take place in the last few weeks of April, making for pretty fair fly-fishing.

The presence of smallmouth bass in the lower reaches of the main river is the well-kept secret of a handful of local anglers. Bronzebacks in excess of 4 pounds are routinely caught downstream from the mouth of Porters Creek. Muddler Minnows and Dace-style streamers are the ticket for catching these bruisers.

Several years ago my dad and I were driving up the gravel road beside the main stream to the old Ramsey Cascade Road. Rounding a curve I spotted a shiny old Jaguar XKE. The vintage jag was stunning. I slowed to get a long look at it. Dad was watching the creek. Down on the stream where most of the flow constricted between large gray boulders to form a deep pool, he spotted two naked young ladies. Insisting that I stop, he leaped from the cab, fetched his fly rod and headed for the creek.

He rushed forward as if they were damsels in distress in need of rescue. Seeing Dad's approach, a lounge-lizard-looking photographer tried to wave him off, shouting "Go on, we're working!" As Dad made his first step down the 90-degree gully, the last thing I heard him yell back at the man was, "It's okay, we're working too." Then Dad's feet went from under him, sending him on a 25-foot spill reminiscent of a water park slide. We never discussed the incident, other than to note that fishing was pretty uneventful that day.

ACCESS: Greenbrier Creek flows under TN 73, 6 miles east of Gatlinburg. Entrance to the park is possible by turning onto the Greenbrier Road at the concrete bridge.

The Greenbrier Road allows stream access by auto as far as the ranger station (.9 mile). This section of road is open year-round. During the fishing season, an additional 2.5 miles of gravel road alongside the stream are also open.

Further access to the main stream is possible via the Ramsey Prong Road Trail, which begins at the end of the road. It generally follows the stream, ending at the junction of Ramsey Prong (1.7 miles). There is no further access to the main stream.

Porters Creek

SIZE: Medium

FISHING PRESSURE: Moderate

FISHING QUALITY: Good

ACCESS: Porters Creek Road

USGS QUADS: Mt. LeConte, NC–TN; Mt. Guyot, NC–TN

PORTERS CREEK IS GENTLE AND EASIER-GOING than the main stream. It would be difficult to be disappointed by a fishless day on this sparkling rivulet. The streamside flora is most engrossing. Probably the most popular to fly-fish of the feeder streams in this watershed, it is not only fairly easy fishing, but getting around on it is not as hazardous as gray boulder jumping other rivulets here.

Porters Creek is primarily a rainbow trout stream, although there are still a few brook trout in the most remote headwater areas. The mouth of the stream is located 3.2 miles upstream from the park boundary. Porters Creek flows off the steep slopes of Mt. LeConte. Its principal tributaries are False Gap Prong, Long Branch, and Cannon Creek. False Gap Prong provides perhaps the best fishing of the three.

ACCESS: Automobile access to Porters Creek is possible using the Porters Creek Road, which begins at the junction of Greenbrier Creek and Porters Creek (Porters Creek flows from the right). This gravel road follows upstream 1 mile to a large parking area. Backcountry campsite Porters Flat (#31; elevation 3,400 feet) is located where fishing ends and climbing up to the Appalachian Trail begins.

The Porters Creek Trail, which starts at the parking area, follows alongside the stream to its headwaters. Fishable tributaries along Porters Creek include Boulevard Creek (1.4 miles), Cannon Creek (1.5 miles), Long Branch (2.4 miles), False Gap Creek (2.75 miles), Kalanu Prong (1.5 miles), Lowes Creek (1.5 miles), and Shultz Prong (1.2 miles)

Ramsey Prong

SIZE: Small

FISHING PRESSURE: Moderately light

FISHING QUALITY: Fair

ACCESS: Ramsey Cascades Trail

USGS QUADS: Mt. Guyot, NC-TN

THE HEADWATERS OF THIS LITTLE STREAM begin at an elevation of around 6,200 feet. It is a nice little brook trout stream. The only drawback is the occasionally crowded trail conditions. When I was in my early teens I would ride my old Honda 90cc bike up to the Cascades, which were open to traffic then (along with other places such as Walnut Bottoms on Big Creek). From there I would fish upstream above the Cascades to the Drinkwater Pool. There I would wolf down a pair of peanut butter and wild strawberry jam sandwiches my mom made (wild strawberry, blackberry, or blueberry picking with Geneva was mandatory as long as I resided under her roof). After washing the sandwiches down with creek water, I would nap on the moss-covered boulders thinking that Bilbo Baggins might emerge from the virgin stands of beech at anytime.

Fishing above the Cascades to the Drinkwater Pool is better now than it was two decades ago, but upstream from these riprap rapids, fishing about the pool remains poor and not worth the effort. According to records dating back almost a century, inherent acrid conditions from leeching iron pyrite have always been a key limiting factor in trout population found in the headwaters. Many are unaware today that the Smoky Mountains were originally known as the Iron Mountains.

ACCESS: The Ramsey Cascades Trail provides access up to the Cascades (2.5 miles). There are no maintained trails upstream from that point. Barefootin' in the creek is the traditional method beyond this point.

Buck Fork

SIZE: Small

FISHING QUALITY: Good, particularly in late summer

ACCESS: Remote

USGS QUADS: Mt. Guyot, NC–TN

BUCK FORK IS A BROOK TROUT STREAM. Eight of the stream's prongs begin at an elevation of more than 5,000 feet. Fishing all day up this stream was like spending a day in Maine or along the highlands of the Gaspe Peninsula in Quebec. Towering fir and spruce shade the sun's rays, as the crystal-clear creek tumbles over moss-encrusted boulders into foaming pools.

ACCESS: The mouth of Buck Fork is located .7 miles from the terminus of the Ramsey Prong Road Trail. Note: It is rough going to the mouth of the stream.

Eagle Rock Creek

SIZE: Small

FISHING QUALITY: Good

ACCESS: Remote

USGS QUADS: Mt. Guyot, NC–TN

EAGLE ROCK CREEK WAS A FAVORITE HAUNT of mountain men during the pre-park era. It was a good brook trout stream. Nine feeder streams begin at an elevation of more than 4,500 feet. Eagle Rock Creek flows into the main stream from the right one mile upstream from the terminus of the Ramsey Road Trail. There are no access trails.

Chapman Prong

SIZE: Small

FISHING PRESSURE: Moderately light

FISHING QUALITY: Fairly good, at its best in late summer

ACCESS: Remote

USGS QUADS: Mt. LeConte, NC–TN

THE CONFLUENCE OF CHAPMAN PRONG AND LOST CREEK forms the starting point of the Middle Prong of the Little Pigeon River. Chapman Prong offers fairly good fishing for speckled trout. The trout here are small, but scrappy and very colorful.

Streams such as this are at their best on rainy days during the hot summer months. A shower starts trout feeding. Ant patterns are lethal during such times.

ACCESS: Chapman Prong is in one of the more remote sections of the Smokies. The stream's mouth is located 1.6 miles upstream from the terminus of the Ramsey Road Trail.

chapter 15

West Prong of the Little Pigeon River System

West Prong of The Little Pigeon River

SIZE: Large to medium

FISHING PRESSURE: Moderate to surprisingly light

FISHING QUALITY: Very good to excellent

ACCESS: Newfound Gap Road

USGS QUADS: Mt. LeConte, NC–TN; Clingmans Dome, NC–TN; Gatlinburg, TN

FOR FLY-FISHERMEN SHORT ON TIME but still looking for outstanding casting for trout and bass, the easily accessed West Prong of the Little Pigeon River is perfect. Despite the fact that its main channel courses along a major throughway in the national park, it still offers excellent fly-fishing for trout and bass.

The West Prong of the Little Pigeon River has been the general over-mountain route of travelers for centuries. Long before white men cast their shadows on these mountains, Native Americans traveled to and fro across the crest of the ridge alongside this stream. During the early 1830s, the Cherokees built a toll road that ran along the same route as Road Prong (thus the branch gained its name). During the Civil War, both armies used the West Prong as a route through the rugged Smokies. Colonel Clingman, the military explorer of the Smokies, also used it as his route when ascending Clingmans Dome, once thought to be the highest point in the eastern United States.

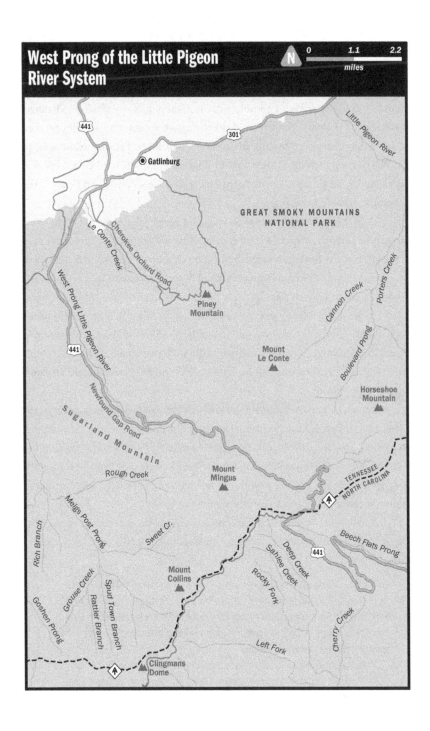

West Prong of the Little Pigeon
River System

N

0   1.1   2.2
miles

441

301

Little Pigeon River

Gatlinburg

GREAT SMOKY MOUNTAINS
NATIONAL PARK

Le Conte Creek

Cherokee Orchard Road

West Prong Little Pigeon River

441

Piney
Mountain

Mount
Le Conte

Cannon Creek

Porters Creek

Boulevard Prong

Horseshoe
Mountain

Newfound Gap Road

Sugarland Mountain

Rough Creek

Mount
Mingus

TENNESSEE
NORTH CAROLINA

Meigs Post Prong

Sweet Cr.

Beech Flats Prong

441

Rich Branch

Deep Creek

Sahlee Creek

Rocky Fork

Cherry Creek

Goshen Prong

Grouse Creek

Rattler Branch

Spud Town Branch

Mount
Collins

Left Fork

Clingmans
Dome

The West Prong's watershed was thoroughly logged to the fir forest line. This area's farming and commerce were well developed. The forest has regained much of its lost stature, but open meadows crisscrossed with hand-laid stone fences can still be found.

The West Prong has one of the steepest descents of any stream in the Smokies, draining some of the highest mountains in the Appalachian range. Upon leaving the park, the stream flows through the center of Gatlinburg, then on to Sevierville, where it joins the Little Pigeon River. Primary tributaries to the West Prong include Dudley Creek, Roaring Fork, LeConte Creek, Walker Creek, and Road Prong. The confluence of Walker Creek and Road Prong is the beginning of the West Prong.

Anglers staying in Gatlinburg or Pigeon Forge will discover that the West Prong offers Smoky Mountain trout fishing with only a minimum amount of fuss. The quality of the fishing is surprisingly good despite its almost urban location. This stream abounds with a large number of 8- to 11-inch fish. Yet I've had more fish in the 16- to 18-inch class buzz my flies here than anywhere else in the park.

At one time, there was a rearing station at what is now the Chimney Tops Picnic Grounds. The stream annually received thousands of rainbow trout. The rainbows have done exceptionally well, reaching 3 to 4 pounds with regularity. Brook trout can still be found in several of the headwater streams, notably Road Prong.

Brown trout have invaded the lower stretches of the West Prong in recent years. Trophy browns are occasionally taken, but rainbows are by far the most numerous. The West Prong can be a treacherous little creek to get around on. Plunge pools are surrounded by deceptively slick huge gray boulders. In addition, the stream is often very swift and turbulent. Accordingly, some stretches seldom see more than one to two fishermen per week.

Smallmouth and rock bass are most common downstream from the Sugarland Rangers Headquarters. Look for these fish in the tails of large pools and along ledges.

ACCESS: The West Prong of the Little Pigeon River is accessible by auto from Newfound Gap Road, which runs alongside the stream to about 4,500 feet. This road connects Gatlinburg, Tennessee, with Cherokee, North Carolina. There is ample roadside parking along the entire route, although traffic may at times be extremely heavy.

No maintained trails offer continuous access to the stream. The National Park Service has in recent years established a number of "quiet walkways" which lead to the stream. It is amazing how few anglers use these

*Great fly-fishing is available just upstream
from the Gatlinburg city limits.*

pathways. There are no backcountry primitive or developed campsites within the bounds of the West Prong of the Little Pigeon watershed.

Dudley Creek

SIZE: Small

FISHING PRESSURE: Light

FISHING QUALITY: Good to fair

ACCESS: At the park boundary from TN 73

USGS QUADS: Mt. LeConte, NC–TN

DUDLEY CREEK IS A SUPER LITTLE TROUT STREAM located only a short drive from Gatlinburg. This stream is fished only occasionally by visiting anglers, probably because of its relatively small size and somewhat obscure location. The stream has a decent population of rainbow trout in its lower reaches, and brook trout can still be found in the headwaters. Fishing was better there a couple of decades ago when I used to slip up this little ribbon of water on afternoons when time was too scarce to venture into the bowels of the park. Still, it is a lot more fun than spending time with your wife pounding the pavement in Gatlinburg to buy things of no particular worth other than the fact they are folksy curiosities.

Novice anglers and even so so-called master casters concede in print that this a difficult stream to fish because of the dense flora. Laurel and rhododendron thickets shroud many fine pools from the reach of all but the most experienced casters. These dense, overgrown sections of Dudley Creek rarely see the fraudulent offerings of the fisherman, especially above the third cascade.

Tributaries of Dudley Creek that warrant mention are Twin Creek and Little Dudley Creek. If you make it that far, please be good enough to keep an eye out for a Rolex watch I lost up there. I would be more than grateful to get it back on my line-mending hand.

There has been some criticism of my past opinion of fishing at Dudley Creek. When I first trekked up this stream, it offered great fishing. However, since the stocking program began, fishing has dulled. Of course, during my most recent trips up this rill, I was stone-cold sober, which may account for past recollections of this little gem. On the other hand, though, perhaps as Herodotus, the Greek historian said: "Those who can do no better should teach the young."

ACCESS: Auto access to Dudley Creek is possible via TN 73. The stream passes out of the park approximately 1.8 miles east of Gatlinburg, and flows alongside the highway. There are no maintained trails inside the park, but an old National Park Service fire road provides excellent access to the stream for a short distance.

Roaring Fork

SIZE: Small

FISHING PRESSURE: Light to moderate

FISHING QUALITY: Excellent

ACCESS: Roaring Fork Motor Nature Trail, Trillium Gap Trail

USGS QUADS: Mt. LeConte, NC–TN

ROARING FORK HAS LONG BEEN ONE OF MY FAVORITE STREAMS in the

Smokies. Located near the heart of Gatlinburg, it offers excellent rainbow and brook trout fishing despite its almost cosmopolitan locale.

Roaring Fork boasts the distinction of having the most drastic descent of any stream its size in the eastern United States. This fact accounts for the loud roar and almost continuous series of cascades and deep pools. These oxygen-rich waters support a prolific population of stone flies. A well-tied stone fly nymph cast into its foaming pools will produce action. Indian Camp Branch and Surry Branch are tributaries that offer good fishing.

ACCESS: Roaring Fork is accessible by auto from the Roaring Fork Motor Nature Trail, a one-way road. It is popular to park at the end of this road and walk in to fish, thus avoiding the drive around the loop.

The Trillium Gap Trail offers further access to the stream. It begins at the Grotto Falls parking area. At 1.5 miles it crosses the stream, and at 4.4 miles arrives at the headwaters of Surry Branch, a tributary of Roaring Fork.

LeConte Creek

SIZE: Small

FISHING PRESSURE: Moderate

FISHING QUALITY: Fair

ACCESS: Roaring Fork Motor Nature Trail, Rainbow Falls Trail

USGS QUADS: Mt. LeConte, NC–TN

LeConte Creek is located alongside one of the most popular foot and horse trails in the Smokies. This fact has not enhanced the fishing. Everywhere, hikers seem to grow like mushrooms. It is a nice little stream to fish, though privacy is elusive. There is a fairly remote reach of the stream from where the trail leaves it to skirt Scratch Britches Ridge that is pretty decent fishing. Additionally, downstream from where the trail first crosses the stream and the Twin Creeks Uplands Research facility is good during early spring when there is average to above average flow. There the gradient is surprisingly mild, and thanks to the Johnny Appleseed Memorial trout-stocking program in Gatlinburg, a few heavy fish find their way. I know, big 'bow are supposed to migrate downstream, but these are hatchery stock, so far removed from the natural world that some of them have actually been observed smoking cigarettes.

ACCESS: Auto access to LeConte Creek is provided by the Roaring Fork

Motor Nature Trail, which follows alongside the stream. Trail access is provided by the Rainbow Falls Trail, which begins off the Cherokee Orchard Road at 4.3 miles, and follows the stream 2 miles to Rainbow Falls. The fishing quality upstream from the falls is poor.

Road Prong

SIZE: Small

FISHING PRESSURE: Moderate

FISHING QUALITY: Excellent

ACCESS: Newfound Gap Road; Road Prong Trail

USGS QUADS: Mt. LeConte, NC–TN; Clingmans Dome, NC–TN

ROAD PRONG IS ONE OF THE BETTER STREAMS forming the headwaters of West Prong. Rainbow trout occupy the lower levels of the stream. The upper reaches hold a fine population of frisky specs. A total of seven tributary prongs begin at an elevation of more than 4,800 feet.

Road Prong passes through the lovely Beech Flats area, considered one of the prettiest sections of the Smokies. There are a number of cascades and pools that can be easily fished by even a novice trouter.

ACCESS: The confluence of Road Prong and Walker Camp Prong is 8.7 miles south of the Sugarland Center, on Newfound Gap Road. There is no further auto access to the stream.

The Road Prong Trail offers access to the creek further upstream. It follows alongside the stream for 3.1 miles, to its headwaters.

Walker Camp Prong

SIZE: Small to medium

FISHING PRESSURE: Moderate

FISHING QUALITY: Poor

ACCESS: Newfound Gap Road; Alum Camp Trail

USGS QUADS: Mt. LeConte, NC–TN; Clingmans Dome, NC–TN

THE CONFLUENCE OF WALKER CAMP PRONG and Road Prong marks the beginning of the West Prong, which seems to have all the necessary qualities of a good trout stream. Unfortunately, the fishing is below par for this watershed.

The headwaters of Walker Camp Prong flow over a formation of acid-bearing shale known as the Anakeesta Formation. For eons Walker Camp Prong flowed over this formation, gradually leaching out and sealing the bulk of the exposed rock's acidic properties. The pH of Walker Camp Prong was always low, but the brook trout and other aquatic life forms found it bearable. When the National Park Service found it necessary to widen Newfound Gap Road alongside the path of the stream, the Anakeesta Formation was unwittingly cut into. The stream was then exposed to this freshly unearthed acid source. To make a bad situation worse, the silty-slatey Anakeesta was crushed into gravel and used as the bed for the new pavement. The aquatic life of this little stream has been damaged by this activity, and the effects will be felt for several lifetimes.

Rainbow trout can be taken in the main stream, and there is still a remnant population of brook trout in the headwaters of the main stream, but overall, fishing here is poor.

Alum Cave Creek, a tributary to Walker Camp Prong, offers mediocre angling for brook trout. It flows into the main stream at a point old-timers call "Grassy Place," a favorite camping spot for mountaineer anglers during pre-park days. Olin Watson, former president of the Smoky Mountains Historical Society, related an amusing story of a fishing trip that took place here around 1910. It seems a group of men from the flatlands decided to spend a few weeks up the West Prong doing a little fishin' and huntin'. At that time, specs were thick as gnats and could easily be caught at any time. One evening, while the day's catch was frying, the jug of moonshine made a round or two around the fire. Now, 'shine often makes for some mighty tall talk, and that evening the subject turned to how many fish a man could eat. As the tale goes, one fellow ate around 80 specs before stopping. He managed to keep the fish down but declined to join the rest of the angling party the next day!

ACCESS: Walker Camp Prong begins 8.7 miles south of the Sugarland Center on Newfound Gap Road. This road offers excellent access to the stream to approximately 4,500 feet in elevation.

Alum Cave Creek flows into the main stream 1.3 miles upstream from the confluence of Walker Camp Prong and Road Prong. Further access is possible via the Alum Camp Trail, which begins at the mouth of the stream.

chapter 16

Little River System

Little River

SIZE: Large

FISHING PRESSURE: Heavy

FISHING QUALITY: Good

ACCESS: Little River Trail

USGS QUADS: Wear Cove, Silers Bald, Clingmans Dome, Gatlinburg

THE UPPER REACHES OF THE LITTLE RIVER, particularly Fish Camp Prong, rank among my favorite fly-fishing destinations in the Great Smoky Mountains National Park. Drifting flies on the gentle glides found on this fair-size stream is about as much fun as man is entitled to have in this life. Trout Unlimited has rated Little River among the top 100 streams in the United States. Much of the stream is easily accessed by opening the door of your truck.

Little River was the site of early pioneer settlements, and the hub of the largest logging operation ever carried out in the Smokies. The Little River Logging Company began cutting operations in 1901, which removed virtually every standing piece of timber by 1938. Those were wild times, because with the logging came a thing seldom seen in the Smokies—hard cash. Logging camps were the sites of numerous duels—and where moonshine flowed free. The scars from this mammoth cutting and subsequent fires are evident even today, although the slopes are gradually recovering their lost splendor.

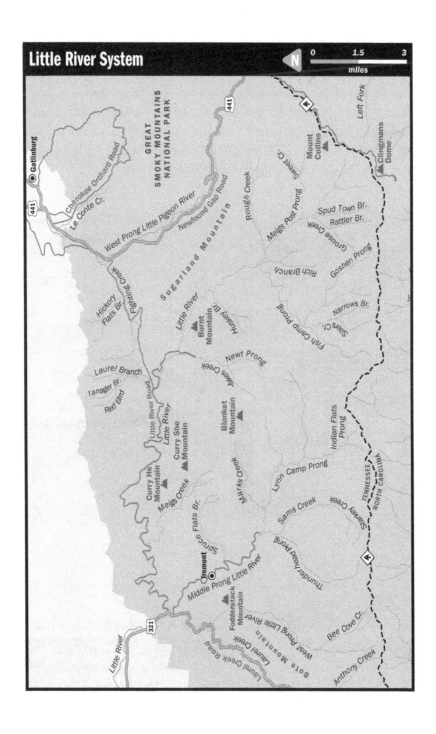

Little River System

All three species of trout now reproducing in the park can be found in the Little River system. The park's largest known brown trout, a hefty 16-pounder, was taken from the East Prong in 1979. Large brown trout in the 3-to-7 pound range are regularly taken from the deep pools of the Little River throughout the year. Yet despite the fact that trophy browns are often taken, rainbow trout are the most abundant. Rainbows that weigh 3 to 4 pounds are occasionally caught, particularly during the early spring and late autumn, but the average rainbow will be 7 to 11 inches long. While brook trout can still be found in this system, most of the brookie water was closed to all fishing in 1975.

H. Lea Lawrence, dear friend of Don Kirk, on one of their frequent fly-fishing trips to the Smokies.

Fishing is good on Little River and its numerous feeder inlets. Fly-fishermen can expect to find sporadic hatches of mayflies and caddis flies, and hatches of large stone flies occur in April and May. Large browns are often taken on a well-tied stone fly nymph pattern.

Anglers should note that during the warm summer months, the main stream and the East Prong of Little River become crowded with fun-seeking swimmers enjoying the stream's cool waters. Fishing becomes nearly impossible when such activity reaches its mid-afternoon peak. The best angling during this time of year is in the early morning and late evening.

A quick look at a map of the Smokies reveals the Little River system is one of the largest in the Smokies, bound on the south by Stateline Ridge, to the east by the Sugarland Mountains, and to the west by Anthony Ridge. There are numerous other ridges and spurs that cut through the Little River Basin. The main stream of Little River is formed by three primary tributaries: the East Prong, the Middle Prong, and the West Prong. All three feeder streams have their own well-developed tributary networks that deserve the investigation of adventurous anglers.

Years ago when my first litter of children were small (Jeff is now 40 years old), we used to take them to Metcalf Bottoms. That portion of Little River alongside the picnic ground was reserved for children under 12 years old to fish. Similar kids' waters were found at Elkmont, the Chimneys, and Bradley Fork. For years these waters were stocked and were, in fact, the last places in the park where the hatchery trucks stopped. The kid zones had no bait restrictions and a two-fish-per-day limit. We would take our wards there and arm them with light spinning tackle and a supply of freshly caught grasshoppers or wasp nest larvae. Sitting on the side of the stream, I would watch Jeff, Shae, and Stephanie systematically work the easy flowing glides of Metcalf Bottoms with the determination of Bering Sea crab fishermen. When Stephanie was 4 years old she managed to toss her bait into the "right spot" along the cliffs on the other side of Little River. As soon as she took up the line, she was fast into a 20-inch brown trout. For several hours thereafter, Shae, who was three years older was confounded with envy.

East Prong of Little River

SIZE: Large

FISHING PRESSURE: Heavy

FISHING QUALITY: Very good, particularly for brown trout

ACCESS: Little River Road (formerly TN 73); all other access is limited to trail use.

USGS QUADS: Clingmans Dome, NC–TN; Wear Cove, TN; Silers Bald, NC–-TN; Gatlinburg, TN

THE EAST PRONG OF THE LITTLE RIVER is often referred to simply as "Little River" by local anglers and in national park literature. Boulders the size of cabins are scattered along its course, plus an abundance of deep pools and long, swift runs. Several of these spots have romantic names the local anglers use to enhance the tales of a day's fishin': The Sinks (officially known as the April Pool), Metcalf Bottoms, the Junction Pool, Indian Head Pool, and the Little River Gorge are all spots Tennessee trout fishermen know by heart. Other spots known only to local anglers are places such as Ole Elmo's Hole and Widow's Pool.

As this is one of the most heavily fished streams in the park, the trout here are often selective; a close inspection of your No.12 Coachman by an 18-incher will certainly put an extra shot of adrenaline into your system.

Mayfly and caddis fly hatches are sporadic and often short-lived. Very few hatches in the Smokies compare with those of the East—though occasionally a lucky angler will stumble upon a surprisingly heavy emergence that entices the trout to feast.

Downstream from Metcalf Bottoms, smallmouth and rock bass are relatively common. The largest rock bass I have seen caught in the Smokies, a 14-inch specimen landed by Vic Stewart of Morristown, Tennessee, was caught in the Junction Pool.

Upstream from the Elkmont Campground, Little River's character changes from that of a small river to a wild, cascading mountain stream. Fast pocket water, plunge pools, and beautiful scenery best describe this section. Beginning beneath Clingmans Dome, at an elevation of more than 5,000 feet, Little River quickly picks up water from other brooks as it rushes down the steep slope. Brook trout prosper in many tributaries (most were closed to all fishing in 1975). More than 29 prongs of the Little River begin at more than 4,600 feet, with 15 beginning at more than 5,000 feet. This is a diverse system with approximately 50 feeder streams draining its basin.

ACCESS: The East Prong of the Little River is easily reached. Upstream from its confluence with the West Prong, for a distance of 14.5 miles, the stream is followed by the Little River Road (formerly TN 73), which winds alongside its junction with the Elkmont Road. Upstream from that point, the Elkmont Road follows the river 1.5 miles to a point just downstream from the Elkmont Campground, a developed area with 340 campsites. The Little River Truck Road, which was closed to automobile traffic in the early 1990s, is now a 1.5-mile foot and bicycle path.

Additional access to Little River is provided by the Little River Truck Road Trail, which begins at the end of the Little River Truck Road and follows upstream. At 2.8 miles, the trail arrives at the mouth of Huskey Branch, a speckle trout stream. At 3 miles, the trail arrives at the junction of the Cucumber Gap Trail. The Little River Truck Road Trail terminates at 4.2 miles at the confluence of Little River and Fish Camp Prong. Access to the main stream is by the Rough Creek Trail, which begins at the end of the Little River Truck Road Trail. The Rough Creek Trail arrives at the junction of Rough Creek and Little River at 4.7 miles (from the terminus of the Little River Truck Road). At this point, the Rough Creek Trail leaves the main stream to continue on alongside Rough Creek. The Rough Creek backcountry campsite (#24, capacity 14; Elevation 2,860′) is located near the junction of the two streams.

Farther upstream, access to Little River is offered by a maintained trail most commonly referred to as the Three Forks Trail. It begins at the junction of Rough Creek and Little River, and follows the main stream to 7.4 miles (from the terminus of the Little River Truck Road). The Three Forks backcountry campsite (#30, capacity 12; Elevation 3,400′) is located near this point. Grouse Creek flows into the main stream near the campsite; it is a fine brook trout stream.

An old, unmaintained path continues upstream alongside Little River (now only a small rill) to 7.9 miles, where the trail then leaves the main stream to continue on alongside Kuwahi Branch (8.4 miles) before ascending Stateline Ridge.

Jake's Creek

SIZE: Small

FISHING PRESSURE: Moderate to light

FISHING QUALITY: Fair to good

ACCESS: Jake's Creek Road; Jake's Creek Trail

USGS QUADS: Gatlinburg, TN

JAKE'S CREEK, A FAIRLY GOOD RAINBOW STREAM, flows into the main stream 200 yards downstream from the Stone Bridge at the upper end of the Elkmont Campground. It is reached by auto along the Jake's Creek Road from the Elkmont Summer Colony, upstream to .4 mile, the trailhead of the Jake's Creek Trail. The trail provides additional access to the stream for another 3 miles.

Fish Camp Prong

> **SIZE:** Moderately small
>
> **FISHING PRESSURE:** Moderate
>
> **FISHING QUALITY:** Good to excellent
>
> **ACCESS:** Little River Truck Road
>
> **USGS QUADS:** Silers Bald, NC–TN

FISH CAMP PRONG FLOWS into the main stream 4.2 miles upstream from the terminus of the Little River Truck Road. Fish Camp Prong and its tributaries, Goshen Prong and Buckeye Prong, are noted brook trout streams. Access is provided by the Fish Camp Prong Trail, which begins near the mouth of Fish Camp Prong. At 3 miles the trail arrives at the Camp Rock backcountry campsite (#23, capacity 8; Elevation 3310'). A short distance from the campsite, Goshen Prong flows into the main stream, and is reached from Goshen Prong Trail, which begins near the mouth of the stream and continues for 4.7 miles, before leaving the stream to ascend Stateline Ridge. The Fish Camp Prong Trail continues alongside the main stream 4.3 miles to the junction of Buckeye Gap Prong. There is no access farther upstream to the main stream of Fish Camp Prong. The Buckeye Gap Trail, which, incidentally, is an unmaintained path, begins here and follows tumbling Buckeye Gap Prong 1.5 miles to the stream's headwaters, before climbing Stateline Ridge. My favorite way to fish this stream is to bicycle up to its mouth, where I then fish. Then I gingerly ride back down the mountain, and while en route, I empty the contents of my backup flasks.

Rough Creek

> **SIZE:** Small
>
> **FISHING PRESSURE:** Moderate
>
> **FISHING QUALITY:** Good to very good
>
> **ACCESS:** Little River Truck Road
>
> **USGS QUADS:** Clingmans Dome NC–TN; Silers Bald NC–TN

ROUGH CREEK, which flows into the main stream of Little River 4.3 miles upstream from the trailhead of the Little River Truck Road Trail, sports a combined population of rainbow and brook trout. It is reached via the Rough Creek

Trail, which begins at the junction of Little River and Fish Camp Prong, then travels upstream .5 mile to the mouth of Rough Creek. The trail then follows Rough Creek 2 miles before leaving the stream. Backcountry campsite: Rough Creek (#24; Elevation 2860')

Middle Prong of Little River

SIZE: Medium

FISHING PRESSURE: Moderately heavy

FISHING QUALITY: Very good to excellent

ACCESS: Accessible by auto from its mouth

USGS QUADS: Thunderhead, NC–TN; Silers Bald, NC–TN; Wear Cove, TN

SEASONED SMOKIES ANGLERS refer to the Middle Prong of the Little River as "Tremont." It has the reputation of producing some of the largest brown trout in the park. A mammoth 12.5-pounder was wrestled from its shallow waters in July of 1980. Not many fish bigger than that are caught here. Rainbow trout are predominant, though brook trout can still be found flourishing in the headwaters. Railway grades dating back to the Little River Lumber Company provide good access to this little stream system.

The confluence of Lynn Camp Prong and the Thunderhead Prong mark the starting point of Middle Prong. Other key tributaries include Spruce Flats Branch and Indian Flats Prong.

ACCESS: Middle Prong is accessible to autos upstream from the mouth along the Tremont Road, located .2 mile from the Townsend "Y" on the Cades Cove Road (also known as the Laurel Creek Road).

The Tremont Road follows the stream, and at 2 miles the paved road ends and a gravel road (no longer regularly open to traffic during the fishing season) continues alongside the stream. At 3.5 miles, Spruce Flats Branch enters the main stream.

Spruce Flats Branch

SIZE: Small

FISHING PRESSURE: Moderate

FISHING QUALITY: Fair

ACCESS: 3.5 miles up from the mouth of Middle Prong

USGS QUADS: Wear Cove, TN

SPRUCE FLATS BRANCH FLOWS into the main stream of the Middle Prong 3.5 miles upstream from the mouth of the Middle Prong. It is a small stream, often difficult to fish, and receives a moderate amount of fishing pressure, particularly near its junction with the main stream. It is accessible via the Spruce Flats Trail, which begins near the mouth of the stream and continues upstream, offering good access to the headwaters. If you make it up to the third waterfall, you have accomplished the task. There is little worth casting to beyond that point.

Thunderhead Prong

SIZE: Small

FISHING PRESSURE: Fair

FISHING QUALITY: Fair to good

ACCESS: Defeat Ridge Trail

USGS QUADS: Thunderhead Mt., NC–TN

THUNDERHEAD PRONG FLOWS from the slopes of Thunderhead Mountain. The stream sports a mixed population of brook and rainbow trout. Sams Creek, a nice tributary of Thunderhead Prong, offers excellent fishing to those seeking an escape from the crowds. The Defeat Ridge Trail begins at the mouth of Thunderhead Prong and follows the stream. At .5 mile the trail reaches the mouth of Sams Creek, and at 2.3 miles leaves the stream for the last time to ascend the ridge.

Lynn Camp Prong

SIZE: Small

FISHING QUALITY: Good

ACCESS: Davis Ridge Trail

USGS QUADS: Thunderhead Mt., NC–TN; Silers Bald, NC–TN

LYNN CAMP PRONG IS A FINE LITTLE TROUT STREAM with an impressive tributary network. It boasts both rainbow and brook trout, though they are seldom more than 12 inches long. Tributaries of Lynn Camp Prong include Panther Creek, a nice rippling stream, Marks Creek, and Indian Flats Prong, an isolated rivulet. All three are small, overgrown but hold trout that rarely see a hook.

The Davis Ridge Trail follows Lynn Camp Prong from its mouth, reaching the mouth of Panther Creek at 2.5 miles. The trail provides excellent access to Panther Creek 1 mile upstream before leaving the creek to climb Timber Ridge. The Davis Ridge Trail continues upstream alongside Lynn Camp Prong, and at 3 miles reaches the confluence of Indian Flats Prong. The Davis Ridge Trail (also known as the Indian Flats Trail) continues alongside beautiful Indian Flats Prong, which offers worthwhile fishing. At 4.7 miles the trail crosses the stream for the last time before ascending Davis Ridge. Backcountry campsite Mark's Creek (#28; Elevation 3490') is located at the mouth of Marks Creek at Lynn Camp Prong.

West Prong of Little River

SIZE: Medium

FISHING PRESSURE: Moderately light

FISHING QUALITY: Good

ACCESS: Auto access via the Cades Cove Road; foot travel via West Prong Trail.

USGS QUADS: Wear Cove, TN; Cades Cove, NC–TN; Thunderhead Mt., NC–TN

MOST ANGLERS WHO FISH THE SMOKIES overlook the West Prong of Little River, yet the stream offers good trout fishing. The roadside portion of the West Prong and its tributary, Laurel Creek, receive the heaviest angling pressure, while the section that passes through the backcountry is relatively untouched. Most anglers bypass the West Prong in favor of more highly touted nearby streams such as Abrams Creek and Little River (the East Prong). When my sons Jeff and Shae were in grade school we frequently made overnight trips to the backcountry campsite here, dining almost exclusively on freshly caught rainbow trout and fried taters.

Rainbow trout have long dominated the main stream of the West Prong. A limited population of specs does exist in a few headwater streams. The West Prong, the smallest of the three prongs that form Little River, is bound by Defeat Ridge, Stateline Ridge, and Bote Mountain. Key tributaries include Laurel Creek and Bee Cove Creek.

ACCESS: The West Prong is accessible upstream from its junction with the East Prong by auto via the Cades Cove Road (also known as the Laurel Creek Road), which follows alongside 2 miles until the stream leaves the road.

Backcountry access is provided by the West Prong Trail (the trailhead is located at the Tremont Center), which crosses a ridge and at 1.7 miles reaches the banks of the West Prong, where the West Prong backcountry campsite (#18, capacity 8; Elevation 1600') is located. This is the trail's only contact with the West Prong.

Meigs Creek

SIZE: Small

FISHING PRESSURE: Moderate to very light

FISHING QUALITY: Good

ACCESS: Meigs Creek Trail and at its mouth at Little River

USGS QUADS: Thunderhead Mt., NC–TN; Silers Bald, NC–TN

OBSERVANT ANGLERS MAY HAVE WONDERED over the years why my previous fishing guides to the Smokies apparently overlooked Meigs Creek. It was a conscious omission, as it was one location I wanted to keep in my pocket. The reasons for this no longer exist, but the story is worth recounting insofar as the statute of limitations has expired.

In 1975 when the NPS put a gridlock on fishing for brook trout in many streams in the Smokies, they issued a new set of regulations in classic NPS agate type. Prior to this, back in the 1960s, Meigs Creek had closed to all fishing, as it was the site of experimental stockings of brook trout from the northeast and subsequent studies and research thereof. When the new regulations were printed, there was no further mention of Meigs Creek being still closed—nor was Meigs Creek even noted. The new regulations did say that in all waters downstream from Elkmont (including tributaries), rainbow and brown that were under 12 inches must be released.

While researching old park records in the damp recesses of the basement at the Sugarland, I saw stream reports that astonished me. Meigs Creek was alive with brook trout—and now no longer closed. One afternoon during early April of 1977, my longtime fishing buddy, Vic Stewart of Morristown, and I hiked from the Sinks along the Meigs Creek Trail. At the creek we began fishing. To our delight, not only was Meigs Creek swarming with the most gullible brook trout in the world, but they were by far the biggest we had ever encountered in the Smokies.

Taking turns fishing pools and runs up the creek, we caught over 100 brightly colored brookies that averaged over 10 inches long. The biggest was a

16-inch buck brookie with a very pronounced, big hook jaw. Of course, we returned them all unhurt, but not until a few photographs were snapped with my old Argus 35mm camera. Vic and I decided this was a place we'd like to return and fish, and there was not one single good reason why this little secret should be shared with anyone.

I broke the vow though. A few weeks later while talking to Sam Venable, then the outdoors editor for the Knoxville *News Sentinel*, about the ongoing progress of my first guidebook to the Smokies, I let the secret slip. At Sam's insistence I took him there where he caught the same fish we had caught, first going up the stream, and then catching them again on the way back down. Sam was hoopin' and hollerin' like he'd found the Lost Dutchman's Mine. He snapped a photo of me holding a 14-incher that ran the next morning in his Sunday column, which began, "Blessed be the bumbling bureaucrats . . ."

Meigs Creek is a pretty ho-hum little run to fish upstream from the 30-foot falls where it empties into Little River. I have not fished it for years, but those who have say the big brookies are now gone. But they were there. I have the pictures to prove it and the scars on my ass to prove some in the NPS were not impressed with my clever detective work.

ACCESS: Meigs Creek is accessible upstream from its junction with the East Prong by auto via Little River Road (formerly TN 73). Backcountry access is provided by the Meigs Creek Trail (the trailhead is located at the Sinks). Meigs Creek Trail makes a 500-foot ascent before taking you down to its first crossing of Meigs Creek .5 mile from the Sinks. Fishable headwater streams are Laurel Branch (which is plenty big enough for anyone to fish), Jay Bird, Red Bird, and Tanager. Interestingly, the mountain folk call the scarlet tanager "the mountain red bird," describing them as "saucy."

chapter 17

Abrams Creek System

Abrams Creek

SIZE: At the mouth, the stream is large; in the Cades Cove area it is medium

FISHING PRESSURE: Moderate to very heavy

FISHING QUALITY: Excellent

ACCESS: TN 72, Happy Valley Road; Rabbit Creek Trail; Cooper Road Trail; Abrams Falls Trail; Anthony Creek Trail

USGS QUADS: Cades Cove, NC–TN; Thunderhead, NC–TN; Calderwood, NC–TN; Blockhouse, TN

OF ALL THE STREAMS in the Great Smoky Mountains National Park, this is my favorite. I have spent many memorable hours on this fine stream, and look forward to many more. Abrams Creek is not only the finest rainbow trout stream in the park, but also the most interesting and unique.

Stream surveys conducted by fishery biologist Steve Moore of the National Park Service confirmed what this writer and many other anglers have long known: this is the most trout-rich water in the national park. The scientific stream survey revealed Abrams Creek has twice as many pounds of trout per surface acre as any other stream in the Smokies. Angling pressure on this stream has gone up significantly over the last 15 years as it has become one of the most popular fishing destinations in the Great Smokies. Abrams Creek also is the top

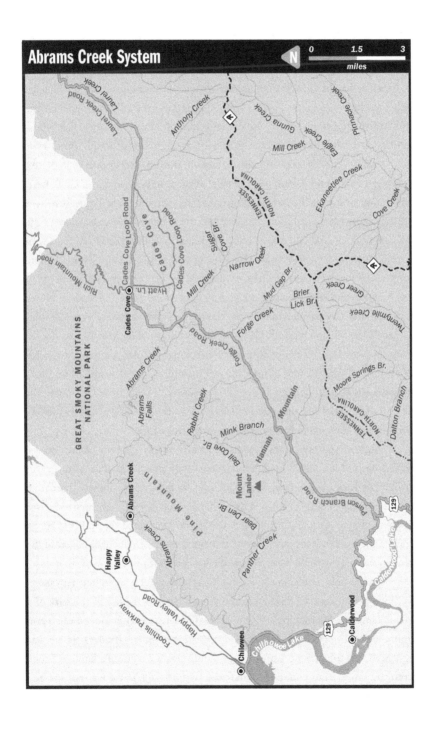

Abrams Creek System

smallmouth and rock bass fishery in the national park. Smallies up to 7 pounds are regularly caught from this stream.

The spring caddis fly hatches here are equal to any found in the southern Appalachian Mountains. Abrams Creek can also boast one of the Smokies' most spectacular hatches of what the old-timers referred to as quadwings, which are either stone flies or caddis flies (or both). It is not only the fly-fishermen who find this stream an inviting haven. The stream is literally alive with forage fish, whose food value to the trout affords the streamer fisherman excellent opportunities.

Abrams Creek is one of many streams in the park still known by its Native American name. Old Abram was the chief of the Cherokee village of Chilhowee, which was located at the mouth of Abrams Creek on the Little Tennessee River. He met an untimely and gruesome death at the hands of a vengeful 17-year-old lad named John Kirk. Old Abram and four other Cherokee chiefs from the neighboring Little Tennessee River area were being held prisoner, as they were thought responsible for the deaths of Kirk's mother and ten brothers and sisters.

John Kirk had received a 275-acre land grand from the state of North Carolina in lieu of pay due him for his service as a quartermaster in the Revolutionary War. Moving west, the Kirks built a cabin on Nine Mile Creek, not far from the site of old Fort Loudoun, a British stronghold overtaken by the Cherokee prior to 1776. The new homestead was on land disputed as Indian Territory near the Great War Path, an ancient trade route extending from Georgia to the Great Lakes. Kirk took advantage of this trade trail, operating a business selling whiskey and firearms to Indians passing along this route.

According to the story, told in my family and in all of the history books, while John and his oldest son, John, Jr., were hunting, a group of traveling braves visited the Kirk cabin where Mrs. Kirk sold them whiskey. Shortly thereafter, the now-drunken braves returned to kill her and ten children. The massacre was discovered upon Kirk's return. John Sevier quickly mustered the militia at Hunters Station (near present-day Maryville) to quell what turned out to be one of the last bloody wars with the Cherokee and East Tennesseans.

In the first confrontations, five Overhill villages, including Hiwassee, were burned in reprisal. Five captured village chiefs were left in the care of a Major James Hubbard. Crossing the Little T, Sevier's militia moved upstream from the mouth of Citico Creek. Met by a delegation of tribal elders, Sevier was informed that the massacre of the Kirk family was the work of a band of Creek from the south. Thus ended the Cherokee War of 1788, but it was not the end of the story.

One version of the story's subsequent events is that Major Hubbard actually invited a group of chiefs that included the famous Old Tassel. Among them were Old Abram (also known as Old Abraham of Chilhowee) and his son. At the goading of Major Hubbard, the younger Kirk entered the lodge where the five chiefs were held (or visiting). In my earlier books I noted that Kirk then killed all five with blows from an ax. Another account says the killings were accomplished with a tomahawk. As it turns out, though, each chief was beheaded by Kirk, who wielded a very short, iron sword. Not long ago I examined the sword, which is still in the family. It is not much more than a poorly balanced, iron butcher knife.

Sevier ordered Kirk hanged for the murder of the Cherokee leaders, but the militiaman then refused to carry out the execution and released Kirk. Sevier went on to become the governor of Tennessee, and my great-great-great-great-grandfather, John Kirk, resettled much farther north in Nolichucky Valley. Over the years I have almost drowned twice on Abrams Creek. Once a sand bar on which I was standing in water that was chest deep literally opened up and sucked me down in the blink of an eye. Another time, while I was in the Horseshoe, I lodged my meaty knee in a sharp crevice. It took the help of Mark Sudeimer to free me from that granite snare.

Abrams Creek's headwaters begin on the slopes beneath the grassy balds of Spence Field and Russell Field. The stream from that point flows into Chilhowee Reservoir. The Abrams Creek watershed is located in the southwest section of the Smokies. Its principal tributaries are Panther, Rabbit, and Mill Creeks. Abrams Creek is basically a rainbow/brown trout fishery. Brook trout have almost vanished from this watershed.

The mouth of Abrams Creek is actually part of the Chilhowee Reservoir impoundment. The first couple of miles upstream from the lake offer only mediocre trout fishing. This section of the stream is often difficult to travel, due to the impoundment and the dense flora around the stream.

It is a common sight in the winter season to view boats full of warmly clad anglers anchored at the mouth of Abrams Creek in the Chilhowee Reservoir. These knowledgeable fishermen brave the sometimes-severe winter weather for a chance at the angling bounty of the rainbow trout spawning run. Winter rains spark the instinctive mating drive of these trout, commonly weighing 3 to 8 pounds, which spend the majority of their lives in the cool depths of the TVA impoundment, waxing fat on forage fish. Before swimming upstream, these hefty milt- and roe-laden trout often spend a day or two at the mouth of the stream, waiting for precisely the right moment before embarking on their quest. It is during this quasi-immobile period at the mouth of the stream that fishermen often score limits of trout of a much greater size than is generally possible during other times of the year. The stream and Chilhowee Reservoir are open to fishing year-round. Anchoring a boat at the mouth of the stream is both legal and profitable.

Abrams Creek at the Abrams Creek Campground offers excellent trout fishing. The stream has many long, green pools, commonly stretching over 300 feet. Here a large number of downed trees litter the stream bank, providing shelter for many wise, old, mossy-back trout. This section of the stream is a favorite haunt of several of the fine local east Tennessee trout fishermen. It is seldom crowded, making this a good bet for a day of solitary fishing.

Upstream from the campground lies an area known as Little Bottoms. This is a somewhat remote section of the stream that offers superior trout fishing for those willing to make the two-mile walk. At Abrams Falls the stream plunges 25 feet into a deep emerald pool. The falls' pool harbors many of the stream's largest trout, and the pool's size allows fly-fishermen plenty of back casting room. Unfortunately for anglers, swimmers and sightseers also find Abrams Falls much to their liking. Early morning and late evenings are usually the only times anglers can find relative peace on this lovely pool.

Abrams Creek upstream from the falls to Cades Cove is Smoky Mountains trout fishing at its finest. The stream forms a small loop above the falls that is .7 mile long and requires nearly half a day to properly fish. Immediately upstream, a second loop known as the Horseshoe rounds Arbustus Ridge. The Horseshoe is 1 mile long, and it is advisable to allow a whole day to fish this sometimes-tricky stretch of creek. Both the falls' loop and the Horseshoe offer superb trout fishing. The stream is subject to heavy fishing pressure from both sportsmen and poachers. Despite this, rainbow trout in the 3- to 4-pound class abound. During May, when several species of caddis fly larvae enter the pupa stage and begin darting about beneath the surface, this section of the creek literally comes alive with feeding action.

During the spring and winter months, the cove section provides good rainbow trout and excellent, if difficult, brown trout opportunities. This area is very overgrown and thoroughly entangled with submerged root structure.

Abrams Creek is better known as Anthony Creek upstream from the Cades Cove Historic Area. Anthony Creek abounds with creel-size rainbow trout. The dense laurel overgrowths surrounding the stream make taking one of these bejeweled little fish a soul-satisfying feat any angler can appreciate. Anthony Creek forks .5 mile upstream from Cades Cove. The Left Prong originates on the northern slopes of Ledbetter Ridge, and the Right Prong flows off the slopes of Spence Field. Both prongs of Anthony Creek offer delightful trout fishing amidst a primeval hemlock forest setting.

That portion of Abrams Creek is one of the most unusual in the park. Known as Tsiya'hi by the Cherokee, which translates to "place of the otters," Cades Cove sits atop a huge limestone bed. It was named for Chief Kade, about whom little is known other than his existence was verified by a European trader named Peter Snider (1776–1867). For many years it was believed Cades Cove was named for Old Abrams's wife, Kate. One of the most unique aspects of Abrams Creek is the metamorphosis the stream undergoes while traversing the Cades Cove Historic Area. As the creek enters the cove, over 60 percent of the stream filters underground and makes a subsurface passage through the limestone before rejoining the stream near the Abrams Falls parking area. This subsurface trek dramatically increases the stream's generally acidic composition of a pH of 6 to 6.7, to a mild pH of 7.1 to 8.3. The remaining surface-flowing portion of Abrams Creek weaves its way through the cove's pasture fields, where hundreds of cattle are grazed. Here the stream receives nutrients from the cattle's waste, which is washed into the stream by rain. These added twists to the stream's composition bring both blessings and problems.

The fecal bacteria from the cattle manure make the water downstream from the cove unfit for human use. The nearly constant presence of the cattle alongside the stream accelerates an already touchy siltation problem. Many gravel spawning beds have been rendered useless by siltation. The silt settles on virtually every rock in the stream, making them as hazardous as ice on a winter's day. Wading Abrams Creek is a dangerous adventure for even the most experienced and daring trout fisherman.

The benefits from the twofold change Abrams Creek is forced to cope with seem to outweigh the problems, at least from the angler's point of view. The added nutrients and the richness gained from the limestone create an ideal habitat for many aquatic invertebrates, particularly the Trichoptera (caddis flies). This radical concentration of macroinvertebrates supports a staggering number of rough, forage, and game fish, especially in the first 4 miles of flow. The obvious reason for this is the exaggerated nutrient base found in this unique stream.

Of all the streams in the Smoky Mountains National Park, only Hazel Creek can rival this stream as an angler's paradise.

ROAD ACCESS: The Abrams Creek watershed is accessible by automobile from several points. Where the stream flows into Chilhowee Reservoir, it is easily reached from TN 72. Access is also available from Abrams Creek Campground, which is located 7 miles north of US 129 on the Happy Valley Road.

At Cades Cove there are two primary points of access to the stream. The Abrams Falls parking area allows access to the stream as it leaves the cove. Access to Anthony Creek can be made from the Cades Cove picnic area. The Cades Cove Loop Road is no longer opened early every morning. It remains closed until noon on Saturdays.

TRAIL ACCESS: At the park boundary, near the mouth of Abrams Creek, there is an old, unmaintained trail that roughly follows the ascent of the stream. This is the only path to the downstream area. This seldom-traveled trail is often difficult to locate and is not recommended for inexperienced hikers. At some points the trail is 700 feet from the stream. At the confluence of Bell Branch, 4 miles upstream from TN 72, the path receives much greater amounts of foot travel. The trail from that point weaves alongside Abrams Creek for 2.8 miles to the Rabbit Creek Trail junction.

From the junction point, the Rabbit Creek Trail becomes the stream's access trail for anglers. It follows the stream to the Abrams Creek Campground. This facility offers primitive campsite accommodations and is easily reached by auto.

Upstream from the campground, the stream is reached by hiking north on the Cooper Road Trail. This trail leaves the stream .6 mile upstream from the campground. At 1 mile the Cooper Road Trail intersects the Little Bottoms Manway. Located at the trail junction is a spacious backcountry campsite known as Little Bottoms (#17, capacity 10; Elevation 1,240'). The Little Bottoms Manway follows the stream up to Abrams Falls Trail. The Falls Trail follows the upstream progress of the stream 2.5 miles to the falls parking area. There is no trail access to Abrams Creek as it passes through the Cades Cove Historic Area.

Anthony Creek, as Abrams Creek is known prior to entering the cove, is accessible from the Anthony Creek Trail. This trail begins at the Cades Cove picnic area. The trail runs adjacent to the stream until the stream forks at 1.5 miles. The Anthony Creek Trail follows the Right Prong of Anthony Creek 2.8 miles before leaving the stream to climb the southern slopes of Cold Water Knob. Located 2.5 miles upstream on the Anthony Creek Trail is the Anthony Creek backcountry campsite (#9, capacity 6; Elevation 3,200'). The Russell Field Trail follows the Left Prong of Anthony Creek upstream 1 mile, then veers right, leaving the stream to ascend Ledbetter Ridge.

Panther Creek

SIZE: Medium to small

FISHING PRESSURE: Light to moderate

FISHING QUALITY: Excellent

ACCESS: Parsons Branch Road

USGS QUADS: Calderwood, NC–TN

PANTHER CREEK IS THE FIRST SIGNIFICANT tributary encountered upstream from the mouth of Abrams Creek. This is an excellent trout stream, holding a large population of rainbow trout. Although only a fair-size stream, Panther Creek offers a wide variety of stream conditions that can tax even a hardened Appalachian trouter. The downstream portion of the creek receives only a moderate amount of fishing pressure, while upstream near the headwaters angling pressure is more intense.

Panther Creek begins its seaward journey beneath the southern slopes of High Point. Bear Den Branch, a tributary of Panther Creek, is worthy of mention to trout fishermen. It flows off the slopes of Pole Cat Ridge and literally swarms with fat, little rainbow trout that seldom see a feathered hook dangling from a willowy fly rod.

ACCESS: Panther Creek is accessible by auto from Parsons Branch Road. This road begins in Cades Cove, off the Loop Road, and crosses Panther Creek at 3.5 miles, at an elevation of 2,540 feet. From this point, anglers are free to fish either upstream or downstream.

The mouth of Panther Creek is reached via an old, unmaintained trail, which is a spur trail from the path that connects the Abrams Creek Campground with TN 72. Panther Creek Manway leaves the Abrams Creek Trail at the first stream crossing and, for a short distance, follows the downstream progress of Abrams Creek. Hikers must then negotiate a hazardous crossing of Abrams Creek at the mouth of Panther Creek. It is often advisable to make this crossing in a rubber raft or canoe. On the other side of the stream, the trail then closely follows the stream for 4 miles before leaving the stream to ascend the southern slopes of Bunker Hill. Bear Den Branch flows into the main stream .4 mile upstream from the trail's last contact with the stream. There is no additional access to the stream until Parsons Branch Road makes contact with the stream at 2,540 feet.

The Hannah Mountain Trail briefly follows along two small tributaries of Panther Creek; however, neither of these small brooks has angling merit. There are no backcountry campsites in the Panther Creek system.

Rabbit Creek

> **SIZE:** Fairly small
>
> **FISHING PRESSURE:** Light
>
> **FISHING QUALITY:** Good
>
> **ACCESS:** Parsons Branch Road; Rabbit Creek Trail
>
> **USGS QUADS:** Calderwood, NC–TN

RABBIT CREEK IS ONE OF THOSE NIFTY LITTLE STREAMS trout fishermen become notoriously sullen about when other anglers query them for its secrets. I have never encountered another angler, or even evidence of their presence, along this rivulet. Rabbit Creek enters Abrams Creek 3.5 miles upstream from the Abrams Creek Campground. Rabbit Creek's icy waters flow from springs located on the sides of Hannah Mountain. Rainbow trout are the dominant species to be found in this stream. There are numerous small tributaries, but none begin at over 2,800 feet. Nearly all of these tiny brooks contain trout.

> **ACCESS:** Rabbit Creek is accessible from Parsons Branch Road. This road begins in Cades Cove and runs alongside the stream for over 1 mile. The stream is reached by foot travel from the Rabbit Creek Trail. This trail begins at the Abrams Falls parking area in Cades Cove. The trail reaches the stream at 4.7 miles. At this stream crossing is the popular Rabbit Creek backcountry campsite (#15, capacity 8; Elevation 1,550′). This is the only contact with the stream for this trail.

Mill Creek

> **SIZE:** Small
>
> **FISHING PRESSURE:** Moderate
>
> **FISHING QUALITY:** Fair
>
> **ACCESS:** Cades Cove Loop Road
>
> **USGS QUADS:** Cades Cove, TN

MILL CREEK FLOWS INTO ABRAMS CREEK at the Abrams Falls parking area. It is most interesting to stand at the junction of these nearly equal-in-size streams and observe the intermingling of their dramatically different waters. Abrams Creek, prior to joining Mill Creek, is a milky, limestone-rich stream. Its bottom is sandy bedrock. Mill Creek, in sharp contrast, is a crystal-clear, acidic, boulder-strewn rivulet typical of most streams in the Smokies. At the confluence, you can easily observe a marked difference in the streams. To the right, the tinted water of Abrams Creek flows on, holding stubbornly to its former character. To the left, Mill Creek's rusty bottom and clear water fight the inevitable clouding. Only after flowing several hundred feet downstream do the two water types intermingle to make their identity indistinguishable.

Mill Creek is a challenging stream of fair fishing quality. Many of the larger fish instinctively move downstream to Abrams Creek, where food is more abundant. Mill Creek is an easy stream to get around on and, as an added bonus, receives only moderate angling pressure. In early spring, a short jaunt up this creek with a good stone fly nymph imitation will make you a firm disciple of small-stream trouting. I highly recommend Mill Creek and its tributaries to those wishing a short, easy fishing trip in the Great Smoky Mountains National Park.

Mill Creek's tributaries flow off McCampbell and Forge Knobs. Mill Creek forks behind the Becky Cable House in Cades Cove. The right prong is known as Forge Creek, and the left prong is Mill Creek. Forge Creek is also worthy of angling merit. This rocky little branch offers fine fishing to those fishermen deft enough to drop a small fly beneath its many foaming cascades. Ekaneetlee Branch, a tributary of Forge Creek, holds a population of rainbow trout. This is a very small creek, but one with a good sprinkling of cascade pools of surprising depth. It is a good stream to depend on for a meal of fresh trout if you plan a backcountry trip in that area.

ACCESS: Mill Creek is accessible by automobile from the Abrams Falls parking area, the Becky Cable House, and the Forge Creek Road, all of which are off the Cades Cove Loop Road. The Forge Creek Road follows the upstream ascent of Forge Creek to 1,929 feet before leaving the stream.

An old, unmaintained road follows Mill Creek for 1 mile, after which there is no other trail access. The old road begins off the Forge Creek Road near the last crossing of Mill Creek.

Forge Creek is accessible from the Gregory Ridge Trail, which begins at the stream's last contact with the Forge Creek Road. This trail follows alongside the stream 2 miles, to 2,600 feet. The Ekaneetlee Manway offers access to Ekaneetlee Branch. This trail begins off the Gregory Ridge Trail behind the Big Poplar, which is about 2 miles from the trailhead. There is a backcountry campsite (#12, capacity 8; Elevation 2,600'), known as Ekaneetlee, .5 mile upstream on the trail. Note: The Ekaneetlee Manway is an unmaintained trail that should only be used by experienced hikers and trout fishermen.

chapter 18

Twentymile Creek System

Twentymile Creek

> **SIZE:** Medium
>
> **FISHING PRESSURE:** Moderately light
>
> **FISHING QUALITY:** Good all season
>
> **ACCESS:** Twentymile Creek Trail
>
> **USGS QUADS:** Tapoco, NC; Fontana, NC

TWENTYMILE CREEK IS ONE of the least-known streams in the park. Local anglers have long considered this their secret preserve. When I used to spend weeks basing out of Fontana Village fishing cross lake streams, Twentymile Creek was my always-in-the-vest backup destination. The stream is located in the extreme southern portion of the Smokies, isolated from almost all commercial development. Visiting anglers should take the time to discover this gem. Twentymile Creek is a productive stream, sporting a scrappy population of rainbow trout in its fast flow. The stream has a nice distribution of deep pools, pocket water, and shallow runs. It is sometimes a challenge to fish, but a well-placed cast will bring rewards.

Twentymile Creek is a rainbow trout fishery, although a rare brown trout, up from Cheoah Lake, will occasionally be taken in the downstream section. Brook trout are as rare here as chicken teeth. Oddly, the rare spec you might catch will be larger than normally found in park waters, and at a lower elevation. The explanation for this is that the state of North Carolina periodically stocks Cheoah Lake with brook trout. Now and then one follows its nose upstream.

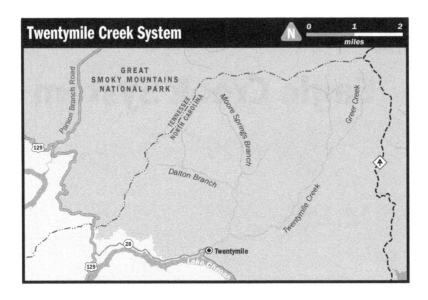

Twentymile Creek is bound by Wolfe Ridge, Greer Knob, and Twentymile Ridge, and flows into Cheoah Lake. It is of medium size, with a small tributary system. Moore Spring Branch and Dalton Branch offer the best feeder stream fishing in this watershed. Moore Springs Branch enters Twentymile Creek .5 mile upstream from the ranger station. Upstream there is no trail access, but 1.7 miles up this tributary, it forks at Dalton Branch, which offers an additional 1.5 miles of fishing. Greer Creek has a bit over a mile of fishable water, joining Twentymile Creek 3 miles upstream from the ranger station. This wooly little run has no trail access, but don't worry. Once you start up this run, the streamside flora is so thick in most places you cannot get out to get lost even if you tried.

ACCESS: The Twentymile Creek Ranger Station is located 2.8 miles east of the US 129/NC 28 junction. Drive past the ranger station to the parking area, where the Twentymile Creek Trail begins. At .6 mile the trail reaches the mouth of Moore Spring Branch and the junction of the Wolfe Ridge Trail.

The Wolfe Ridge Trail follows Moore Spring Branch, and at 4 miles arrives at the Wolfe Ridge backcountry campsite (#95, capacity 8; Elevation 2,360'). The mouth of Dalton Branch is near this campsite.

The Twentymile Creek Trail continues along Twentymile Creek, and at 1.8 miles arrives at the Twentymile backcountry campsite (#93, capacity 14-Elevation 1,880'). At 4.5 miles the trail leaves the stream for the last time to ascend to Shuckstack Fire Tower.

chapter 19

Eagle Creek System

Eagle Creek

SIZE: Medium

FISHING PRESSURE: Moderately light to heavy

FISHING QUALITY: Very good, particularly upstream from Pinnacle Creek

ACCESS: Fontana Lake; Eagle Creek Trail

USGS QUADS: Fontana Dam, NC; Thunderhead, NC–TN; Cades Cove, NC–TN; Tuskeegee, NC

WHEN MY FIRST TROUT FISHING GUIDE to these streams was published, Eagle Creek was one of the most overlooked waters in the national park. That has changed significantly over the last 15 years. Fishing pressure is up, but the quality of fishing in these waters remains high.

Eagle Creek is nestled in a secluded valley in the southwest corner of the Great Smoky Mountains National Park. Its remote location has spared the stream's trout the daily ritual of scanning every morsel for a hidden hook. It receives only a moderate amount of angling pressure, and there are few signs of overuse anywhere in this area. The backcountry campsites are clean and not trampled.

Brook trout still have a few good strongholds in the Eagle Creek watershed, notably Gunna Creek and Asgini Branch. This watershed was not as heavily logged as the nearby Hazel Creek Valley, thus the flow was not defiled by such

154

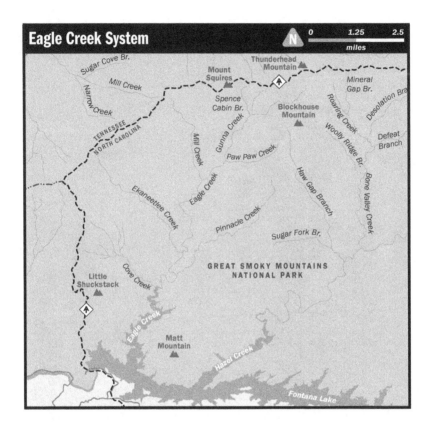

lethal logging byproducts as silt and tannic acid (from the decomposing tree bark and slash). Although it is only a matter of conjecture, many knowledgeable anglers feel the strong presence of the rainbow trout in the stream is partially responsible for the deterioration of the brook trout fishery.

In recent years, a few brown trout have immigrated into the main stream from Fontana Lake. Their presence is insignificant compared to that of the abundant rainbow trout, which have dominion over the main stream up to Pinnacle Creek. Rainbow trout fishing is very good here. Occasionally you hear moronic banter about steelhead running up Eagle Creek from Fontana Lake. Here's the deal. A steelhead is a rainbow that spent some time in the Pacific Ocean. Occurrences of rainbow trout with mysterious pasts have been stocked in lakes everywhere in southern Appalachia. Perhaps the best-known winter upstream spawning run was during the 1950s, from Watauga Lake into a little feeder stream known as Doe Creek. The run arose unexpectedly, and left almost as mysteriously.

Shae Kirk landing a nice rainbow trout.

The lower reaches of Eagle Creek sport a limited smallmouth and rock bass fishery. These fish are found upstream from the mouth of the stream for at least 3 miles. Like on other waters, during mid- to late-spring a certain percentage of the brown bass in Fontana Lake go upstream to spawn and then return to the lake.

Eagle Creek is bound by Jenkins Ridge, Stateline Ridge, and Twenty Mile Ridge. It flows into Fontana Lake a short distance from the dam. Eagle Creek's tributaries of interest to fishermen are Lost Creek, Pinnacle Creek, Ekaneetlee Creek, Tub Mill Creek, and Gunnas Creek.

ACCESS: No roads lead to the Eagle Creek watershed, as it was permanently sealed off during World War II by Fontana Lake's impoundment of the Little Tennessee River. Crossing the lake by boat is the most popular means

Greg Ward wet wading Eagle Creek.

of visiting Eagle Creek. Light boats equipped with small outboard motors can be rented from the operators of the Fontana Village Resort Marina. Additionally, the operators of the marina will be happy to make arrangements with fishermen to take them to the mouth of the stream and later pick them up. I have made use of this handy service on a number of occasions, and I highly recommend it.

Anglers wishing to visit Eagle Creek, but preferring to keep both feet on solid ground, will discover that Lost Cove Trail offers the easiest access to Eagle Creek by auto. This route makes it necessary to begin on the Appalachian Trail crossing of Fontana Dam. Traveling north along the Appalachian Trail 3.7 miles to Sassafras Gap, the trail reaches the junction of the Lost Cove Trail. The Lost Cove Trail descends down the ridge to the right, and at 3 miles reaches the Lost Cove Creek backcountry campsite

Big rainbow

(#90, capacity 12; Elevation 1,760'), a lakeside camp near the mouth of Eagle Creek. Upstream access is provided by the Eagle Creek Trail, which begins at the mouth of the stream and follows alongside the creek. The trail rounds Horseshoe Bend at .5 mile and reaches the mouth of Pinnacle Creek at 1 mile, which is also the site of the trailhead for the Pinnacle Creek Trail. The Eagle Creek Trail continues upstream alongside the main stream to the confluence of Ekaneetlee Creek at 2 miles, where the Lower Ekaneetlee backcountry campsite (#89, capacity 8; Elevation 1,880'), a superb fishing camp, is located. Continuing upstream, the Eagle Creek Trail reaches the Eagle Creek Island backcountry campsite (#99, capacity 10;

Elevation 2,880') at 3.5 miles, then continues its upstream climb and at 5 miles reaches the confluence of Tub Mill Creek and Gunna Creek. This is the beginning point of Eagle Creek proper. The Big Walnut backcountry campsite (#97, capacity 10, Elevation 2,400'), the last camping spot along the trail, is located here. The Eagle Creek Trail continues upstream alongside Gunna Creek (see Gunna Creek in this chapter).

Pinnacle Creek

SIZE: Small

FISHING PRESSURE: Light

FISHING QUALITY: Fair

ACCESS: Remote; Pinnacle Creek Trail

USGS QUADS: Fontana Dam, NC; Thunderhead, NC–TN

PINNACLE CREEK IS PROBABLY the most overlooked feeder stream in the Eagle Creek system. It holds a few good rainbow trout, and there is a nice campsite upstream that makes a fine, secluded fishing base.

ACCESS: The Pinnacle Creek Trail provides good access to the stream. It begins at the mouth of Pinnacle Creek and follows alongside the stream. At 1.5 miles the trail arrives at the Pinnacle backcountry campsite (#88, capacity 8; Elevation 2,200'). The trail continues along the stream for 2.8 miles, where it leaves the stream and ascends to Pickens Gap.

Ekaneetlee Creek

SIZE: Small

FISHING PRESSURE: Light

FISHING QUALITY: Excellent

ACCESS: Remote

USGS QUADS: Fontana Dam, NC; Cades Cove, NC–TN

EKANEETLEE CREEK IS A FINE LITTLE TROUT STREAM that flows alongside an ancient Native American pathway. There is a good population of speckle trout above the 2,900-foot mark, with rainbows filling the gap between the main stream and that point.

Big Tommy Branch and Adams Hollow Branch, tributaries of Ekaneetlee Creek, are a sure bet for a day of good fishing.

ACCESS: The Ekaneetlee Manway provides very good access to the stream. Ekaneetlee Creek flows into Eagle Creek 2 miles upstream from Fontana Lake. The trail begins at the mouth of the stream and follows alongside to its headwaters before ascending to Ekaneetlee Gap. Note: This is an unmaintained trail that is usually kept open by fishermen; however, inexperienced backcountry travelers should exercise caution if they decide to visit here.

Tub Mill Creek

SIZE: Small

FISHING PRESSURE: Light

FISHING QUALITY: Very good

ACCESS: Remote

USGS QUADS: Cades Cove, NC–TN

TUB MILL CREEK FLOWS TOGETHER with Gunna Creek to form Eagle Creek. It has a well-developed tributary network that sports both rainbow and brook trout. Asgini Branch and Lawson Gant Lot Branch are tributaries of Tub Mill Creek that offer good fishing.

ACCESS: Tub Mill Creek flows into the main stream 5 miles upstream from Fontana Lake. The stream is reached at this point from the Eagle Creek Trail. No maintained trails lend access upstream from the mouth of the stream.

Gunna Creek

SIZE: Small

FISHING PRESSURE: Light

FISHING QUALITY: Excellent

ACCESS: Remote; Eagle Creek Trail

USGS QUADS: Cades Cove, NC–TN; Thunderhead, NC–TN

GUNNA CREEK IS THE UPSTREAM EXTENSION of the main portion of Eagle Creek. It holds a mixed population of rainbow and brook trout. Its extreme headwaters were closed to all fishing in 1975 to protect the brook trout, which prosper there. Massive hemlocks grow alongside the stream, many covered with cool, green growths of thick moss that help make this a delightful place to fish.

Greg Ward battling a big rainbow in the middle of Gatlinburg.

Paw Paw Creek and Spence Cabin Branch, tributaries of Gunna Creek, hold populations of colorful speckle trout.

ACCESS: The Eagle Creek Trail follows alongside Gunna Creek upstream from its confluence with Tub Mill Creek. The trail passes by the mouth of Paw Paw Creek at 6 miles (upstream from Fontana Lake), then follows alongside this lovely mountain brook 8 miles before leaving, to later terminate on the ridge at the Appalachian Trail.

chapter 20

Hazel Creek System

Hazel Creek

SIZE: Large

FISHING PRESSURE: Moderate to very heavy in the lower portion; relatively light to moderate in the upper portion above 2,500 feet

FISHING QUALITY: Excellent

ACCESS: Fontana Lake; Hazel Creek Trail

USGS QUADS: Tuskeegee, NC; Thunderhead, NC–TN; Silers Bald, NC–TN; Noland NC–TN

HAZEL CREEK HAS BEEN TERMED the crown jewel of trout fishing in the Great Smoky Mountains National Park. It's been touted by most major outdoor publications as long as fishing in these mountains has found its way into sporting journals. Hazel Creek has all the qualifications to claim being the finest freestone stream in the southern Appalachian Mountains. Alas, since my first books on fishing in the Smokies came out, I have been blamed for the avalanche of fly-fishermen spending thousands more hours here than during the 1970s. My only defense is to blame Brad Pitt, whom, if I might humbly suggest, had a bit more to do with the current fly-fishing craze than did Kornbread Kirk.

One of the secrets of this stream's excellent fishing is the abundant insect life. Caddis flies dominate, although you will find that prolific hatches of Stenonema mayflies get the attention of trout during the summer. The lower portion, dominat-

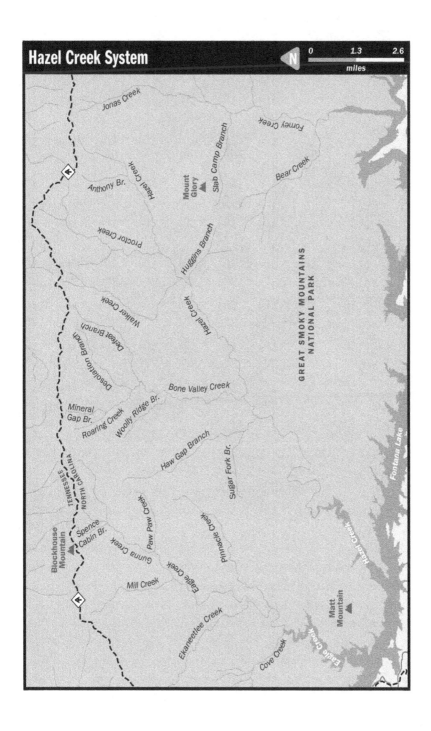

A youthful Don Kirk with a bragging-size brook trout caught at the upper reaches of Hazel Creek.

ed by rainbow and brown trout, is highly productive for large terrestrial imitations such as the grasshopper and jassid. Here, the stream rushes past old homesteads and fragrant orchards, forming many long, slow pools, perfect for floating a cinnamon ant pattern. I feel nothing will put the adrenaline in your system faster than a lightning-fast strike from a trout coaxed from one of these beautiful pools.

Brookies can be found in the main stream beyond an elevation of 3,040 feet, one of the lowest elevations for brookies in a major streamshed in the Smokies. Hazel Creek has one of the loftiest tributary systems in the park. These headwater streams provide some of the finest brook trout habitat in the Smokies.

The lower reaches of Hazel Creek not only hold trout but also healthy populations of largemouth, smallmouth, and rock bass. This is one of the very few places in the Great Smoky Mountains National Park where largemouth bass can be caught by fly-fishermen.

Hazel Creek is located in the southeast section of the Smokies and is bound by Welch Ridge and Jenkins Ridge. Its headwaters are located beneath the slopes of Stateline Ridge, and from there the stream flows into Fontana Lake. Primary tributaries of Hazel Creek are Sugar Fork, Bone Valley Creek, Walker Creek, and Proctor Creek. The gradient of the mid- to lower-reaches of Hazel Creek is one of the mostly leisurely of park streams. The creek and its tributaries in many instances are flanked by flats where crops were tended not so long ago.

The Hazel Creek watershed was one of the most heavily devastated in the Smokies. The Ritter Logging Company removed virtually every stand of virgin timber from the valley in an operation that took nearly 20 years. The loggers laid rail lines almost 13 miles up Hazel Creek to enable them to haul the fallen giants to the sawmills. Proctor was a booming sawmill town of more than 1,000 people, and was the center of the valley's life.

Upon receiving stewardship of the Smokies, the National Park Service found many residents reluctant to abandon their mountain homesteads. Even today, you may encounter groups of mountain folk on the trail, carrying floral arrangements to be placed on the graves of loved ones buried in the park, an annual event for the people who still feel a part of these mountains of their birth.

The forest has regrown nicely under the protection of the National Park Service. The area has an abundance of plant life and, not too surprisingly, many varieties of domestic plants. Hazel Creek can boast of one of the park's few beaver colonies. There are no beaver dams on the stream, but the busy beaver have downed a large number of trees alongside the stream, which provide badly needed cover for trout.

One of my most memorable visits to the lower reaches of Hazel Creek occurred in late April of 1978, when I crossed the lake from Fontana Village in the company of Soc Clay. Perhaps the most colorful figure in a business that is spangled with colorful figures, Clay was from northern Kentucky where he made a living as a freelance writer of hunting and fishing stories, but is now the Poet Laureate of Kentucky. He and H. Lea Lawrence, who was also along with us that day, are the two most animated characters I knew in those days although their styles were radically different from each other: Lea never stopped talking, and Soc never allowed you to stop laughing.

*Big browns and smallmouth bass abound
in the lower reaches of Hazel Creek.*

A direct descendent of Henry Clay of Kentucky politics, Soc has an incredible ability to keep the challenges of life in manageable perspective. Carried by Luther Turbin, manager of the Fontana Village Resort Marina, Soc and I peered across the bow of the boat into the thick fog hanging over Fontana Lake until we arrived at the mouth of Hazel Creek. I was chilled to the bone, but not Soc, who was wearing a jacket made with something he referred to in passing as GORE-TEX. He was even kind enough to tell me that once I became a well-known personage in the outdoor writing racket, I would probably be able to "obtain" as he called it, samples. Shortly thereafter in my writing career, I learned that the term "obtain" was pretty synonymous with "beg for," "scam," and "extort," gear from manufacturers, which is why when I'm asked how much something I am fishing costs, I usually respond truthfully that I have no idea.

Soc and I made our way up to the Saw Dust Pile, where a hitherto unseen thermos bottle appeared from this fishing vest. Caught off guard, I lamented to Soc that I wished my paltry wisdom had been such as to have had the presence of mind to also have brought coffee. Soc bent over in one of those horse laughs he is so famous for, then looked up at me and said, "By gawd, Kirk, you're really new at this, aren't you? Do you really think I would carry coffee this far up a damned mountain? This here is Maker's Mark—bona fide Kentucky brown water."

Reducing the contents of the foot-tall thermos to a pittance, Soc fished in one direction, and I in other. A couple hours later we met back at the lake. I had a field dressed limit of rainbow trout that all exceeded 10 inches. Soc's creel was bulging too, but not with trout. He had been gathering morel mushroom and plucking ramps. Soc and I still remain in fairly close contact today.

Steve Claxton is perhaps the best-known modern guide on Hazel Creek. He has fished these waters from his home base in Bryson City for the better part of five decades, and has been an outfitter on the stream since the early 1990. Most of his guided trips occur from a base camp at the edge of Fontana at the mouth of Hazel Creek where his clients fish upstream as far as Bone Valley and bit beyond.

"There is certainly more pressure on Hazel Creek these days than there was when I was a young fellow fly-fishing there," says Claxton, who is without question the best known of the guide service owners who operate within the park. "Oddly enough though, during the last couple few years, fishing pressure seems to have decreased a bit. I credit this with negative impact of the draught years of 2007 and 2008, and that Fontana Village Marine increased the fee for delivering anglers to the mouth of Hazel Creek from $100 per float-boat load of fishermen, to $50 a person."

"Fishing on the Hazel Creek during October when the brown trout spawn is truly world class. About a mile upstream from the Saw Dust Pile is what we call the Brown Pool. I have seen brown trout weighing 5 to 10 pounds in bunches of two dozen more fish at a time then," Claxton says.

ACCESS: All roads leading into Hazel Creek were closed during World War II when Fontana Lake was impounded. The isolation has helped spare the stream and enabled it to maintain high-quality fishing.

Crossing the lake by boat is perhaps the easiest and most popular way to visit Hazel Creek. For a modest sum, the operators of the Fontana Village Resort Marina provide transportation across the lake by arrangement. One really nice feature of going this route is being relieved of worrying about the safety of your boat.

You may encounter a variety of strange-looking vehicles on these trails that appear to be a cross between a wheelbarrow and a bicycle. These versatile contraptions, known as "Smoky Mountain pushcarts," are constructed of lightweight materials, such as tubular aluminum, and tires from ten-speed bicycles. Such backcountry rarities as coolers full of perishable foods, lanterns, cots, and big tents are transported up the stream in these rigs by local fishermen unwilling to compromise their fishing trips with the usual backcountry fare of freeze-dried foods and cramped hiking tents.

The Hazel Creek Trail follows the stream. The trailhead is located near the mouth of the stream on Fontana Lake. The Proctor backcountry campsite (#86, capacity 20; Elevation 1,680'), located .5 mile upstream from the lake, is a popular base camp. Upstream from this site is the "Horseshoe," noted for its excellent trout fishing.

At 3.3 miles is the Sawdust Pile backcountry campsite (#85, capacity 20-Elevation 2,000'), also popular with backcountry fishermen. The poetic "Brown Pool" is nearby. Its famous waters have been the sight of the day's last cast for countless anglers.

At 5 miles the trail reaches the junction of Sugar Fork and the trailhead of the Sugar Fork Trail. Located nearby is the Sugar Fork backcountry campsite (#84, capacity 8; Elevation 2,160'), which is well-suited as a fishing camp. At 5.6 miles the trail arrives at the mouth of Bone Valley Creek, also the trailhead for the Bone Valley Trail and the site of the Bone Valley backcountry campsite (#83, capacity 20; Elevation 2,280'). At 8.6 miles the trail reaches the Calhoun Camp backcountry campsite (N.P.S. #82 capacity 15; Elevation 2,720') and continues to the junction of Hazel Creek and Walker Creek at 9.5 mile.

The trail upstream from the Proctor Creek site becomes steeper and more difficult to travel. At 13.5 miles the trail reaches the old Hazel Creek Cascades backcountry campsite. located at an elevation of more than 4,000 feet, well into the heart of the brook trout fishery. The trail upstream from the cascades is steep, though open and passable. In recent years the NPS has frequently closed backcountry campsites at Hazel Creek (and other wilderness areas) for a number of reasons. Often it is due to rogue bear activity, but other reasons are often cited.

Sugar Fork

SIZE: Small

FISHING PRESSURE: Fairly light

FISHING QUALITY: Very good

ACCESS: Hazel Creek Trail; Sugar Fork Trail

USGS QUADS: Tuskeegee, NC; Thunderhead, NC–TN

SUGAR FORK IS THE FIRST SIGNIFICANT feeder stream encountered up Hazel Creek. It is a nice little stream—although often overlooked by anglers—offering excellent rainbow trout fishing, with an abundance of cascades that provide interesting fishing almost any day of the year.

Haw Gap Branch and Little Sugar Fork are tributaries of angling merit.

ACCESS: The Sugar Fork Trail starts 5 miles upstream from the lake. At .5 mile the Sugar Fork Trail reaches the mouth of Haw Gap Branch and the junction of Haw Gap Trail. The Haw Gap Trail offers access to the branch.

At 1.7 miles the trail arrives at the junction of Little Sugar Fork. A short distance upstream from this point, the trail leaves the stream.

Bone Valley Creek

SIZE: Medium

FISHING PRESSURE: Moderately light

FISHING QUALITY: Excellent

ACCESS: Bone Valley Trail

USGS QUADS: Tuskeegee, NC; Thunderhead, NC–TN

ANYONE TAKING THE TIME to visit the Hazel Creek area should spend at least one day exploring and fishing Bone Valley, which came by its name in the late 1880s, when an unexpected and severe late-spring blizzard hit the area. Cattle, already brought up from the valley, were caught in the midst of the storm's fury. In their efforts to stay warm, the cattle huddled together, one on top of the other. Their efforts failed, and huge stacks of bones were left to bleach in the summer sun. Henceforth, the area was known as Bone Valley.

Bone Valley Creek enters the main stream 5.6 miles upstream from the lake and offers excellent rainbow and brook trout fishing. It is a good-size stream with a challenging mixture of riffles and pools.

Noteworthy tributaries of Bone Valley Creek include Wooly Branch, a good little trout stream, although very overgrown; Defeat Branch, a personal favorite, sporting both rainbow and brook trout; Desolation Branch, a brook trout stream; and Roaring Fork, a popular brookie stream.

ACCESS: The Bone Valley Trail begins at the mouth of the stream, 5.6 miles upstream from Fontana Lake. The trail follows alongside the stream and reaches the Hall Cabin at 1.7 miles at the end of the maintained portion of the trail, where an unmaintained path continues upstream. At the mouth of Desolation Branch the trail then begins following alongside the small tributary.

Walker Creek

SIZE: Small

FISHING PRESSURE: Light

FISHING QUALITY: Excellent

ACCESS: Unnamed path

USGS QUADS: Thunderhead, NC–TN

WALKER CREEK IS A SMALL, often overlooked trout stream of very good fishing quality. The trout here are of average size, but are not nearly as leader shy as the fish in the main stream. There are rainbow trout in the lower section of the stream, but above the falls the stream is all speckle trout.

ACCESS: The stream's mouth is 9.5 miles up stream from Fontana Lake. The stream is only accessible via an unmaintained path that begins at the mouth of the stream and follows alongside to its headwaters.

Proctor Creek

SIZE: Small

FISHING PRESSURE: Light

FISHING QUALITY: Excellent

ACCESS: Unnamed path

USGS QUADS: Thunderhead, NC–TN

PROCTOR CREEK OFFERS ANGLERS a chance to fish in a stream abounding with lively trout amidst an exceptionally beautiful forest setting. This is a popular trout stream, and barbless hooks are definitely in order for all sportsmen.

Proctor Creek flows into the main stream 10.5 miles upstream from the lake. This stream has a well-developed tributary system. Long Cove Creek and James Camp Branch are favorites among anglers.

ACCESS: The stream's mouth is 10.5 miles upstream from Fontana Lake. There is an excellent unmaintained path that follows alongside the stream to its headwaters.

chapter 21

Forney Creek System

Forney Creek

SIZE: Medium

FISHING PRESSURE: Moderate to light

FISHING QUALITY: Excellent

ACCESS: Fontana Lake; Forney Creek Trail

USGS QUADS: Noland Creek, NC; Silers Bald, NC–TN, Clingmans Dome, NC–TN

CONTRARY TO RUMORS that have circulated in the national sporting press in recent years, Forney Creek is not the weak sister of Hazel Creek. In fact, some local anglers like it better than Hazel Creek, which currently gets considerable fishing pressure.

Forney Creek is well known to anyone who has spent time fishing in the Smokies, although it has not received the attention given several of the more highly publicized fishing spots. Its remote location, plus its proximity to two of the most famous streams in the park—Hazel Creek and Deep Creek—spare it from the burden of excessive angling pressure. Local anglers from Tennessee and North Carolina are often about the only folks you will encounter fishing this sparkling stream.

The Forney Creek watershed was one of the most thoroughly devastated valleys in the Great Smoky Mountains National Park. It was the site of an

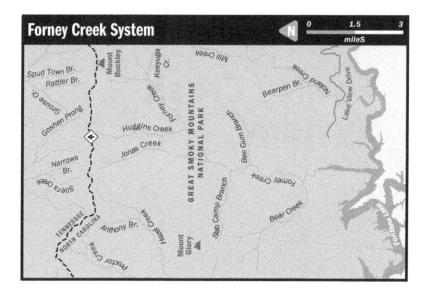

intensive logging operation that clear-cut the coves and slopes without mercy. A massive forest fire that occurred during the mid-1920s, fed by the slash left behind by the loggers, consumed what remained of the valley's flora. As with many of the clear-cut sections of the Smokies, this one has slowly regrown under the protective sanctions of the National Park Service, yet deep scars heal slowly. Hikers and fishermen should not depend on old maps of this valley, since the devastation of the past altered many of the old trails.

As was the case with most of the streamsheds, it was not acquired by the NPS at the time of the creation of the Great Smoky Mountains National Park. However, the remaining, inhabited lower reaches of the valley were made booty by TVA raiders who later gave the seized land to the NPS. Considering that I personally regard Forney Creek with its accelerated gradient and modest fishing pressure as the best fishing on the North Carolina side of the park, I have to wink at those past indiscretions.

Forney Creek possesses an exceptional population of frisky, colorful rainbow trout. Each summer a number of trophy-size 'bows are taken from this stream, although the majority of the fish fall into the 7- to 10-inch range. The exception to this is late October to mid-November when the lower reaches have become popular among those seeking leviathan brown trout during their spawning time. (The Forney Creek Outlet Bay on Fontana Lake offers very good fishing for winter-run spawning rainbows.)

In recent seasons angling pressure at Forney Creek has peaked, and for good reason.

Brook trout can still be found in the stream's upper reaches. They are a fragile remnant population that under no circumstances should be disturbed. Habitat destruction dating back to the logging era, and competition with rainbow trout have placed the future of the brookie in this watershed in grave danger.

The lower reaches of Forney Creek are silly with 2- to 4-pound small-mouth bass, and rock bass up to 1 pound. These fish are most commonly caught from the stream from June through September. Forney Creek is located in the southeastern section of the Smokies. It is bound by Forney Ridge, Stateline Ridge, and Welch Ridge, and empties into Fontana Lake. Forney Creek has a well-developed network of tributaries, including Bear Creek, Advalorem Branch, Bee Gum Branch, Slab Camp Branch, Whitemans Glory Creek, Jonas Creek, Hugging Creek, Little Steeltrap Creek, and Steeltrap Creek.

> **ACCESS:** There is no auto access to this stream; you reach it via boat, foot travel, or horseback. It is popular to visit this watershed by horseback, which allows for fast travel and ease in carrying gear. Several of the backcountry campsites along Forney Creek accommodate horseback travelers.

Upstream from Fontana Lake, you'll find the Forney Creek Trail, which begins at the mouth of the stream. Located approximately 100 yards upstream is the Lower Forney backcountry campsite (#74, capacity 12; Elevation 1,720'), an excellent fishing camp. At .6 mile upstream the trail arrives at the junction of Bear Branch and the trailhead of the Jumpup Trail. The Bear Creek backcountry campsite (#73, capacity 15; Elevation 1,800') lies west of the stream junction.

The junction of Forney Creek and Bee Gum Branch is located upstream 2.6 miles. This is also the location of the trailhead for the Bee Gum Branch Trail, and nearby is the CCC Camp backcountry campsite (#71, capacity 12 campers/horses; Elevation 2,180'). At 3.3 miles the trail arrives at the junction of Slab Camp Branch, and at 4.1 miles is the junction of Jonas Creek. This is also the location of the trailhead of the Jonas Creek Trail and the Jonas Creek backcountry campsite (#70, capacity 12; Elevation 2,400').

Huggins Creek flows into the main stream 5.3 miles upstream. The Huggins backcountry campsite (#69, capacity 12; Elevation 2,800'), also referred to as the Monteith campsite, is located near the stream's fork. The Forney Creek Trail passes a sign 6.9 miles up that indicates the direction of the Steeltrap backcountry campsite (#68, capacity 8; Elevation 3,960'). The trail crosses Little Steeltrap Creek (which is a wildly productive stream to fish) at 7 miles, leaving the main stream of Forney Creek to travel along the gentle slopes of Wild Cherry Ridge. Near 8.8 miles the trail fords Steeltrap Creek and resumes its streamside ascent of the ridge alongside Forney Creek. The trail continues to furnish excellent access to Forney Creek to about the 9.7-mile mark, where it then leaves Forney Creek for the last time, to later terminate 1 mile from Clingmans Dome. Forney Trail makes seven crossings of the creek along its route. At the mouth of the stream where it enters Fontana Lake is the backcountry campsite Lower Forney (#74; Elevation 1,720')

Bear Branch

SIZE: Small

FISHING PRESSURE: Light

FISHING QUALITY: Very good

ACCESS: Remote

USGS QUADS: Noland Creek, NC

BEAR BRANCH IS A SMALL STREAM that offers fair fishing for stream-bound rainbow trout. It cannot be said this is the finest stream in the Forney Creek watershed. Most of the rainbow trout taken in this stream are below creel size (averaging 5 to 7 inches in length).

> **ACCESS:** Bear Branch is accessible upstream from its confluence with Forney Creek via the Jumpup Ridge Trail. The trailhead is located at the mouth of Bear Branch .6 mile upstream from Fontana Lake. It provides intermittent access to the stream for 2 miles. The trail reaches Poplar Flats at 2.8 miles and leaves the stream at that point. Backcountry campsite Popular Flats (#75; Elevation 2,800') is a fine base camp if you are content to focus your efforts on this diminutive little rill.

Bee Gum Branch

SIZE: Small

FISHING PRESSURE: Light

FISHING QUALITY: Fairly good

ACCESS: Remote

USGS QUADS: Noland Creek, NC

BEE GUM BRANCH IS A DECENT LITTLE TROUT STREAM. There are a fair number of cascades and pools holding rainbow trout. The stream is heavily overgrown with laurel and rhododendron, making fishing difficult.

> **ACCESS:** Bee Gum Branch flows into the main stream 2.8 miles upstream from Fontana Lake. Fair access to the stream is provided by the Bee Gum Branch Trail. For the first 2.3 miles, the stream is often several hundred yards from the trail. At 2.8 miles, the trail leaves the stream to ascend Forney Ridge.

The lower reaches of this stream offer great fishing.

Jonas Creek

SIZE: Small

FISHING PRESSURE: Light

FISHING QUALITY: Very good

ACCESS: Remote

USGS QUADS: Silers Bald, NC–TN

JONAS CREEK IS A DANDY LITTLE TROUT STREAM. Numerous deep holes harbor some fine rainbows. You will probably have the entire stream to yourself any time you decide to wet a line there. As an added dividend, there are several tributaries in this little valley that are very worthwhile to fish. Adventurous anglers can find side streams working alive with trout that seldom see more than a dozen bronzed hooks per year. Two feeder streams of merit are Scarlett Ridge Creek and Little Jonas Creek.

ACCESS: The Jonas Creek Trail provides access to the stream. The trailhead is located 4.1 miles upstream from Fontana Lake near the mouth of Jonas Creek. At 1.3 miles, the trail forsakes the main stream and continues upstream alongside Little Jonas Creek, then at 1.7 miles it crosses Yanu Branch, leaving Little Jonas Creek. The trail then makes a series of switchbacks until 2.7 miles, where it comes within 50 feet of Yanu Branch, before leaving to ascend Welch Ridge.

Huggins Creek

SIZE: Small

FISHING QUALITY: Very good

ACCESS: Remote

USGS QUADS: Silers Bald, NC–TN

HUGGINS CREEK IS AN EXCELLENT EXAMPLE of the plight of the southern Appalachian brook trout. As late as 1975, fish and wildlife surveys showed populations of brook trout in Huggins Creek. Closed to fishing at that time, in 2006 it was reopened to fishing. Little Huggins Creek and three other prongs to Huggins Creek begin at an altitude of more than 4,800 feet. Brook trout futures appear to be safe investments for now.

ACCESS: Huggins Creek flows between Suli Ridge and Loggy Ridge. There is an unmaintained trail that begins near the mouth of the stream and follows alongside to the headwaters.

chapter 22

Noland Creek System

Noland Creek

SIZE: Medium

FISHING PRESSURE: Moderate near the mouth of the stream, somewhat less intense farther upstream

FISHING QUALITY: Very good

ACCESS: North Shore Road; Noland Creek Trail

USGS QUADS: Clingmans Dome, NC–TN; Bryson City, NC–TN; Noland Creek, NC; Silers Bald, NC–TN

DESIGNED FOR THE STOUT OF SOUL AND BODY, this tough-to-get-around-on rivulet is one of the best-kept secrets in the Great Smoky Mountains National Park. It hosts all of the usual suspects, including trout and bass, which are present in good numbers and size.

The Noland Creek Valley seems to impart tranquility and peace of mind. Most of Noland's headwater streams flow through stands of virgin forest, making fly-fishing here a delight.

The overpowering beauty of this valley has not been forgotten by its former residents. The area's rural dwellers were reluctant to leave their homes when the park was created. Former landowners and their descendants frequently come here to fish and walk among the tall trees they refer to with misty eyes as the "old home place."

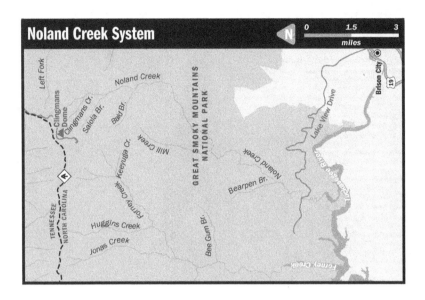

During the prepark era, the Noland Creek watershed was a remote farming community. The families living here in the hollows and coves of the valley supported themselves raising corn and cattle. Corn not needed for bread or winter cattle feed usually found its way through the copper lining of a still. Making mountain "corn likker," or moonshine, was not only an honored art in the mountains of the South, but a reliable source of hard cash. During lean times, which were common in this area, it often helped put shoes on the children's feet.

Fishing on Noland Creek is very good. The upper reaches are made up of fast runs, pocket water, and plunge pools, while the lower reaches of Noland Creek widen out to lend it to modestly genteel fly-fishing. In recent years, brown trout have established themselves in the lower sections of the main stream. Fly-fishermen using big stone fly nymph or streamer-pattern flies take occasional trophy browns from Noland Creek.

Rainbow trout are common from the mouth of the stream to about an elevation of 4,000 feet, and average 7 to 11 inches. But don't be too surprised by the surge of a 16-incher if you drop the right offering in the right spot at the right time.

Brook trout flourish in the headwaters of several streams. Anglers planning to fish the backcountry should make a point of bringing along flies tied on barbless hooks, or pliers for crimping down barbs. I find it amusing that at least one so-called insider notes that fishing at Noland Creek is not as good as that of

Crowds are never a problem at remote Noland Creek.

Forney Creek. I can assure you, were I to take him blindfolded to ether stream he not only would not know which he was fishing, but which was better fishing. He could, however, tell you where pet cemeteries and hoodlum hangouts were before the days of the park.

Noland is an oddity of sorts in a number of ways. Locals universally agree that summer fishing is better than spring fishing because the stream stays so cold. While it is not noted as a producer of big trout, its lower reaches hold lots of big trout that regulars to these waters catch with disturbing consistency on a variant of the Royal Coachman with a blue band substituted for the traditional red band.

Noland Creek is located in the southeast section of the Great Smoky Mountains National Park. It is one of the smallest major streams flowing out of the Smokies into Fontana Lake. It is bound by Forney Ridge, Stateline Ridge, and the Noland Divide. The principal tributaries of the main stream include Bearpen Branch, Mill Creek, Bald Branch, Salola Branch, and Clingmans Creek.

ACCESS: Noland Creek flows into the Tuckasegee River branch of Fontana Lake. It is accessible by auto from North Shore Road (which can be reached via US 19 through Bryson City), which crosses the Noland Divide and reaches the stream at approximately 7 miles. More and more these days, this route is referenced as the Lakeview Drive while the route the road would have taken has been dubbed Lakeshore Trail.

The Noland Creek Trail provides further stream access. The trailhead is located near the Noland Creek Bridge, off the highway. The trail travels alongside the stream and arrives at the confluence of Bearpen Branch and the Bearpen Branch backcountry campsite (#65, capacity 12; Elevation 2,040′) at approximately 1.7 miles. The trail continues upstream and at 4 miles reaches the junction of Mill Creek in the Salola Valley, the site of the Mill Creek Horse Camp backcountry campsite (#64, capacity 20; Elevation 2,540′) and the trailhead of the Springhouse Branch Trail.

At 6 miles the trail arrives at the Jerry Flat backcountry campsite (#63, capacity 10; Elevation 2,920′), and at 7.2 miles the Upper Ripshin backcountry campsite (#62, capacity 12; Elevation 3,160′). The trail continues upstream alongside Noland Creek until reaching the confluence of Sassafras Branch at 8.8 miles, where it leaves Noland Creek to ascend the Noland Divide.

The Bald Creek backcountry campsite (#61, capacity 12, reservations needed; Elevation 3,560) is located 200 yards upstream from the confluence of Sassafras Branch near the junction of Bald Branch and Noland Creek. Upstream from the Bald Creek site, the main stream is accessible by an un-maintained path that closely follows the stream to its confluence with Salola Branch at 10 miles. Clingmans Creek flows into the main stream at 10.8 miles. The Lower Noland Creek backcountry campsite (#66, boats only; Elevation 1,702′) is located along the Noland Creek embayment of Fontana Lake one mile downstream from where the Lakeview Drive crosses Noland Creek.

Bearpen Branch

SIZE: Small

FISHING PRESSURE: Light

FISHING QUALITY: Fair

ACCESS: Remote

USGS QUADS: Noland Creek, NC

BEARPEN BRANCH IS PURELY A RAINBOW TROUT FISHERY. Fishing pressure on this small stream is light, despite its proximity to the North Shore Road. There are several unnamed tributaries that sport a few trout. Anglers should note that the terrain surrounding this little stream is very rugged.

ACCESS: The mouth of the branch is located 1.7 miles upstream from the Noland Creek Trail starting point; there are no streamside trails.

Mill Creek

SIZE: Small

FISHING PRESSURE: Light

FISHING QUALITY: Good to fair

ACCESS: Remote

USGS QUADS: Clingmans Dome, NC–TN; Silers Bald, NC–TN

MILL CREEK IS ONE OF THE MOST IMPORTANT streams flowing into Noland Creek. It enters the main stream in the lovely Salola Valley, which was a busy community before the park was established, and later the site of a ranger station. The lower portion of the stream is dominated by rainbow trout, but the headwaters still contain a healthy population of speckle trout.

Springhouse Branch, a noteworthy tributary of Mill Creek, flows into the main stream a short distance upstream from the Mill Creek Horse Camp site. It passes through a virgin forest and contains only rainbow trout. It's not a place I would try again if that says anything about this creek.

ACCESS: The Springhouse Branch Trail offers limited access to Mill Creek and Springhouse Branch. It begins near the mouth of Mill Creek, and travels alongside the stream. At .7 mile upstream the trail crosses Mill Creek, and from that point continues up the Springhouse Branch. At 1.2 miles the trail leaves the stream to ascend Forney Ridge.

Bald Branch, Salola Branch, and Clingmans Creek

SIZE: All are small

FISHING QUALITY: Very good to excellent

ACCESS: Remote

USGS QUADS: Clingmans Dome, NC–TN

THESE WERE SOME OF THE MOST POPULAR brook trout streams in the park. The ease of descending from Clingmans Dome has proved to be something less than a blessing. All three rivulets were closed to all fishing in 1975 to protect the brook trout stock. While I usually resist noting closed and open waters, Salola Branch was reopened along with a bevy of other formerly closed park waters in 2006.

ACCESS: There are no maintained trails offering access to any of these streams. Bald Branch flows into the main stream 9 miles upstream from Fontana Lake, or 4.5 miles from the Clingmans Dome Road. Salola Branch flows into the main stream 10 miles upstream from Fontana Lake, or 3.5 miles from the Clingmans Dome Road. Clingmans Creek flows into the main stream 10.8 miles upstream from Fontana Lake, or 2.7 miles from the Clingmans Dome Road.

chapter 23

Deep Creek System

Deep Creek

SIZE: Large

FISHING PRESSURE: Moderately heavy near the Deep Creek camp-ground, moderate in the backcountry

FISHING QUALITY: Very good to excellent

ACCESS: Deep Creek Road Trail

USGS QUADS: Bryson City, NC; Clingmans Dome, NC–TN

FEW STREAMS IN THE GREAT SMOKY MOUNTAINS National Park have a richer fly-fishing tradition than Deep Creek. It is one of the more highly publicized streams in the Smokies. Trophy brown trout weighing more than 10 pounds have been wrestled from its emerald-green pools. Few things can compare with a 16-inch rainbow emptying the line from your reel as it flees down one of Deep Creek's swift runs. In recent decades Deep Creek has gained quite a reputation for large brown trout, especially in the late fall months when spawning action reaches its crescendo.

Brook trout still flourish in the headwater streams. You will begin to encounter these aquatic jewels at an elevation of approximately 3,600 feet. It is good to carry several fly patterns tied on barbless hooks, or pliers for crimping down the barbs on your flies, when fishing the backcountry here. A safely returned

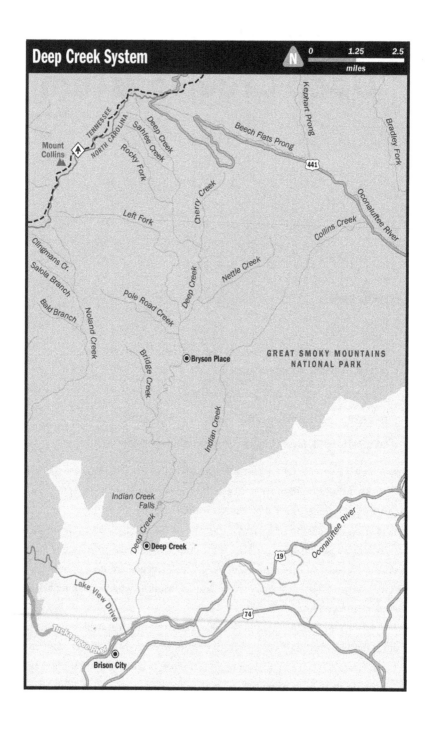

brook trout has an excellent chance of survival, whereas an injured spec might never recover from an encounter with a barbed hook.

As is the case with virtually every large streamshed in the national park, the lower reaches of Deep Creek abound with seldom-cast-to smallmouth and rock bass. Smallies up to 5 pounds are caught here by the handful by local anglers aware of the presence of these spunky gamesters.

This valley was spared some of the wholesale destruction loggers levied on the majority of the watersheds of the Smokies. Deep Creek's rough terrain made getting the lumber out uneconomical, although valuable species such as poplar, walnut, and cherry were selectively cut. However, the lower reaches of Deep Creek were settled by mountain families who lived there in relative peace for generations.

Deep Creek was the favorite haunt of Horace Kephart, the famous Bryson City resident and early advocate for the creation of a national park in the southern Appalachian highlands. Kephart made many trips up this stream, recording his experiences in his writing. This was also the favorite fishing spot of the mountaineer fishing guide Mark Cathey. Cathey guided numerous parties into this valley and delighted in showing the elite anglers of the East his awesomely deadly "dance of the fly."

Much has been written about Cathey's legendary figure-eight dancing fly act, which he loved to perform for anglers from all over the world who visited his favorite stream. In his well-known book, *Hunting and Fishing in the Great Smokies*, Jim Gasque described the dance as follows:

> . . . he (Cathey) jigged and danced his dry fly on the surface all about him without apparent effort to retrieve. He retrieved only when a fish was on, but that was frequent. It was a distinct departure from the conventional method of making the cast and allowing the fly to float down the current. . .

He made the fly wobble and dance on the surface by an almost invisible wrist movement that kept the rod tip trembling and shaking constantly.

Clearly Mark Cathey and probably other anglers from the Great Smoky Mountains in those days understood the deadly value of the currently popular notion of fishing a dry fly as a living insect. When in the vicinity of Bryson City, it is worth looking up Mark Cathey's tombstone, which reads, "Mark Cathey, beloved hunter and fisherman, was caught by the Gospel hook, just before the season closed for good."

Deep Creek was the favorite haunt of the legendary Mark Cathey.

Deep Creek is fortunate to possess a rich aquatic insect community. May-fly hatches are heaviest during the early spring and late summer. In addition, Deep Creek is noted for its large population of stone flies. The only drawback to fishing Deep Creek is the steady stream of tube-riding fun-seekers who system-atically filter down the last mile or so of the stream. The lower section (in park) is nearly impossible to fish in the summer months due to floaters in inner tubes. Above Indian Creek no tubers are allowed, and the fishing gets better upstream. Deep Creek is bound by Thomas Ridge, Stateline Ridge, and the Noland Divide. Its principal tributaries are Indian Creek, Bridge Creek, Pole Road Creek, the Left Fork, Nettle Branch (or Creek), Cherry Creek, Rocky Fork, and Sahlee Creek.

Mirth, remarkable exaggeration, and worse are prominent in the lore of fly-fishing in the Smokies. The story of Abner the Fly-Fishing Ape of Deep Creek is passed along by Carl Lambert, Cherokee storyteller and former director of the Cherokee CETA Program. Also known as the wild monkey of the Smokies, an ape named Abner was an astute specimen that is said to have escaped from a carnival sideshow that was visiting Cherokee in the 1920s. A well-versed panhandler, according to folks in Deep Creek, little Abner sometimes arrived on their porches shivering during cold weather.

An amiable guest, Abner would stay a few days until the cold snap broke before returning to wherever it was he called home in the park. Come spring, Abner always disappeared, although he would be spotted now and then fly-fishing on Deep Creek, and even Hazel Creek. Despite his reputation for stealing coolers of beer and potato salad at the Smokemont Camp Ground, park rangers tended to turn a blind eye to Abner's antics. Being dry fly purists, they admired the fact that Abner did not use live bait when fishing park waters, which was a plus in the eyes of the rangers. Abner is said to have been fond of dangling Thunderhead flies over pools, while he hung by his tail from trees, wearing his signature tweed Stetson.

Abner was also renowned for his efforts to protect the bears of the park from illegal hound hunting. He would allow the Plotts to chase him until he was ready to tree. Just when the hounds thought they had put a bear cub up a balsam, Abner would drop down on the back of the biggest dog and ride him like a polo pony until the hound dropped from exhaustion. He pushed his luck a bit too far one night, galloping by a hunter who swears he put enough buck shot in the ape to kill a 400-pound bear. Perhaps it was true, as thereafter no one ever saw Abner the Fly-Fishing Ape of the Smokies.

My personal favorite fly-fishing stretch at Deep Creek is Bumgardner Bend, a semi-remote section of the stream that requires just enough effort to visit to keep the faint of heart at bay. While not very noteworthy as a fishing creek, Juneywhank Falls are worth the short walk to see and even sling a fly. To get there from the Deep Creek trailhead parking area, follow the well-marked trail .25 mile uphill to Juneywhank Falls. The roar of the falls can be heard even before you reach it. An 80-foot cascade of water starts above you and runs under a log footbridge with handrails, and meets up with Deep Creek at the bottom of the trail. There are two theories regarding the name of this branch and falls. Some say it was named for a Mr. Junaluska "Juney" Whank, who is said to be buried near the falls. However, "Juney Whank" is also a Cherokee phrase, which has been translated to mean "place where the bear passes." Like with much of the lore and fishing opinions, you pick which one you like the best.

ACCESS: Deep Creek has auto access from the Deep Creek Campground, located south of Cherokee via US 19 through Bryson City (from Bryson City the route is well-marked). Access upstream from the campground is provided by the Deep Creek Road Trail. This auto trail begins at the campground and terminates in 2.2 miles at the trailhead of Deep Creek Trail.

The Deep Creek Hiking Trail follows intermittently alongside the stream, and at 2.6 miles (from the Deep Creek Campground) arrives at the Bumgardner Branch backcountry campsite (#60, capacity 10; Elevation 2,120'). This is a small campsite, located 100 feet from the stream. At 5.3 miles is the McCracken Branch backcountry campsite (#59, capacity 6; Elevation 2,320'), a popular fishing camp. At 5.5 miles is the Nicks Nest Branch backcountry campsite (#58, capacity 6; Elevation 2,360'), and at 6.1 miles is the Bryson Place backcountry campsite (#57, capacity 20-Elevation 2,360'). The Burnt Spruce backcountry campsite (#56, capacity 10; Elevation 2,450') is located .3 mile upstream from the Bryson Place site.

Pole Road Creek is located at 7 miles and is the site of the Pole Road backcountry campsite (#55, capacity 15; Elevation 2,410'), which is also the trailhead of the Pole Road Trail. At 7.4 miles the Left Fork of Deep Creek flows into the main stream, and at 8 miles is the Nettle Creek backcountry campsite (#54, capacity 8; Elevation 2,600'), a popular streamside camp. Beetree Creek joins the main stream at 8.4 miles, and at 10.4 miles the trail passes the Poke Patch backcountry campsite (#53, capacity 12; Elevation 2,410'). The confluence of Deep Creek and Rocky Fork is located at 11.6 miles, and at 12.5 miles is the junction of Sahlee Creek. The trail continues alongside the stream to 4,060 feet before ascending Thomas Ridge.

Indian Creek

SIZE: Medium

FISHING PRESSURE: Moderately heavy

FISHING QUALITY: Good

ACCESS: Indian Creek Trail; Deep Creek Campground

USGS QUADS: Bryson City, NC; Smokemont NC–TN; Clingmans Dome, NC–TN

INDIAN CREEK IS A MEDIUM-SIZE STREAM that offers good fishing. The headwaters of this stream lie tucked between the steep grades of Thomas Ridge and Sunkota Ridge. The Bryson City Bachelor, Uncle Mark Cathey, was the last private deed holder of the property in the vicinity of where Indian Creek empties into Deep Creek up to the falls. In his days, when the lower reaches of the Indian Creek were largely flanked by open fields, the creek was larger and in all likelihood

Smallmouth bass are an overlooked quarry common to the lower reaches of Deep Creek.

offered better fishing than it does today. The large pool at the base of the falls has been mislabeled the Cathey Hole so long that, for all practical purposes, most modern-era fly-fishermen believe it is so. Doubtless Cathey would be amused, as these were his so-called backyard waters, but there is little evidence he preferred it to other runs in the Deep Creek drainage. However, it makes for a good story around a campfire when telling ghost stories about him and Kephart.

Brown trout are occasionally landed in the extreme downstream portion of Indian Creek, although rainbows are the stream's dominant species. Brookies have all but vanished from the streamshed.

Indian Creek is a popular fishing spot, and the trail leading to the stream is often crowded with sightseers, who find the walk to Indian Falls irresistible. My personal favorite area where I have spent dozens of afternoons without seeing another angler is where Indian Creek dashes through a rough gorge that is located approximately two miles upstream where the road ascends the slopes well beyond the creek. The Deep Creek watershed has received a lot of ink over the last two decades, and accordingly it can be a bit crowded on weekends. Indian Creek offers a great respite from competing anglers as well as being worth checking if Deep Creek is high or roily.

ACCESS: The mouth of the stream is located 2.2 miles from the campground. The Indian Creek Trail provides access to the stream. It follows alongside the stream to the falls, and at 4 miles leaves the stream. An unmaintained path provides further access to the stream. In recent years the NPS has established two designated backcountry campsites along Indian Creek where in earlier versions of this book there were none. Backcountry campsite #46 (Deep Creek/Indian Creek; Elevation 2680') is located approximately 4 miles upstream from the terminus of a gravel NPS maintenance road. Backcountry campsite #51 (Deep Creek/DeeplowGap; Elevation2700') is the other newly designated site.

Pole Road Creek

SIZE: Small

FISHING PRESSURE: Moderate to fair

FISHING QUALITY: Very good

ACCESS: Pole Road Trail

USGS QUADS: Bryson City, NC; Clingmans Dome, NC–TN

POLE ROAD CREEK IS A SMALL, but respectable, trout stream. The population is composed primarily of rainbows, but a fragile community of brook trout can be found in the headwaters. The trout in this stream are surprisingly wary of anglers.

ACCESS: The Pole Road Trail provides access to Pole Road Creek. It begins at the mouth of the stream, which is located 7 miles upstream from the campground, after a ford of Deep Creek. The trail follows alongside the stream for 2 miles before leaving to ascend Sassafras Gap. Backcountry camping is available at Pole Road (#55, capacity 15; Elevation 2410') .

The Left Fork of Deep Creek

SIZE: Medium

FISHING PRESSURE: Moderate

FISHING QUALITY: Very good; at its best from late spring through early fall

ACCESS: Unmaintained Trail (see Access)

USGS QUADS: Clingmans Dome, NC–TN

THE LEFT FORK IS ONE OF THE LARGEST TRIBUTARIES in the Deep Creek watershed. The mouth of the stream (.4 mile upstream from the Pole Road trail-head) is sometimes difficult to locate from the Deep Creek Trail. Some local anglers tout the Left Fork as their most frequent choice when they reach the forks, despite the fact it is tough to get about on. If you are a history buff, there are old loggers dams a couple of hours of fishing upstream from the mouth of the Left Fork.

The lower reaches of the stream are dominated by rainbow trout. The headwaters support a good population of brookies. Five prongs of this stream begin at an elevation of more than 4,800 feet, and to most experienced Southern trout fishermen, that spells specs. If you plan on fishing this area, include an overnight stay at backcountry campsite Pole Road (#55, capacity 15; Elevation 2410'), which requires reservations. Noteworthy tributaries of the Left Fork are Bearpen Branch and Keg Drive Branch.

ACCESS: The best method for reaching this stream is to fish upstream from Pole Road Creek to the mouth. The mouth of the stream is 7.4 miles upstream from the campground. There is an old, unmaintained trail that follows the stream, but it is at times difficult to locate.

Nettle Creek

SIZE: Small

FISHING QUALITY: Fair to poor

ACCESS: Remote; Deep Creek Campground

USGS QUADS: Clingmans Dome, NC–TN

NETTLE BRANCH, WHICH IS KNOWN AS NETTLE CREEK in many publications and on some maps, is a pretty little run of fast water with average-size rainbow trout and brookies in its upper levels. It drains the steep southerly slopes of Thomas Ridge and enters Deep Creek at a popular backcountry campsite. There are no records of anything more than game trails along this stream. The lower reaches of Nettle Branch get some pressure due to its proximity to a camping area. However, you do not have to work your way far upstream through the laurel chokes to find seldom-cast-to trout. Stay in the creek up and down this rivulet to ensure a certain return to the main trail along Deep Creek.

ACCESS: The mouth of the stream is located 8 miles upstream from the campground. The stream has no access trails. Backcountry campsite Nettle Creek (#54, capacity 15; Elevation 2600') is located at the mouth of the creek. Reservations are not required.

Beetree Creek

SIZE: Small

FISHING QUALITY: Fair to poor

ACCESS: Remote; Deep Creek Campground

USGS QUADS: Clingmans Dome, NC-TN

BEETREE CREEK WAS ONCE A PRODUCTIVE BROOK TROUT STREAM. It is located in one of the loveliest coves in the Smokies. Massive poplars and hemlocks tower above the stream like eternal guardians. Unfortunately, in recent years, the quality of fishing on this stream has eroded, making it a poor choice.

ACCESS: The mouth of the stream is located 8.4 miles upstream from the campground. The stream has no access trails.

Rocky Fork

SIZE: Small

FISHING PRESSURE: Moderate to light

FISHING QUALITY: Good

ACCESS: Remote; Deep Creek Campground

USGS QUADS: Clingmans Dome, NC–TN

ROCKY FORK IS A PICTURESQUE MOUNTAIN BROOK. Tumbling cascades and cool, clear pools are an open invitation to fishermen. It has a combination of rainbow and brook trout at the mouth of the stream, but as one progresses upstream, it quickly becomes a purely brook trout residence.

This is one of the better brook trout streams that was not closed in 1975, but anglers should be forewarned that this is a backcountry stream, located in an fairly remote section of the park. When you decide to fish in such a place, you must depend on yourself. Should you be injured, it could be days, weeks, or even longer before another human being casts a shadow on your face.

ACCESS: The mouth of the stream is located 11.6 miles from the campground; however, anglers should note that the distance from Newfound Gap is 2.8 miles. The stream has no access trails.

Sahlee Creek

SIZE: Small

FISHING QUALITY: Good

ACCESS: Remote; Deep Creek Campground

USGS QUADS: Clingmans Dome, NC-TN

SAHLEE CREEK SUFFERS FROM BEING too easily reached from Newfound Gap. Partially as a result of this, the stream was closed to all fishing in 1975. It was the only stream in the Deep Creek watershed that was ever closed to fishing in the name of protecting the specs. A beautiful stream with an unusual number of deadfalls crisscrossing it, Sahlee Creek is a physically tiring stream to fish.

ACCESS: The mouth of the stream is located 12.5 miles upstream from the campground; however, anglers should note the distance from Newfound Gap is 1.9 miles. There are no streamside trails.

chapter 24

Oconaluftee River System

Oconaluftee River

SIZE: Large

FISHING PRESSURE: Moderately heavy to heavy

FISHING QUALITY: Very good; the lower reaches of the stream are noted for producing trophy brown trout

ACCESS: Newfound Gap Road

USGS QUADS: Clingmans Dome, NC–TN; Mt. Guyot, NC-TN; Smokemont, NC-TN; Bunches Bald, NC; Luftee Knob, NC–TN

THE OCONALUFTEE RIVER IS NOTED as a good brown trout stream, as well as the most overlooked, high-octane smallmouth bass fishery in the park. The stream is large, with an abundance of long, slow runs and deep pools. Browns exceeding 12 pounds have been wrestled from the crystalline waters of this river. Late fall is a favorite time for local anglers, who employ a wide variety of large stone fly nymphs to entice large browns. One fly I was shown, however, appeared to be an imitation of a large "tobacco worm." Constructed of raffia, the fly was dyed a deep green and tied on a No. 4 long-shanked hook. I attempted to trade for one of the odd-looking flies, but its owner, Jim Mills, one of Cherokee's most successful brown trout fishermen, told me that upon receiving this pattern from an old mountain man years before, he had promised to never give a copy of the fly to anyone.

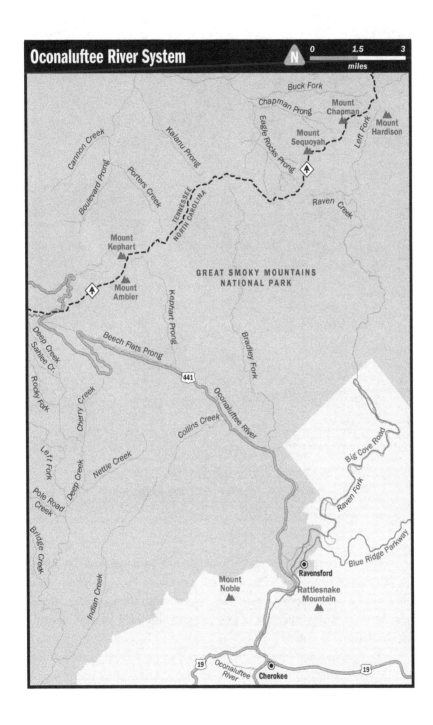

Oconaluftee River System

Buck Fork

Chapman Prong

Mount Chapman

Mount Hardison

Eagle Rocks Prong

Mount Sequoyah

Left Fork

Cannon Creek

Kalanu Prong

Boulevard Prong

Porters Creek

TENNESSEE

NORTH CAROLINA

Raven Creek

Mount Kephart

GREAT SMOKY MOUNTAINS NATIONAL PARK

Mount Ambler

Kephart Prong

Deep Creek

Sahlee Cr.

Beech Flats Prong

Bradley Fork

Rocky Fork

Cherry Creek

441

Oconaluftee River

Collins Creek

Big Cove Road

Left Fork

Deep Creek

Nettle Creek

Pole Road Creek

Raven Fork

Bridge Creek

Blue Ridge Parkway

Indian Creek

Mount Noble

Ravensford

Rattlesnake Mountain

19   Oconaluftee River   Cherokee   19

0   1.5   3

miles

The Oconaluftee River is home to many big brown trout.

Despite the presence of brown trout in the Oconaluftee River, the adaptable rainbows are the primary trout of the watershed. Their eagerness to eat almost any time food appears makes them favorites with average anglers. Brook trout, however, still prosper in a large number of headwater streams, particularly the Raven Fork system.

The Oconaluftee River is deeply rooted in the human history of the Great Smoky Mountains. The Smokies were the cultural heart of the Cherokee Nation, whose domain once extended from the mountains of northern Georgia throughout the entire southern Appalachians. Prior to contact with white settlers, the Cherokee civilization was considered to be the most advanced of any eastern North American native people. Primarily farmers, their prowess in combat kept their neighbors in awe. The word "oconaluftee" in Cherokee means "by the river." Most local anglers simply refer to it as the Luftee, as too many syllables can be tough to navigate when not in a necessarily solid state of sobriety.

White settlers, attracted by the valley's fertile soil, first carved out homesteads in the 1790s. Later, during the mid-1830s, the federal government ordered the forced removal of all remaining Native Americans to the west of the Mississippi River. The result of this action inflicted on the Cherokees has been named the "Trail of Tears." A small band of Cherokees numbering about 1,000 refused to obey the order and retreated to the more remote sections of the Smokies. Later, the survivors of those who refused to leave were able to purchase the land that we now know as the Qualla Reservation.

The Oconaluftee River watershed is located in the center of the Smokies on the North Carolina side of the park. The river proper is formed by the confluence of Beech Flats Prong and Kepart Prong. Other key tributaries include Raven Fork, Collins Creek, and Bradley Fork. Raven Fork and Bradley Fork both have exceptionally well-developed tributary networks that are of considerable interest to anglers.

ACCESS: The park section of the main stream of the Oconaluftee River runs alongside the Newfound Gap Road (formerly US 441) for 10.4 miles, to the junction of Kepart Prong and Beech Flats Prong.

Raven Fork

SIZE: Medium

FISHING PRESSURE: Local horse-riding anglers use this stream on a fairly regular basis, but overall it does not receive a great deal of pressure

FISHING QUALITY: Good

ACCESS: Remote

USGS QUADS: Smokemont, NC–TN; Mt. Guyot, NC–TN

RAVEN FORK IS UNIQUE BECAUSE it flows out of the park, then comes back in. Its headwaters begin beneath the fir-lined ridges of Balsam Mountain and Stateline Ridge. A total of 11 prongs of Raven Fork's main stream begin at an altitude of more than 5,000 feet, with the majority of these feeder streams merging above 4,200 feet.

This is a rugged area, a fact that helped protect the streamshed from the wholesale logging that hurt many of the watersheds in the Smokies. Choice market trees, such as walnut and cherry, were selectively removed from the region, yet much of the valley remained intact. Over the years I have made perhaps a half dozen safari trips back to its magical headwaters. If you plan to do so as well, I strongly recommend the Sherpa guide service I use to ensure you have all of the necessary amenities for a casual visit to the sure-enough "back of beyond."

The stream's native brook trout were possibly spared because of two circumstances: remoteness and fishing pressure. Fewer than 2,000 rainbow trout were stocked in Raven Fork. In contrast, the neighboring Oconaluftee River received over a quarter of a million rainbows. It has been theorized that this has been a factor in explaining the population densities of the brook trout in the two adjacent streams. Raven Fork is one of the finest remaining brook trout waters in the southern Appalachians. It was named in honor of "Kalanu," one of the Cherokee Nation's most revered war chiefs, who resided along the banks of this stream.

Raven Fork enters the Qualla Reservation near the Big Cove area, then near its confluence with the Oconaluftee River flows back into the park. At the time of this writing, the regulation of that portion of Raven Fork in the park belongs to the Qualla Reservation. Directly upstream from the Qualla Reservation, Raven Fork flows through a section known as "The Gorge," which is considered to be one of the most rugged and primitive areas in the eastern United States. The water jets over weathered gray boulders, pausing in the depths of foaming pools before racing on. This section of the stream offers very good fishing, but it should never be attempted alone.

ACCESS: The park portion of Raven Fork is one of the most remote areas in the entire Smokies. To reach Raven Fork, one must drive to the Cherokee Reservation. Big Cove Road, located off the Newfound Gap Road in Cherokee, is the easiest route. Follow Big Cove Road, which travels along scenic Raven Fork, about 9 miles to the junction of Raven Fork and Straight Fork. Big Cove Road continues upstream along Raven Fork, and Round Bottom Road enters from the left, leading up Straight Fork. Anglers wishing to follow Raven Fork should take Round Bottom Road, alongside Straight Fork, and at 1.2 miles pass through the park's boundary gate. At 2.5 miles, Round Bottom Road arrives at the trailhead of the Enloe Creek Trail.

The trail offers the easiest access to the upstream sections of Raven Fork. It travels for a short distance along sparkling Hyatt Creek, and at 2.7 miles arrives at the junction of the Raven Fork Trail. The Raven Fork Trail descends the ridge alongside the gushing waters of Enloe Creek to the banks of Raven Fork. Located at the junction of Enloe Creek and Raven Fork is the Enloe Creek

Fly-fishing is outstanding throughout the Oconaluftee watershed.

backcountry campsite (#47, capacity 8; Elevation 3,620'), which is a super base fishing camp where reservations are required. It is nestled among some of the most spectacular cascades in the Smokies. Downstream from the campsite, Raven Fork is accessible by a path that roughly follows the stream.

Upstream from the campsite, the Raven Fork Trail winds along the swift waters of the stream. At 2.5 miles, the trail reaches the abandoned Big Pool backcountry campsite. The Right, Middle, and Left prongs of Raven

Fork all merge here, forming a large, expansive pool, perfect for floating a dry fly. The trail leaves the stream to ascend Breakneck Ridge. Backcountry campsite McGee Spring (#44, horse/camper; Elevation 5,040') is accessible via the Hyatt Ridge Trail (3 miles to campsite). This lovely parcel of relatively flat land affords the luxury of walking downhill to get in a stream to then fish back upstream to the waiting comforts of camp. It is located in a surprisingly quaint little cove alongside a spring that trickles to enter near the Three Forks area. There is no trail along the branch, so avoid the urge to stray far in pursuit of morel mushrooms or ramps, both of which are worthy accompaniments to eggs eaten with freshly caught trout. During late summer the accumulation of horse droppings makes the aroma of springtime ramps something to covet.

Straight Fork

SIZE: Small

FISHING PRESSURE: Light to moderate

FISHING QUALITY: Good

ACCESS: Round Bottom Road

USGS QUADS: Luftee Knob, NC–TN

STRAIGHT FORK OFFERS GOOD TROUT FISHING opportunities to those seeking a nice stream with limited road access. True to its name, the creek is pretty much a linear southward shoot through steep hollow. Standing in one spattering of pocket water you can see upstream where you will be fishing in an hour. The lower reaches of the stream are chock-full of rainbow and brown trout, while the upper reaches, though small, are home to brook trout. It is a decent-size trout stream, and fishing pressure is largely limited to local anglers. Round Bottom Road provides access to the stream, traveling 3.5 miles to the Round Bottom Picnic Grounds. There are no further maintained trails upstream from the picnic grounds. This is a tributary of Raven Fork, which is a tributary of the Oconaluftee River. Please be aware that where Straight Fork flows over tribal land, you better be a member of that club to fish. The park boundary is well marked. Straight Fork is a nifty combination of easy fishing with easy access. I rate it two flasks.

Mingus Creek

SIZE: Small

FISHING PRESSURE: Moderate

FISHING QUALITY: Marginal to fair

ACCESS: Roadside; Remote

USGS QUADS: Smokemont, NC

MINGUS CREEK DRAINS THE SOUTHEAST SLOPES of Newton Bald before its downward dash bends abruptly to the east where it parallels the southern border of Great Smoky Mountains National Park for 2 miles to reach the Oconaluftee River. Mingus Creek is a small trout stream that enters the Luftee a short jaunt upstream from the Oconaluftee Visitors Center. An unmarked slave cemetery is located on the flat on the right side of the creek that dates back to when this run of water was known as Spillcorn Creek. It is a decent enough little trickle where rainbow hold court, but brown trout occasionally show up, especially during their autumn spawning time. Brook trout are found in the headwaters along the trail that ultimately ascends to Newton Bald (which is no longer a bald). Over a dozen feeder streams merge with Mingus, but the only one of any note is Madcap Branch, which enters from the left 2 miles up the trail.

The name Mingus took hold as a result of the old grist mill built long ago, which is still located within sight of the mouth of the creek on the Oconaluftee River. Demonstrations are still held from late spring to fall at the mill, which was rehabilitated by the National Park Service down to its redwood millrace in 1968. According to some sources, hikers are discouraged from using the nearby Mingus Creek Trail. No longer included on park maps, the trail passes a law-enforcement target range as well as the water-supply treatment area for the town of Cherokee, making it neither safe nor pleasant to walk on.

Couches Creek

SIZE: Small

FISHING PRESSURE: Moderate

FISHING QUALITY: Marginal

ACCESS: Remote

USGS QUADS: Smokemont, NC

COUCHES CREEK IS A SMALL TROUT STREAM that is often overlooked for greener pastures elsewhere. It is picturesque, though scenery cannot entirely satisfy the desire to catch fish. Frankly, were this book not the tell-all, be-all cornucopia of secret fishing knowledge, I would not in good conscious mention this rill in the same sentence as "fishing."

Bradley Fork

SIZE: Large at its junction with the Oconaluftee; smaller a short distance upstream from that point

FISHING PRESSURE: Heavy

FISHING QUALITY: Excellent

ACCESS: Smokemont Campground Road; Bradley Fork Trail

USGS QUADS: Smokemont, NC; Mt. Guyot, NC–TN

MANY NORTH CAROLINA TROUT FISHERMEN feel that the lower reaches of Bradley Fork provide some of the better, if not the best, trout fishing in the Smokies. It holds large brown trout and colorful rainbow trout in abundance, and sports an impressive population of native speckle trout. Its size permits relatively easy casting room for fly-fishermen and spinner enthusiasts alike. The stream annually produces mayfly hatches that capture the imagination of both anglers and trout. The lower reaches of the main stream are often crowded due to the stream's reputation and proximity to the most popular campground in the Smokies. Anglers willing to walk a couple of miles upstream will be rewarded with relief from the crowds and better fishing.

It is not particularly difficult to fish; Bradley Fork is not shrouded in a cast-resistant canopy. Some hacks say it has clearer water than elsewhere in the park. Since I cannot tell the difference in the clarity of cheap gin and expensive gin, I can only say that my vision, along with my palate, may have become impaired over the years. These days I need reading glasses to snake a tippet through the eye of my #28 and smaller flies.

Bradley Fork's feeder streams offer good fishing and are lovely. Among these outstanding rivulets are Chasteen Creek, Taywa Creek, Gulf Prong, and Chasm Prong. The main stream of Bradley Fork begins at the confluence of Gulf Prong and Chasm Prong. It is bound by the steep ridges of Richland Mountain and Hughes Ridge. Bradley Fork empties into the Oconaluftee 6.5 miles upstream from the park boundary, near the Smokemont campground. The Smokemont Campground has 180 campsites, and is often crowded.

ACCESS: Bradley Fork is accessible from its mouth to the upper end of the Smokemont Campground by auto from the Smokemont Campground Road. Upstream from the campground, access is limited to horse and foot travel.

The Bradley Fork Trail, one of the finest in the Smokies, follows the stream to its headwaters. The trailhead is located at the end of the Smokemont campground. At 1.2 miles, you will find the confluence of Chasteen Creek, also the site of the well-developed Lower Chasteen backcountry campsite (#50, capacity 15) and the trailhead of Chasteen Creek Trail.

The Bradley Fork Trail continues on, and at 4.1 miles arrives at the junction of Taywa Creek, also the starting point of the Taywa Creek Trail. At 4.3 miles, the Bradley Fork Trail passes the junction of Tennessee Branch, a fishable little feeder stream, and at 5.2 miles arrives at the Cabin Flats backcountry campsite (#49, capacity 20; Elevation 3060'). It is a nice spot, although it can become very muddy during certain times of the year.

Upstream from the campsite, the stream is reached via a path that is not maintained, which continues upstream alongside the stream. At 6.3 miles is the confluence of Gulf Prong and Chasm Prong. At this point, the path leaves the stream to ascend Balsam Ridge.

Chasteen Creek

SIZE: Small

FISHING PRESSURE: Moderately light

FISHING QUALITY: Good

ACCESS: Chasteen Creek Trail

USGS QUADS: Smokemont, NC–TN

CHASTEEN CREEK FLOWS INTO BRADLEY FORK 1.2 miles upstream from the Smokemont Campground. It offers good rainbow trout fishing, and occasionally brown trout action. The Chasteen Creek Trail, which begins near the mouth of the stream, offers access to the stream. It runs alongside the creek and at 2.2 miles arrives at the Upper Chasteen backcountry campsite (#48, capacity 15; Elevation 3,320'). The trail continues on beside the creek for 3 miles before the stream becomes too small to fish. The Lower Chasteen backcountry campsite (#30, capacity 15 horses/15 campers; Elevation 2,360') is a less desirable option during hot weather if you are not particularly fond of the aroma generally associated with stables.

Taywa Creek

SIZE: Small

FISHING PRESSURE: Light

FISHING QUALITY: Fair to good

ACCESS: Taywa Creek Trail

USGS QUADS: Smokemont, NC–TN

TAYWA CREEK IS THE SECOND SIGNIFICANT feeder flowing into Bradley Fork upstream from the Smokemont Campground. The lower reaches of Taywa Creek hold brightly hued rainbow trout, while the headwaters are held by speckle trout. The creek is reached via the Taywa Creek Trail, which begins near the mouth of the stream and follows alongside the stream for 1.5 miles.

Chasm Creek and Gulf Prong

SIZE: Both are very small

FISHING PRESSURE: Light

FISHING QUALITY: Good

ACCESS: Remote

USGS QUADS: Mt. Guyot, NC–TN

THESE TWO MOUNTAIN RILLS MERGE to form the starting point of Bradley Fork. Both are primarily brook trout streams. The forest through which these aquatic gems flow is one of the loveliest in the Oconaluftee Valley. There are no maintained streamside trails offering access, but upstream progress via the streambed is usually possible.

Collins Creek

SIZE: Small

FISHING PRESSURE: Light

FISHING QUALITY: Very good

ACCESS: New Found Gap Road; Collins Creek Trail

COLLINS CREEK IS A SURPRISING LITTLE MOUNTAIN CREEK that offers very good fishing. I have never fished this stream without a nice fish taxing my tackle. I cannot say if this is an extraordinary stream or just a place where "lady luck" smiles on me. On several occasions during his last years, my neighbor, Harry Middleton, and I sat and chatted about the Smokies. Middleton penned *On the Spine of Time* (published in 1991), which is perhaps the finest work ever written on fishing the Smokies. I was quite flattered to learn from Middleton that he credited his discovery of the outstanding Collins Creek to the accolades I have always given it in print. His house and mine were but slingshot shooting range apart in Homewood, a suburb of Birmingham, Alabama, where Jesse James is said to have once frequented to buy horses. Harry was a couple of years older than I and had approximately four times the talent I possessed. At his suggestion, management at Southern Progress where he worked, handling the outdoor beat for *Southern Living*, contacted me to start up a new publication they were launching called *Cooking Light*. Again, I was flattered, but had considerable moral trepidation at turning my back on cooking with butter and lard. Harry understood.

> *Sooner or later you've got to let loose of certainty's hand and leap. Jump. Believe in something, like mountains and mountain streams, trout and mountain people.*
>
> —Harry Middleton, 1949–1993

An added bonus to fishing Collins Creek is the fact that it flows through a beautiful virgin forest upstream from the Newfound Gap Road. The lower reaches of the stream hold brown and rainbow trout, while up in the headwaters brookies hold dominion.

ACCESS: The mouth of Collins Creek is reached by auto from the Newfound Gap Road, 8.8 miles upstream from the park boundary. Immediately upstream from its mouth, Collins Creek passes through the Collins Creek Picnic Area. Beyond the picnic ground, access is limited to an unmaintained path, known as the Collins Creek Trail, for a distance of 2.6 miles.

Kephart Prong

SIZE: Small

FISHING PRESSURE: Moderately light

FISHING QUALITY: very good to excellent

ACCESS: Kephart Prong Trail; Grassy Branch Trail; Sweet Heifer Creek Trail

USGS QUADS: Smokemont, NC; Mt. Guyot, NC–TN

KEPHART PRONG WAS NAMED IN HONOR of Horace Kephart, the Smokies' famous outdoor writer. An early fellow trout bum, Kepart had the good fortune of not only fishing these streams during their heyday, but also dying with his boots on. His demise was closely associated with moonshine, an automobile, and a tough-to-navigate-while-too-happy curve. If you are a fisherman, there is a lot to be said about going with your boots on and not on the urine-soaked sheets of a hospital bed. Should we who fish these waters be so lucky to go out like real men as did Kephart and Hemingway. IV-free departures are a blessing.

There was once a trout and bass rearing station located alongside this stream during the early years of the National Park. Today, the stream offers anglers fair fishing for rainbows. The brookies have disappeared from this streamshed.

ACCESS: Kephart Prong is accessible at its mouth by auto via the Newfound Gap Road, 10.4 miles upstream from the park boundary. The Kephart Prong Trail offers additional access to the stream. Its trailhead is located near the mouth of the stream, off the highway. It follows upstream alongside Kephart Prong and at 2 miles arrives at the Kephart shelter (capacity 14). Here, the Kephart Prong Trail ends and the Grassy Branch Trail and the Sweet Heifer Creek Trail begin. Both offer further access to tributaries of Kephart Prong.

Beech Flats Prong

SIZE: Small

FISHING PRESSURE: Moderate to light

FISHING QUALITY: Fair to somewhat poor

ACCESS: Newfound Gap Road

USGS QUADS: Smokemont, NC; Mt. Guyot, NC–TN

BEECH FLATS PRONG IS, in truth, the upstream extension of the main stream of the Oconaluftee River. It is a scenic little rivulet, though not a particularly outstanding trout stream. The stream flows over a formation of acid-bearing shale known as the Anakeesta Formation. For eons, Beech Flat Prong flowed over this formation, gradually leeching out and sealing the bulk of the exposed "hot" rocks' acidic properties. The pH of Beech Flats Prong was always low, but the brook trout and other aquatic life forms found it bearable and prospered. When the National Park Service thought it necessary to widen Newfound Gap Road alongside the path of the stream, the Anakeesta Formation was unwittingly cut into. The stream was then exposed to this freshly unearthed acid source. To make a bad situation worse, the Anakeesta was crushed into gravel and used as the bed for the new pavement. The aquatic life of this little stream has been damaged by this act, and the effects will be felt for several lifetimes. Kanati Fork is the nicest of the little tributaries of Beech Flats Prong, which in terms of fishability includes almost a half dozen streams that include Huskey Creek, Aden Branch,

Peruvian Branch, Minnie Ball Branch, Mine Branch, and Jack Bradely Branch. These come together in a relatively short distance, and it's just about impossible not to sample one or two of them.

It is where, in an easy single outing, you can accomplish the coveted Smoky Mountains TTT (tri-trout triumphus), or all three species trout. Also referred to as the Triple T, it is sort of like the coveted sheep grand slam, which was later hijacked by turkey hunters. Having hunted my share of sheep and goats as well as turkey and gophers, as Dan Quayle was told he was not Jack Kennedy, shooting a pile of dumb birds that sleep in trees or burrowing gophers is no grand slam. Gimme a break! Hunters Jack O'Connor and Mark Cathey would laugh their asses off at this bastardization of the venerated term, "grand slam." Now that is what I call back of beyond.

ACCESS: The Newfound Gap Road follows alongside the route of Beech Flats Prong for 2.8 miles. Upstream from the highway's last contact with the stream, a National Park Service road parallels the stream to its headwaters.

Kanati Fork

SIZE: Very small

FISHING PRESSURE: Light

FISHING QUALITY: Very good

ACCESS: Kanati Fork Trail

USGS QUADS: Smokemont, NC–TN

KANATI FORK, A TRIBUTARY OF BEECH FLATS PRONG, is a small stream often overlooked by anglers. It flows into Beech Flats Prong, the headwaters of the Oconaluftee River It offers great fishing for native brook trout. "Kanati" is Cherokee, meaning "lucky hunter." Anglers wishing to try their luck here should by all means use barbless hooks or crimp down the barbs of the flies used. Kanati Fork is accessible by auto at its mouth via the Newfound Gap Road. It enters the main stream 10.6 miles upstream from the park boundary. The Kanati Fork Trail lends suspect (at best) access to the stream beyond that point. Its trailhead is located near the mouth of the stream and provides fair access for a very short distance. If you are of a mind to dabble flies here, ignore Kanati Fork Trail. In terms of stream access, it is as useless as tits on a boar hog. It's a well-above-average brookie stream, at least in terms of sheer numbers and having fun to boot. It rates a solid one flask.

chapter 25

Cataloochee Creek System

Cataloochee Creek

SIZE: Large

FISHING PRESSURE: Moderate to light

FISHING QUALITY: Excellent; particularly good early and late in the season

ACCESS: New Cataloochee Road

USGS QUADS: Dellwood, NC; Cove Creek Gap, NC; Bunches Bald, NC; Luftee Knob, NC

IT TOOK CONSIDERABLE SOUL-SEARCHING on my part before I decided to include this stream. It is so quiet and peaceful there that I almost did not want to let other fly-fishermen in on the secret of its outstanding trout and bass angling opportunites. Now there are dozens of guides who offer guided trips to the Cataloochee, so suffice it to say the cat is out of the bag.

The Cataloochee Valley lies in one of the most remote sections of the Great Smoky Mountains National Park and is often referred to as the "Forgotten Far East." Catalooch was the most common name given this 10,000-acre valley prior to the federal park's recreation. Located off the established tourist path, Cataloochee has limited facilities—a ranger station and a primitive campground (28 campsites, located alongside the stream)—but a well-developed trail system. The Cataloochee Primitive Campground makes an ideal base camp for anglers wishing to sample Cataloochee's smorgasbord of trout streams.

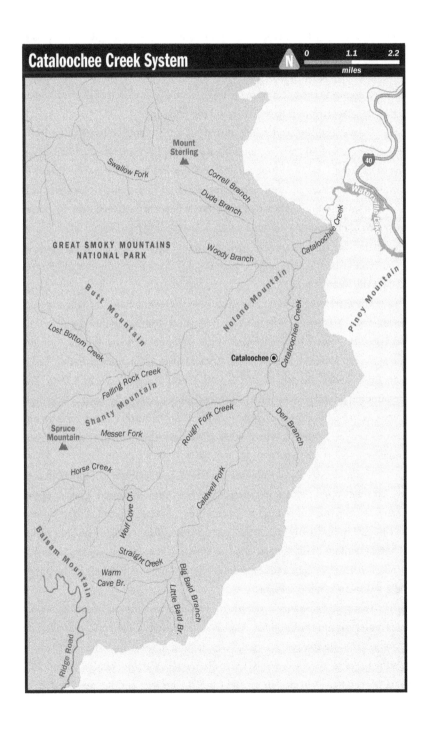

Cataloochee Creek System

N

0   1.1   2.2
miles

Mount Sterling

Swallow Fork

Correll Branch

Dude Branch

Woody Branch

GREAT SMOKY MOUNTAINS
NATIONAL PARK

Butt Mountain

Noland Mountain

Cataloochee Creek

Piney Mountain

40

Waterville Lake

Cataloochee Creek

Lost Bottom Creek

Falling Rock Creek

Shanty Mountain

Cataloochee

Spruce Mountain

Messer Fork

Rough Fork Creek

Den Branch

Horse Creek

Caldwell Fork

Wolf Cove Cr.

Balsam Mountain

Straight Creek

Warm Cave Br.

Big Bald Branch

Little Bald Br.

Ridge Road

When it comes to Cherokee names, they are as elusive and changing as the names of trout flies everyone and his brother from the hills say they were the first to tie and fish. The Cherokee who found this piece of heaven called it "Gadalutsi," which according to one translation means "fringe sticking straight up" in reference to the tall, mountain-top balsams. Many say that the word refers to the row after row of ridges that crowd the horizon.

Located off the established tourist path, Cataloochee has limited facilities—a ranger station and a primitive campground (28 campsites, located alongside the stream)—but a well-developed trail system. The Cataloochee Primitive Campground makes an ideal base camp for anglers wishing to sample Cataloochee's smorgasbord of trout streams. Lots of decent folk lived here, and there are reams of information on them detailing everything from whom among them was left-handed to the names of their old hound dogs. This is a fishing book, so if you want to find out the precise location of J. Clark Correll outhouse, you are reading the wrong book.

The Cataloochee system is more like the combination of four separate streams, which converge within a relatively short distance within the cove. The main stream flows 7 to 8 miles within the park, before leaving to later empty into Walters Lake (also known as Waterville Lake), an impoundment of the Pigeon River under the control of Carolina Power & Light's Walters Dam. The surrounding property is owned by Progress Energy, a corporation that is as mysterious as its name sounds. You may not be able to actually contact them to buy lakeside property, but if you trespass, you may get an opportunity to meet their attorneys in court.

The main stream of Cataloochee Creek and a number of its tributaries flow through open fields and dales, often laced by weathered, gray, split-rail fences, an ever-present reminder of the sturdy farmers who toiled in this green cove in past times. Many local streams are named after families who once resided here. Reunions of old Cataloochee families, held here every August, unite 400 to 500 former residents and their descendents—a human heritage that bonds these mountains to the present.

This pastoral stream is not nearly so rough-and-tumble as are the majority of waterways in the Smokies. Anglers from upstate New York will feel quite at home here; the stream has a generous helping of long, slick runs, perfect for floating a sparsely dressed dry fly. Once discovered, Cataloochee becomes a personal Mecca that provides an escape from the crowds and hurried lifestyle of the outside world.

The main stream of Cataloochee Creek is populated by a mixture of rainbow and brown trout, with trophies occasionally taken of each. Terrestrials such as jassids, grasshoppers, and several other seasonal land insects are extremely important to the diet of these trout, particularly where the stream flows past open fields. Once, while fishing below the campground, I was lucky enough to be on the stream while one of the fields was being mowed. With every pass of the mowing tractor, a wave of fleeing grasshoppers would spangle the surface of the creek. The Hip's Hopper I used that day accounted for more than 50 creel-size trout (both rainbow and brown) within a two-hour period (all were released). I would never venture into this valley without an assortment of terrestrial imitations. The lower reaches of Cataloochee Creek are alive with smallmouth bass in the 3- to 5-pound class. These fish are common in the stream to its mouth at Waterville Lake.

Elk can now be seen here as well as elsewhere in the park where elk have been restored. I giggle a bit at this when I recall the the many meetings and interviews in the 1970s that I had with Tennessee Wildlife Resources Agency, U.S. Fish and Wildlife Service, and NPS about the possibility of returning elk to the Smokies. They all told me it was impossible. Conversely, a few years later when the same people began the red wolf restoration program, I publicly said they were crazy. Well, today we have elk in the park; the red wolf program is no more.

My strangest experience in the Smokies occurred at Cataloochee River downstream form the valley. Rounding a bend while fishing, I came upon some Cherokee circled around a large pool. Most were waist deep, while at the edge of the creek older women tended kettles suspended over fires. They were catching crawdads, which they delivered to the women who were cooking the catch as it was delivered.

Walking up to the gathering, I was pretty much ignored, until the brother of a Cherokee friend of mine, Adam Thompson, recognized me. He greeted me and showed me crawdad cornmeal mush (Selu'sa Anista Tsisdvna) being cooked up. Its taste was reminiscent of a bland lobster Newburg. I was told that this was, among other things, a traditional Thanksgiving Day dish. Adam had often taken me into mountains to talk to tribal herbalists who spoke little or no English. It was always a treat.

The Cataloochee Basin is bound by the Cataloochee Divide, Mt. Sterling Ridge, and the Balsam Mountains. Its key tributaries include Little Cataloochee Creek, Caldwell Fork, and Palmer Creek, all possessing well-developed tributary systems that deserve the attention of anglers.

Full-bellied rainbow trout are common here.

ACCESS: Getting to this remote area requires a long drive over a gravel road. Approaching from the west along I-40, take the Waterville exit (No. 451) and cross the Pigeon River. Turn left at the end of the bridge and follow the paved road 2 miles to an intersection. Here, turn left onto a gravel road (formerly known as NC 284) and continue on to the Cataloochee Valley (approximately 23 miles).

Upon reaching the valley, the New Cataloochee Road follows alongside the stream for 3 miles, arriving at the campground. The confluence of Palmer Creek and Caldwell Fork is located a short distance upstream. The confluence of these two streams marks the starting point of Cataloochee Creek.

Little Cataloochee Creek

SIZE: Medium to small

FISHING PRESSURE: Light

FISHING QUALITY: Good

ACCESS: Old NC 284; Little Cataloochee Creek Trail

USGS QUADS: Cove Creek Gap, NC

LITTLE CATALOOCHEE CREEK IS A MINIATURE VERSION of the main stream, not dominated by a long, all-encompassing single creek, but rather the result of several small streams converging within a short distance to form a medium-size trout stream. Little Cataloochee Creek's headwaters begin well above 5,000 feet, on the steep slopes of Mt. Sterling. Rainbow trout are most common in the lower and middle reaches of the stream, with brook trout still occupying the upper portions.

Tributaries of Little Cataloochee Creek that are of angling merit include Coggins Branch, Conrad Branch, and Andy Branch for rainbow trout, and Correll Branch and Woody Branch for brook trout.

ACCESS: Old NC 284 travels alongside Little Cataloochee Creek upstream from its confluence with the main stream to .3 mile, where Correll Branch enters Little Cataloochee Creek. The road continues alongside Correll Branch for 3,600 feet, before leaving the stream.

Trail access to the main stream of Little Cataloochee Creek is available via the Little Cataloochee Creek Trail. To reach the trailhead, drive 4.5 miles past the intersection of Old NC 284 and the Cataloochee Road (in the direction of Mt. Sterling). At that point there is a sign that reads "Little Cataloochee Baptist Church, 2 miles." This is the starting point of the Little Cataloochee Creek Trail, which, for the first 1.5 miles, travels through a lovely forest setting. At 1.5 miles, the trail arrives at Little Cataloochee Creek (the only contact the trail has with the main stream), then travels on past Little Cataloochee Creek, and at 2.2 miles arrives at Coggins Branch. The trail follows Coggins Branch 2.6 miles before leaving the stream to climb Noland Gap.

Caldwell Fork

SIZE: Small

FISHING PRESSURE: Moderate near the campground; farther upstream the pressure decreases

FISHING QUALITY: Fish are small but plentiful

ACCESS: Caldwell Fork Trail

USGS QUADS: Bunches Bald, NC; Dellwood, NC

THE CONFLUENCE OF CALDWELL FORK AND PALMER CREEK forms the starting point of Cataloochee Creek. Caldwell Fork is the smaller of the two streams, flowing off the Cataloochee Divide. It contains rainbow and brown trout in its lower reaches, and a remnant population of specs in a few headwater areas. Over ten prongs of this stream begin at more than 4,400 feet; however, the rainbow trout, the most abundant game fish in the watershed, are the dominant species the entire length of the main stream. McKee Branch, a small tributary, maintains a population of brookies.

Caldwell Fork receives a moderate amount of fishing pressure immediately upstream from the campground. The quality of the fishing is good, but most of the fish are under creel size (5 to 8 inches).

Fishable tributaries of Caldwell Fork include McKee Branch, Big Bald Branch, and, during the spring, Warm Cove Branch.

The lower reaches of this watershed are home for tackle-busting smallmouth bass.

ACCESS: The Caldwell Fork Trail follows the main stream from its confluence with Palmer Creek. The trailhead is located off the New Cataloochee Road near the mouth of the stream. Upstream at .8 mile, Den Branch flows into the main stream, the starting point of the Booger Man Trail, a loop that rejoins the Caldwell Fork Trail at 2.5 miles near the confluence of Snake Branch.

McKee Branch is located at 3 miles, and at 3.5 miles the trail arrives at the Caldwell Fork backcountry campsite (#41, capacity 10; Elevation 3,360′), located near a large, open field known as the Deadening Fields. Anglers will find this section of the stream particularly suited for the use of hopper flies during the summer.

The trail continues upstream alongside Caldwell Fork. At 4.4 miles, Double Gap Branch enters the main stream. The Double Gap Trail offers access to Double Gap Branch, a very small branch of questionable fishing merit. Shortly after passing over Double Gap Branch, the trail becomes known as the Big Poplar Trail. At 5 miles it leaves the stream for the last time, to climb a small ridge, later terminating on the Rough Fork Trail.

Palmer Creek

SIZE: Medium

FISHING PRESSURE: Moderate to light

FISHING QUALITY: Very good to excellent

ACCESS: Palmer Creek Trail

USGS QUADS: Bunches Bald, NC; Luftee Knob, NC

THE MAIN STREAM OF PALMER FORK sports a mixture of rainbow and brook trout upstream from an elevation of 3,000 feet. Downstream from that point, it holds rainbow trout and an occasional wayward brown. Palmer Creek offers anglers very good trout fishing on a number of very beautiful and productive feeder streams; Rough Fork, Pretty Hollow Creek, Lost Bottom Creek, Beech Creek, and Falling Rock Creek all hold populations of brightly hued speckle trout. Each has its own little tributary system that can be a delight to explore.

The springs that form Palmer Creek, once known as Indian Creek, begin on the sides of the Balsam Mountains at an elevation of more than 5,200 feet. From there, the stream picks up a steady flow of water from feeder streams as it tumbles down. It passes through former grassy glades and old home sites, before passing over the gentle terrain of the cove.

ACCESS: The main stream of Palmer Creek is accessible by auto for 1.6 miles upstream from the campground. Upstream from the confluence of Rough Fork, the

Palmer Creek Trail provides further access. The trailhead is located on the right side of Palmer Creek, 1.6 miles above the campground. It traces alongside the stream, and at 1.5 miles Pretty Hollow Creek flows into the main stream. This is also the site of the starting point for Pretty Hollow Gap Trail (see Pretty Hollow Creek later in this chapter).

The Palmer Creek Trail continues alongside the main stream 2.6 miles, where Lost Bottom Creek enters. The confluence of Beech Creek and Falling Rock Creek is located at 3.1 miles. The combination of the two streams signals the beginning of Palmer Creek. The Palmer Creek Trail continues alongside Falling Rock Creek for a very short distance before leaving the stream.

Rough Fork

SIZE: Small

FISHING PRESSURE: Moderate

FISHING QUALITY: Good

ACCESS: Old Palmer Chapel Road; Rough Fork Trail

USGS QUADS: Bunches Bald, NC; Dellwood, NC; Cove Creek Gap, NC

ROUGH FORK FLOWS INTO THE MAIN STREAM near the Palmer Creek Trail starting point. Rough Creek, once known as Ugly Creek, offers good fishing for rainbow trout. It is accessible upstream from its mouth via the Old Palmer Chapel Road. The road continues upstream alongside Rough Fork for .9 mile, where it terminates. The Rough Fork Trail lends additional upstream access. The trailhead is located at the end of the road. At 2 miles, the trail arrives at the Big Hemlock backcountry campsite (#40, capacity 10; Elevation 3,100'), an excellent fishing camp. The trail continues upstream alongside Rough Fork only a short distance beyond the campsite. It is one of the unique streams in the Smokies in terms of appearance and how it is fished. Where Rough Fork snakes tenderly through the old Caldwell homestead reminds me of a number of streams I have fished over the years in Pennsylvania and New York. In this meadow setting you need to work pretty hard to lose a fly to the trees. It leaves the timbered ridges as a dashing sport of a lass, then in the vales spreads lazily like the hind side of my fourth wife.

Pretty Hollow Creek

SIZE: Small

FISHING PRESSURE: Moderate

FISHING QUALITY: Good

ACCESS: Pretty Hollow Gap Trail

USGS QUADS: Luftee Knob, NC–TN

PRETTY HOLLOW CREEK FLOWS INTO THE MAIN STREAM 1.5 miles upstream from the trailhead of the Palmer Creek Trail. The Pretty Hollow Gap Trail follows the stream. The trail begins off the Palmer Creek Trail near the mouth of Pretty Hollow Creek, and at .2 mile arrives at the Pretty Hollow backcountry campsite (#39, capacity 20; Elevation 3,040'), also known as the Turkey Gorge Horse Camp. The trail continues upstream alongside the stream to the 3-mile mark, at which point it leaves the stream.

chapter 26

Big Creek System

Big Creek

SIZE: Large

FISHING PRESSURE: Moderate

FISHING QUALITY: Fair (fishable miles: approximately 11)

ACCESS: State Road 1332; Big Creek Trail

USGS QUADS: Waterville, NC–TN; Luftee Knob, NC–TN

PERHAPS THE STREAMSHED that is visited the least by nonlocal anglers, Big Creek offers mixed-bag fishing, with trout in all waters, and smallmouth bass in the lower reaches downstream from the campground. Insofar as it is located only 10 minutes from I-40, that is a bit ironic.

Big Creek is without a doubt one of the most beautiful streams in the Smokies. I have found that even on fishless days it is hard to leave this stream unfulfilled. The stream cascades down the mountain over massive gray boulders, forming deep plunge pools, slows momentarily, then rushes on to the next stop. An added attraction is the fascinating varieties of moss and lichen one finds attached to scores of streamside boulders.

Big Creek is located in the northernmost section of the Smokies. It is bound by Mt. Cammerer, Mt. Sterling, and Mt. Guyot, and flows into the Pigeon River. Primary tributaries include Swallow Fork, Gunter Fork, Yellow

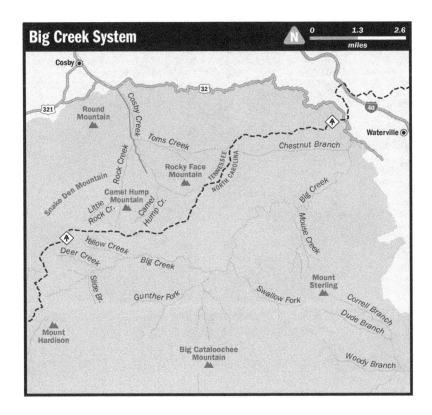

Creek, and Deer Creek.

The Big Creek watershed was thoroughly logged between 1909 and 1918, but under the protection of the National Park Service the forest has regained much of its original beauty. Further development has been halted, and some access and facilities have been curtailed in recent years. Despite these efforts, however, this is a popular area due to its proximity to I-40. The quality of fishing on Big Creek does not quite match the scenery. Most of the fish are small (5 to 8 inches), because Big Creek is not an exceptionally fertile stream capable of maintaining a population of trophy-size trout. Anglers should also note that the terrain surrounding Big Creek is rugged, so getting about is strenuous, and can be dangerous if care is not taken.

This is not a creek where it is advisable to leap from the side of the trail to the water. You can easily get hurt. There is no shortage of old narrow-gauge railroad track in the stream either. No one can pass the Blue Hole, or, as North Carolina flatlanders call it, the Midnight Hole. During a moment of questionable

*Big Creek is one of the roughest places to fish
in the Great Smoky Mountains National Park.*

sanity, I carried my scuba gear up Big Creek Trail where I donned said gear to have a little fun in the deep pool. I sat there on the bottom of the pool for almost an hour observing life under the surface. Frankly, I was a bit disappointed, not seeing lots of brisk action on the scoured clean bottom. There were some trout, one lunker measuring perhaps 11 inches long, but it, like the rest of the residents, appeared to live a pretty mundane life in the pool, which I measured to be no more than 10 feet deep during periods of normal flow. Having spent time at the bottom of Blue/Midnight Hole, it shall henceforth be called Kirk Hole. After all, my name is etched into a boulder at the bottom of this oversized plunge pool beneath the 6-feet-high falls.

It was pretty and fun, but the aesthetics outweigh the results, which pretty well sums up the lower reaches of Big Creek. I've had some pretty good fishing trips there, but just as many that were humbling.

During the early 1970s I partially supported my fly-fishing habit by taking wedding pictures. Among the fiascos which I chronicled was the wedding of my fishing buddy, George, who was marrying a gal whose clan hailed from Big

Creek. George was 30 years old, and this was his third attempt at marital bliss. The bride was 15 years old. Due to losses playing Rook at Fort Knox, a speakeasy in the vicinity of Cosby, I owed George money.

When I arrived at the one-room church, a pickup pulled up and an old fellow got out of the truck and proceeded to the backdoor of the church, where he was fumbling with the door lock when I arrived. Clad in a soiled cotton shirt with some sort of dark dress jacket, he sported a 10-day-old beard. He looked as though his hair had been done by the hair stylist for the movie *Deliverance*. Assuming he was the caretaker, I inquired as to when the pastor might arrive. "Sonny, I's here," he said. He informed me that he had been bear hunting, but since he was a reliable man of the cloth and the bride's family faithfully tithed, the scheduled hitching was to be done. It was the apex of 1970s disco era. George's guests were attired in pastel polyester leisure suits and dresses that would have made Dolly Parton blush. Following the ceremony they all planned to go honky-tonking at the Village Barn in Knoxville. In contrast, the bride's family was slightly built and dressed all in black. It was a stark meeting of two cultures little known to each other.

After the bride was escorted down the aisle, suddenly a loud crack from the pastor's large Bible being slammed shut filled the air. Tucking his Bible under his elbow, without saying a word or looking up, the preacher pace back and forth before the couple. On his third pass, he stopped in front of George. Putting his index finger on the groom's nose, he began questioning, "Do you love her?" "Is there anyone else?" Just as unexpectedly, he departed George to once more paced back and forth, only to stop before the bride. He queried her with the same questions of truth and fidelity. She too was able only to nod her head. The preacher then raised both arms and shouted, "You're married." Now, that's country!

ACCESS: Big Creek is accessible by auto, by way of I-40 at the Waterville exit (No. 451). Cross the Pigeon River (in reference to a large paper mill a short distance upstream, for years the locals referred to it as the "Dead Pigeon") and turn left. The entrance to the park is approximately 2 miles away. From the park boundary, a gravel road follows upstream .2 mile to the Big Creek Ranger Station. The stream is located 100 to 200 yards from the road most of the time. This road continues on to the Big Creek Primitive Campground (.5 mile), the end of the auto trail.

The Big Creek Trail provides further access to the stream. It begins off the gravel road a few hundred feet from the campground, and from that point follows alongside the stream, offering fair-to-good access to anglers. At 5.2 miles the trail reaches the junction of Swallow Fork, and at 5.6 miles arrives at the Walnut Bottom backcountry campsites (Lower Walnut Bottom #37, capacity 20; Elevation 3,000'; reservations needed, and Upper Walnut Bottom #36, capacity 20 campers/20 horses; Elevation 3,040'). Walnut Bottom is a superb fishing camp located on a flat, tree-covered area. This site allows easy exploration of several feeder streams flowing into the main stream nearby, and is the only backcountry campsite in the Big Creek basin. Walnut Bottom is also the end of the Big Creek Trail. The Yellow Creek Trail begins at Walnut Bottom and runs alongside Big Creek. At 6.3 miles (from the Big Creek Campground), the Yellow Creek Trail arrives at the junction of Gunter Fork, the starting point of the Gunter Fork Trail. Old maps of the Smokies refer to Big Creek upstream from this point as Mt. Guyot Creek, a name infrequently used today. At 9 miles, the stream reaches the junction of Yellow Creek. There is no maintained trail access to the upper main stream. Deer Creek flows into the main stream at 9.6 miles.

Mouse Creek

SIZE: Small

FISHING PRESSURE: Light to very light

FISHING QUALITY: Fair

ACCESS: At its mouth at Big Creek

USGS QUADS: Luftee Knob, NC–TN

MOUSE CREEK IS A HAVEN for those seeking absurd adventure. It is the first tributary to enter Big Creek. It flows into the main stream .5 upstream from the Midnight Hole. It's easy to spot, as there is a 35-foot cascading falls that announces its presence. I made one trip up that cliff to see what was up there in 1969, and shall not return. It is a treacherous climb to get above the falls, where you can catch even smaller rainbow trout than in the main body of the creek.

ACCESS: Climb the falls and travel the creek if you are dumb enough to try.

Swallow Fork

SIZE: Small

FISHING PRESSURE: Moderate to light

FISHING QUALITY: Fair, at its best in mid-summer

ACCESS: Swallow Fork Trail

USGS QUADS: Luftee Knob, NC–TN

SWALLOW FORK IS THE FIRST SIGNIFICANT TRIBUTARY encountered while traveling up Big Creek. It flows into the main stream 5.2 miles above the campground. This stream has a combination of rainbow and brook trout. John Mack Creek and McGinty Creek, tributaries of Swallow Fork, offer good brook trout fishing. A total of seven prongs begin at an altitude of more than 4,400 feet. Swallow Fork is a lovely little stream, well known for its canopy of impressive hemlocks, plus scenic waterfalls that roar like never-ceasing lions.

ACCESS: The Swallow Fork Trail begins near the mouth of the stream and follows upstream 2.5 miles before leaving the stream to ascend Pretty Hollow Gap. The Walnut Bottom backcountry campsites are located near the mouth of the stream.

Gunter Fork

SIZE: Small

FISHING PRESSURE: Light

FISHING QUALITY: Fair

ACCESS: Gunter Fork Trail

USGS QUADS: Luftee Knob, NC–TN

LOCATED 6.3 MILES ABOVE CAMPSITE, Gunter Fork flows through some of the most beautiful forests in the park and could be termed by anglers as the perfect size trout stream, because it is large enough to allow comfortable back cast room for the average fly-fisherman, and small enough to cross at will.

Gunter Fork sports both rainbow and brook trout in its numerous pools and little "pockets." Fishing on this stream reaches its peak during the last weeks of May.

ACCESS: The Gunter Fork Trail provides good access to the stream, beginning at Walnut Bottom and running concurrently with the Yellow Creek Trail for .5 mile to the mouth of Gunter Fork, where it then turns upstream alongside Gunter Fork for 2 miles before parting company.

Yellow Creek

SIZE: Small

FISHING PRESSURE: Closed

FISHING QUALITY: Good; the hot summer months are usually productive

ACCESS: Yellow Creek Trail

USGS QUADS: Luftee Knob, NC–TN

BEFORE IT WAS NECESSARY TO CLOSE Yellow Creek due to the precarious status of the brook trout in the park's waters, this was one of the most popular speckle trout streams in the Smokies.

The old mountain men of the Cosby area were extremely fond of crossing the mountains from Tennessee and descending alongside this stream with a cane pole and a can of red worms. For these rural farmers, late summer was the time to "make camp" in the mountains, sometimes for weeks, until their crops were ready for harvest. Nightly, great fish fries were held, in which hundreds of speckle trout were consumed, and jars of moonshine were passed around the fire. Those were the days!

ACCESS: Yellow Creek is accessible at its confluence with Big Creek from the Yellow Creek Trail. There is no maintained trail that lends further access to the stream.

Deer Creek

SIZE: Small

FISHING QUALITY: Fair

ACCESS: Remote

USGS QUADS: Luftee Knob, NC–TN

DEER CREEK IS A REMOTE BROOK TROUT STREAM. My only experience on this stream involved a meeting with a large black bear. I came face-to-face with the bruin as I haphazardly rounded a lush rhododendron bush. He was equally startled, but appeared to maintain better bladder control through the entire ordeal. Since that time, I have stayed away from this productive little stream.

ACCESS: There are no trails to this stream. Its mouth is located .6 mile upstream from the junction of Yellow Creek and Big Creek.

chapter 27

Minor Streams of the Smokies

BESIDES THE MAJOR WATERSHEDS, anglers may also fish a number of small streamsheds that begin within, but do not flow into, a larger system prior to departure from the park. They vary in size from hard-to-find Tabcat Creek, which flows from the extreme southern end of the park, to Parson Branch, a respectable-size creek with excellent auto access. Many of these little streams are seldom fished by anyone other than local anglers, although most offer fair to very good angling. These streams are broken down into two sections—Tennessee and North Carolina. Most should be considered early-season picks; it is not uncommon for these streams to shrink to little more than a trickle during the dry periods of summer.

Tennessee

Cosby Creek

SIZE: Small

FISHING PRESSURE: Moderate

FISHING QUALITY: Fair

ACCESS: TN 32; Cosby Campground Road; Cosby Creek Trail

USGS QUADS: Luftee Knob, NC; Hartsford, TN

*Small but productive, these seldom-visited creeks
are true gems in the rough.*

FEW PLACES IN THE SOUTHERN APPALACHIANS compare with the colorful community of Cosby. In years past, this hilly hamlet laid a valid claim on the distinction of being the "Moonshine Capital of the World." Today, the storied corn-mash distillery businessmen are difficult to locate, having forsaken running 'shine for other forms of livelihood. The movie *Thunder Road*, starring a young Robert Mitchum, was from a story that originated here.

Cosby Creek is a small stream draining a surprisingly large basin bound by the lofty peaks of Mt. Cammerer and Mt. Inadu. The creek's lower reaches are populated by rainbow trout, while brookies still hold sway over the headwaters. This is one of the more scenic streams in the park, cascading over moss-encrusted boulders and passing under a canopy of hemlocks. Fishing quality is fair to poor where the creek flows past the Cosby Campground, a developed area offering 230 campsites. The middle and headwater reaches, including the tributaries of Crying Creek, Tom's Creek, Inadu Creek, and Rock Creek, offer slightly better opportunities.

Cosby Creek downstream from the park is regularly stocked with rainbow trout by the state. The storied Colonel M.M. Bullard, upon whose farm the Ramp Festival began, ran this area for decades. Ramps are pungent, wild leeks that grow in abundance in the park during the spring. In 1955, the Ramp Festival was attended by President Harry Truman. Other guests have included Tennessee Ernie Ford, Eddie Arnold, Roy Acuff, Bill Monroe, Minnie Pearl, and Brenda Lee. The Colonel was well connected politically and always involved in some sort of newsworthy adventure. In the late 1970s he hooked up with Jim Fowler of the then well-known television show *Mutual of Omaha's Wild Kingdom*. It premiered in 1963 with host Marlin Perkins, who allowed the younger Jim to wrestle the crocs and cats before the camera. Fowler lived in Cosby for a couple of years. One October while returning from fishing Greenbrier, I stopped by Bullard's Apple Barn where the Colonel sold the fruit from his extensive orchards. Picking up a handful of Golden Grimes to munch, I went to pay. Running the cash register was Jim Fowler of *Wild Kingdom* fame. I don't know why, but I found that odd at the time.

ACCESS: Cosby Creek flows under TN 32, 20 miles east of Gatlinburg, adjacent to the entrance to the park at the Cosby Campground Road. Upstream access from the park boundary to the campground is available via Cosby Campground Road, which travels alongside the creek.

Low Gap Trail (formerly known as Cosby Creek Trail) follows the stream after it leaves the road (the trailhead is located in the southeast corner of the Cosby Campground) for 1 mile before leaving the creek for the last time.

Indian Camp Creek

SIZE: Small

FISHING QUALITY: Very good

ACCESS: Laurel Springs Road; Indian Camp Creek Trail

USGS QUADS: Jones Cove, TN; Mt. Guyot, TN

INDIAN CAMP CREEK, one of the most popular brookie streams in the park prior to the 1975 Brook Trout Moratorium, flows past nearby Albright Grove, where a magnificent virgin stand of poplars towers. Although Indian Camp Creek will probably remain closed to all fishing for some time, anglers are urged to make the 3-mile hike back to this wonderland to view the splendor of an uncut southern forest.

ACCESS: The Indian Camp Creek Trail lends access to a portion of Indian Camp Creek. The trailhead is located off Laurel Springs Road, a gravel road that has a junction with TN 73 15.3 miles east of Gatlinburg. The trail crosses Cole Creek and Maddron Creek, tributaries of Indian Camp Creek, before reaching the main stream at 2.7 miles. Driving from Gatlinburg, as you pass the 15-mile mark, you will observe the Rainbow Ranch, a pay-to-fish pond on the right. Laurel Springs Road enters the highway near this establishment. The trailhead is a few hundred yards beyond.

Dunn Creek

SIZE: Small

FISHING QUALITY: Good

ACCESS: TN 73

USGS QUADS: Jones Cove, TN; Mt. Guyot, TN

SIX PRONGS OF THIS LOVELY RIVULET begin at an altitude of more than 4,400 feet among the steep slopes of Pinnacle Lead. Brook trout are still fairly common in the upper reaches of this little branch.

An old-timer from the Cosby community told me that at one time as many as 15 moonshine stills operated along this branch and its prongs during the late 1940s.

ACCESS: No maintained trails cross or follow the stream, although there was at one time an old path alongside it for several miles.

Webb Creek

SIZE: Small

FISHING PRESSURE: Light

FISHING QUALITY: Fair to questionable

ACCESS: TN 73

USGS QUADS: Jones Cove, TN; Mt. Guyot, TN–NC; Gatlinburg, TN

WEBB CREEK DIFFERS FROM THE MAJORITY of waters described, because its flow within the Great Smoky Mountains National Park consists of several small brooks that later merge with the main stream outside the park. The main stream of Webb Creek leaves the park 13.5 miles east of Gatlinburg, passing under TN 73 as a small brook, having originated between the steep slopes of Snag Mountain and Pinnacle Lead. A number of very small feeder streams flowing out of the park pass under TN 73 to enter Webb Creek downstream from the park boundary. These streams include Texas Creek, a very small waterway with two prongs extending more than 4,000 feet in elevation; Nosy Creek, one of the largest of the feeder streams, with four prongs that each pass the 4,000-foot mark; Redwine Creek and Timothy Creek, both very small but lovely brooks; and Soak Ash Creek. Most of these waters have rainbow trout averaging less than 7 inches in length.

ACCESS: Webb Creek is reached from the park boundary upstream only by moving along the trailless creek. The creek flows under TN 73, 13.5 miles east of Gatlinburg.

Hesse Creek

SIZE: Medium

FISHING PRESSURE: Light

FISHING QUALITY: Fair to good

ACCESS: Fairly remote

USGS QUADS: Kinel Springs, TN; Blockhouse, TN

HESSE CREEK IS THE LARGEST of the streams noted in this chapter, draining one of the most unique and least-visited regions of the Smokies. Hesse Creek Valley is often referred to as the Hurricane, probably because of severe blow-downs that have occurred here in the past.

The Hurricane is best known for its caves and unusual flora. Logged in the early part of the 19th century by the Little River Logging Company, Hesse Valley has today regrown nicely. Fishermen will notice the unique, lush, switch canebrakes growing along the streams. The cane, actually a species of bamboo, *Arundinaria tecta*, was especially favored by old-time fishermen as excellent material for making fishing poles.

The quality of fishing in this watershed is fair to very good. There are plenty of trout here, although they average less than 8 inches in length. Note-worthy tributaries of Hesse Creek include Cane Creek and Bread Cane Creek.

Note: National Park Service regulations forbid the removal of any plant (or part thereof) from the park, so forget any notion you might have of making a fishing pole from these canes.

ACCESS: There is no easy way to enter the Hurricane. All routes require a moderate amount of foot travel. Hesse Creek, upon leaving the Great Smoky Mountains National Park, flows through a lovely rural area known as Miller Cove. The Miller Cove Road (which has a junction with TN 73 near the intersection of the highway and the Foothills Parkway) deadends 1 mile from the park boundary. An old, unmaintained path continues upstream alongside Hesse Creek. Cane Creek (which originates in the park) enters the main stream at .7 mile from the right (another unmaintained path begins at its mouth and follows the upstream ascent of Cane Creek, later having a junction with the Cooper Road Trail).

The path continues alongside Hesse Creek, entering the park at 1 mile, and at 1.3 miles arrives at the mouth of Bread Cane Creek. The Bread Cane Creek Trail follows alongside Bread Cane Creek to its headwaters, before terminating at 2.5 miles at the Cooper Road Trail. There are not trails upstream of Hesse Creek.

Tabcat Creek

SIZE: Small

FISHING PRESSURE: Light

FISHING QUALITY: Fair

ACCESS: Unnamed Path

USGS QUADS: Calderwood, TN–NC

TABCAT CREEK IS ONE OF THE LEAST-KNOWN trout streams in the national park. Early spring is the best time to venture up this seldom-trampled stream, as it is quite small. During the dry periods common to the late summer, it often appears to nearly dry up. Rainbow trout about 6 to 9 inches long are plentiful. Tributaries that can be fished include Bunker Hill Branch and Maynard Creek. It's tough going anywhere you try at this dash of water.

> **ACCESS:** Tabcat Creek flows into Calderwood Lake 2.5 miles south of the mouth of Abrams Creek on TN 72. There is an old, unmaintained path that begins at the park boundary and follows Tabcat Creek to the confluence of Bunker Hill Branch, later reaching Bunker Hill.

Parson Branch

SIZE: Medium

FISHING PRESSURE: Relatively light

FISHING QUALITY: Fair

ACCESS: Parson Branch Road

USGS QUADS: Calderwood, TN–NC; Tapoco, TN–NC

PARSON BRANCH IS THE SORT OF STREAM a trout fisherman passes on a Sunday drive with the family, and swears to return and fish later on, but never does. The stream holds a good population of rainbow trout, most of them fairly small. Black Gum Branch, a tributary of Parson Branch, also offers fair fishing. It is a bit larger than most rills in the park that carry the name branch.

> **ACCESS:** Parson Branch flows into Calderwood Lake after leaving the park. The Parson Branch Road, a one-way gravel road originating off the Cades Cove Loop Road, provides excellent roadside access to most of the main stream, following the stream from its headwaters to the park boundary.

Fighting Creek

SIZE: Small

FISHING PRESSURE: Light

FISHING QUALITY: Fair to poor

ACCESS: Sugarland parking lot

USGS QUADS: Sevier County, TN

PURPOSEFULLY LEFT OUT OF MY EARLIER BOOK at the request of Walter Cole, Fighting Creek is a mediocre little trickle of minor importance to most serious fly-fishermen. To Cole, though, it was his boyhood fishing spot. He has been dead for decades now, so perhaps he will not be overly offended by my mention of Fighting Creek. It's easy wading and slow fishing.

ACCESS: The stream is most easily accessed from the NPS's Sugarland Headquarters. It enters the West Prong of the Little Pigeon a short distance away. Upstream from the Sugarland there is no trail access, but you can always hear traffic on the Little River Road that passes through the valley a stone's throw to your left.

North Carolina

Chambers Creek

SIZE: Small

FISHING PRESSURE: Moderately light

FISHING QUALITY: Good

ACCESS: Remote

USGS QUADS: Noland Creek, NC; Tuskeegee, NC

CHAMBERS CREEK OFFERS FAIRLY GOOD TROUT FISHING opportunities for those wishing to make the trip across Fontana Lake. There is an excellent backcountry campsite (Chambers Creek, #98, capacity 10; Elevation 1,800') that serves fishermen nicely as a base camp. The stream is populated with rainbow trout, with brook trout reputed to be in the extreme headwater reaches. The North Fork and the West Fork merge .7 mile upstream from Fontana Lake to form Chambers Creek. Both forks offer good trout fishing.

ACCESS: Chambers Creek is located between Forney and Hazel Creeks. It is most often visited by crossing Fontana Lake and is easily recognized by the long cove that cushions it from the main body of the lake.

An unmaintained fisherman's trail ascends the creek. Upon reaching the junction of the north and west forks at .7 mile, the trail also forks, with footpaths following both small rivulets for a short distance. The best access is via the newly completed Lakeshore Trail, which crosses Chambers Creek 12 miles from the Noland Creek parking area. I recommend taking a boat.

Lands Creek

SIZE: Small

FISHING PRESSURE: None

FISHING QUALITY: Perhaps the best in the park

ACCESS: At the mouth of stream at the Tuckasegee River

USGS QUADS: Swain County, NC

ASK YOURSELF THIS: "Who the hell ever heard of or fished Lands Creek?" Yes, it's a park stream that has trout—but no public access. If you really want to fish there, it's a five-flask venture. The nearby casino is a better bet for not losing your shirt and dignity.

Mount Sterling Creek

SIZE: Small

FISHING PRESSURE: Little to none

FISHING QUALITY: Good to very good

ACCESS: Along NC 284

USGS QUADS: Cove Creek Gap, NC

WHILE OF LITTLE INTEREST to most fly-fishermen, Mt. Sterling Creek is a decent little rill that is not only fun to fish, but can be productive, especially during mid-spring. Most of the fishable portions of Mt. Sterling Creek roughly follow along NC 284, a gravel road that kinda, sorta connects Cosby, Tennessee, with the Cataloochee area. There is roughly a mile of fishable water when there is enough water to make it possible.

Peachtree Creek

> **SIZE:** Small
>
> **FISHING PRESSURE:** Little to none
>
> **FISHING QUALITY:** Poor to worse
>
> **ACCESS:** By boat
>
> **USGS QUADS:** Swain County, NC

OKAY, CAMPERS, HERE'S THE MISSION. If you can locate the mouth of this creek, it is your peach to eat. It is a diminutive flow that enters the Tuckasegee River arm of Fontana Lake at almost a fishable size. The Road to Nowhere crosses Peachtree Creek, but is so small the odds are great you will miss it even if you are looking for it. Must more be said?

Cooper Creek

> **SIZE:** Small
>
> **FISHING PRESSURE:** Light
>
> **FISHING QUALITY:** Good
>
> **ACCESS:** Cooper Creek Trail
>
> **USGS QUADS:** Smokemont, NC

COOPER CREEK IS A NOISY LITTLE RIVULET tucked between two better-known watersheds, the Oconaluftee River and Deep Creek; it offers pretty fair angling for rainbow trout. Cooper Creek is relatively small, but those looking for an out-of-the-way locale in which to wet a line should not mark this little gem off their list.

> **ACCESS:** The Cooper Creek Trail (it is no longer listed as an official NPS trail) offers good access to the most productive reaches of the stream. Its trailhead is located .4 mile upstream from the termination of the Cooper Creek Road, which has a junction with US 19 5.5 miles southwest of Cherokee.

The trail travels along the route of the stream 1.8 miles before leaving the creek. An unmaintained path continues alongside the stream for a distance. A gate blocks upstream traffic where the Cooper Creek Trout Ponds are located on private property. Qualla Reservation property flanks the trail at this point. Getting permission to briefly trespass to get to park waters is recommended and often granted by the pond owners.

chapter 28

Fontana and the Finger Lakes

FONTANA LAKE HAS BEEN A POPULAR FISHING destination since it was created. For fly-fishermen who love remote locations, it has served as an effective deterrent to easy access to several large streamsheds. Wine connoisseurs fond of New York State white and sparkling wines probably believe the United States' only "finger lakes" are those glacial afterthoughts found in the Empire State. Not so, and if you don't believe this, just look at the Great Smoky Mountains National Park's southern edge.

Found here are Fontana Lake and three slender, snaking lakes: Cheoah, Calderwood, and Chilhowee, the Finger Lakes of the South. The latter are owned and operated by Tapoco, a subsidiary of the Aluminum Company of America (or Alcoa). Little lodging is found along the 27-mile length of the Finger Lakes of the South alongside US 129 and US 19, although lodging is abundant along Fontana Lake

Fontana Lake

PERCHED ALMOST 2,000 FEET ABOVE SEA LEVEL, Fontana Lake is one of the "highest" impoundments in the seven-state Tennessee Valley Authority (TVA). This 10,530-surface-acre lake sits wedged between the Great Smoky Mountains National Park and the Nantahala National Forest. During the summer, when the surrounding countryside is dominated by forest green and cloud-dotted pale blue skies, this emerald-green lake appears natural, sometimes giving the impression of being a jewel in a fine piece of jewelry.

Fontana Lake is a result of the impoundment of the Little Tennessee River, which drains into western North Carolina. Construction on Fontana Dam began overnight following the United State's entrance into World War II in late 1941. Many thousands of acres of bottomland and ridge country were purchased from local residents, many of whom were less than willing to turn over family holdings to the federal government. Much of the acreage became the lake, although 44,204 acres acquired from the mountain folk were later deeded over to the Great Smoky Mountains National Park.

The completed Fontana Dam construction project left the construction center of Fontana Village to become a ghost town. Since WWII a number of tourist-oriented corporations have operated Fontana Village. I have stayed at Fontana Village many times over the years and have made return trips to this old backwoods construction camp. The worker cabins and cottages have been remodeled and are now guest lodging. The old cafeteria still serves up homemade fruit pies and biscuits 'n' gravy, as it did daily 60 years ago. Once I was there when Jodie Foster was making *Nell*, and Dan Ackroyd and Jack Lemmon were also filming there.

Fontana Village's other unique attribute is its proximity to the finest treasure house of the Southern highlands. One has only to walk a few hundred feet from any point here to enjoy the region's lush flora. The Appalachian Trail passes directly through the village, and other trails and noteworthy backcountry destinations are easily reached from this place.

Fontana Lake offers angling for walleye, white bass, rainbow and steelhead trout, muskie and tiger muskie, catfish, largemouth bass, brown trout, red breast bream, crappie, and, of course, smallmouth bass. Fontana Lake, with its steep, rocky shoreline and year-round cool water temperatures, is a picture-perfect bronzeback habitat. Bronzebacks in the 10- to 14-inch class are the usual fare, but 3-pound smalljaws are always a possibility, and tackle busters in the 4- to 6- and even 7-pound class inhabit every rocky point.

Cheoah Lake

CHEOAH WAS THE FIRST IMPOUNDMENT BUILT on the Little Tennessee River, predating the creation of the Tennessee Valley Authority. The old dam, which

Breecher Whitehead with a rainbow trout caught from the trash lines of Chilhowee Lake, just downstream from Calderwood Dam.

is visible where US 129 crosses Calderwood Lake near Tapoco, is the site of the famous "dam jump" scene in the 1994 movie *The Fugitive.*

Cheoah Lake extends approximately 10 miles behind 189-foot-high Cheoah Dam. Much of the lake is silt-filled, with its winding main channel and the area near the Santeetlah Powerhouse being the lake's deepest zones.

Trout are the lake's primary game fish, and this lake is stocked regularly by the state of North Carolina with rainbow, brown, and brook trout.. Twelve- to 16-inch rainbows and browns are common, and larger browns up to 5 to 7 pounds are available in good numbers. The brookies usually do not grow longer than a foot, but by Southern stream standards this is large.

Cheoah Lake's major feeder streams are Lewellyn Branch, a small tributary that enters the lake near the US 19 Bridge and Twenty Mile Creek. The lake begins immediately downstream from Fontana Dam's tailrace, and accounts for approximately 595 surface acres. Its headwaters are actually a tailrace river. Fly-fishing streamers, dries, or nymphs works well.

Calderwood Lake

CALDERWOOD LAKE IS ONE OF THE SOUTH'S least-known gems. Located between Cheoah and Chilhowee on the Little "T," this 536-acre impoundment offers superb trout fishing. Tennessee and North Carolina stock this lake with brook, rainbow, and brown trout, but fishing pressure is light. Big brown and rainbow trout in excess of 10 pounds are often caught.

Calderwood Dam stands 213 feet high, but is less than 200 feet across. The lake is deep, with depths more than 190 feet in the lower end along the river channel, which winds over 8 miles back through rugged, remote ridges. The Tennessee/North Carolina state line bisects this lake less than 2 miles downstream from Cheoah Dam. A long-standing reciprocal agreement between these two adjoining states honors both states' fishing licenses on the entire lake and Slickrock Creek. The lake's northern shoreline is NPS domain. Its south shore is largely bounded by the Nantahala and Cherokee National Forests. Calderwood Lake is the most remote and difficult to access of the Smoky Mountains Finger Lakes. Roadside access from US 129 is only available immediately downstream from Cheoah Dam at the two-lane highway's intersection with a gravel road, which leads off US 129 to Calderwood Dam. The latter is a steep roadway, difficult to pass during inclement weather.

Chilhowee Lake

THE THIRD "FINGER LAKE" is Chilhowee, a 1,747-acre impoundment of the Little Tennessee River. It is the most diverse, accessible, and popular of the Finger Lakes, although in recent years its edges have been taken over by motorcycle gangs. The dam stands 68 feet high, but it backs up a lake over 9 miles long. At its widest point, Chilhowee Lake is almost a mile across; five times wider than either Calderwood or Cheoah at their widest points. This is a remarkably shallow mountain lake, seldom topping more than 50 feet deep, and usually less than 20, with 10-foot-deep water being very abundant along the shoreline. Chilhowee's

Joe Manley, the best-known old-time angler of the Smokies with a big muskie caught from the Little Tennessee River below Calderwood Dam before the creation of Chilhowee Lake.

headwaters are wedged between two vertical rock cliffs that are well worth boating up the lake to view. Its primary feeder streams are Tallassee Creek, which enters along the south shore, draining the Cherokee National Forest.

Fly-fishermen will be delighted to discover that this lake offers season-long summertime long rod trout action in the trash line. Trash, or debris, lines beginning at the base of Calderwood Dam form from shoreline to shoreline. Viewed from above, these trash lines resemble "bathtub rings" as they slowly wash down the lake, disappearing approximately 5 miles downstream.

These so-called trash lines hold large numbers of beetles, bees, and other terrestrial foods that are of considerable interest to Chilhowee Lake's big rainbow trout. Trout cruise these trash lines, gingerly picking off insects. Fly flickers using large nymphs or beetle patterns sit in the bow of their boat or canoe and watch the lake's mirror-like surface for an approaching feeder.

Once a trout begins prowling a debris line, it will follow it from one end to the other, rhythmically surfacing every 10 to 20 feet. The trick is to gauge your quarry's surface pattern and attempt to drop your fly where the fish will probably surface next. Admittedly, this is a hit-or-miss angling technique, but it can be very effective. One nearby Maryville fly-fisherman who has been flicking to the trash-line trout for many years confided he took over 30 trout in excess of 20 inches from Chilhowee Lake in a single month

Map Data
THERE ARE NO INDIVIDUAL MAPS of Cheoah, Calderwood, and Chilhowee Lakes. A good map depicting Fontana and the Finger Lakes is available from TVA by writing the TVA Map Sales, Haney Building, Chattanooga, TN 37401. USGS quadrangles of these lakes are as follows: Cheoah Lake—Fontana Dam, NC, Tapoco, NC; Calderwood Lake—Tapoco, NC, Calderwood, NC; Chilhowee Lake—Calderwood, NC.

chapter 29

Fly-Fishing Gatlinburg According to Ward

by Greg Ward

ſTANDING KNEE DEEP IN GIN-CLEAR WATER you observe a hole teeming with 20 to 30 rainbow trout that are 12 to 20 inches long or longer. Quickly, you cast your favorite dry fly several feet above the fish, anticipating the drift over the pod. A simple mend makes your fly skitter across the surface triggering a mad rush at the fly. One of the bigger fish beats the others and gulps your offering. Lifting your rod tip you notice the sheer weight of the fish and hope your 5x tippet will hold. The fish executes some spectacular jumps and runs that end at your side. As you reach down to release the fish you hear applause from the many tourists watching from the sidewalks of Gatlinburg, Tennessee.

Of course, you're fishing stocked waters: where else will you find a hole teeming with 20 to 30 1- to 3-pound trout? The City of Gatlinburg has one of the top municipal stocking programs in the nation. They turned their old sewer plant into a trout-rearing facility in 1981. City elders committed early on to stocking fish larger than the 7-to-9 inches-long trout as is the norm. As a result, the average fish in Gatlinburg waters is 12 inches or better. Officials decided to stock on Thursdays and close the waters to fishing so the fish can acclimate for a day. I really like this rule. As a youth, I watched cars line up behind the state's stock trucks; every place the stock truck stopped, two to three cars pulled over, and anglers cast at fish that had been released only seconds earlier. A half dozen grown men taking their seven-fish limits within an hour of a hole being stocked did not leave many trout to catch until the stock truck rolled around again two weeks later. Then, of course, those same cars would be there to trail the stock trucks again; I hope they at least ate the fish.

From 1981 to 1996, Gatlinburg's program consisted of weekly stocking from late March through November; few trout were stocked during the winter. This all changed in 1997. City officials had been considering a delayed-harvest program and implemented the catch-and-release portion of their program to coincide with the winter months. December through March is single-hook, artificial lures only, catch-and-release on all Gatlinburg waters. I was a little reluctant at first. My clients like a mess of fish now and then, and I worried that most anglers didn't know how to properly release a fish.

My first guided trip during the delayed-harvest season washed all my concerns away. My client caught and released five rainbows over 20 inches as well as five others that were all better than 14 inches! The gentleman compared his afternoon catch in Gatlinburg to his best day fishing Alaska. I was also very impressed and have taken advantage of the program with other clients. Neither I, the City of Gatlinburg, nor George W. Bush makes the weather, but when the weather is right and the fish have fed well during the heat of summer in the trout-rearing facilities, there are ample numbers of big fish for delayed harvest.

The latest addition to the program is a handicapped access ramp to a concrete landing along the West Prong of the Little Pigeon River located in the youth-only waters at Herbert Holt Park. Maps of Gatlinburg's corporate waters are readily available, which include all the rules and regulations. Access is easy when staying at one of the many motels, hotels, cabins, and condos along the river. The city has many parking lots throughout, and River Road has free parking along the stream.

Many of the flies I recommend for wild trout will work for stocked trout streams. My clients often catch wild trout in Gatlinburg, and, to my surprise, a client caught a Southern Appalachian Brook Trout from Gatlinburg waters in the spring of 2010. I have fished these waters since 1969 and never landed a wild brook trout. The ambient water temperature has dropped enough over the years to support wild brookies at such low levels. I have caught many wild rainbows in Gatlinburg waters, but the brookie in 2010 was a first.

During catch-and-keep season, you can use live bait, but remember single hooks are the law. The daily limit is five fish, and a trout stamp as well as a city permit is required along with your fishing license. The streams are closed every

Thursday for stocking. Gatlinburg waters, which include the West Prong of the Little Pigeon River, start just south of traffic light #10 in Pigeon Forge and end at the National Park boundary just south of traffic light # 10 in Gatlinburg. Three tributaries also included in Gatlinburg corporate waters are LeConte Creek, Roaring Fork, and Dudley Creek from the National Park boundary to their confluence with the West Prong.

Twelve and under youth-only waters are located at Mynatt Park on LeConte Creek, and at Herbert Holt Park on the West Prong at the trout-rearing facility. Playgrounds, rest rooms, and a picnic area, including pavilions, are located at both youth water sites. A two-fish limit is the rule on youth waters, and, remember, Herbert Holt Park has the only handicap access to a free-flowing stream east of the Mississippi.

LeConte Creek youth waters are easy to access at Mynatt Park and the GSMNP boundary, but access to the general waters of LeConte Creek can be a little trickier. The stream's confluence with the West Prong is located at Ober Gatlinburg. The effort required to access LeConte Creek can be rewarding if tight water is your thing. Roaring Fork is small as well and offers a challenge. The confluence of Roaring Fork and the West Prong is located downstream of Morton's Antiques on the Parkway in Gatlinburg.

I cut my teeth fishing Roaring Fork at the ripe age of 6. You can access Roaring Fork along Roaring Fork Road or park at Roaring Fork Baptist Church and access the road from their parking lot. The GSMNP boundary is located upstream at Tree Tops Condominiums. Dudley Creek follows Highway US 321 and the East Parkway. It flows along US 321 from the National Park boundary near Gatlinburg-Pittman High School and goes under US 321 at First Baptist Church of Gatlinburg, then runs through backcountry only to reemerge at the confluence with the West Prong at Herbert Holt Park. All three tributaries are small streams. High-sticking is the way to go when fly-fishing any of our smaller waters. No need to cast when you can present your fly just as easily holding your 9-foot rod up high and letting the fly ride the surface. Be prepared to put a few flies in the trees when you miss the fish or the fish misses your fly.

The West Prong offers a little more room. The GSMNP boundary is located at the dam just above traffic light #10 and River Road at the Gatlinburg Water Plant. It flows along River Road to traffic light #5 at Ripley's Aquarium of the Smokies, then flows along the Parkway all the way to just downstream of the third bridge in the Spur (what the locals call the 5-mile stretch of road connecting Gatlinburg and Pigeon Forge) prior to entering Pigeon Forge. Gatlinburg corporate waters technically end at the confluence of Gnatty Branch, which is located approximately 250 yards below the last bridge in the Spur along Highway US 441 North.

Summer Flies

BASE YOUR FLY SELECTION for stocked waters on the seasons just as you do for wild trout. The lower elevation and wide open spaces of Gatlinburg warm the water in the summer, making it the hardest season to fish. While the wild trout in the Smokies are enjoying a feeding frenzy, the stocked trout at lower elevation become quite lethargic. Consecutive days of 90-degree-plus weather along with a lack of rain can be as hard as winter fishing at high elevations. The fish won't bite. I use several different tricks to wake the fish from their slumber. Twitching or skittering a large fly across the top can generate a strike, but slowly drifting tiny nymphs may be your best bet. Sizes 12 and 10 Adams along with size 14 and 12 Ausable Wulff, including terrestrials—hoppers, ants, and crickets—will work on top for stocked trout. Some anglers use fat brown flies that simulate the pellets used in rearing facilities and hatcheries. Nymphs of choice include sizes 18, 16, 14, 12 Inchworms, Prince Nymphs, Tellicos, Pheasant Tails, Crow Flies, and yellow, brown, and black Wooly Worms. My favorite streamers are sizes 8 and 6 black, brown, and olive Wooly Boogers and, of course, a correctly tied Muddler Minnow. Streamer fishing is much like fishing inline spinners. Stripping them across the current is by far better than going against the current. I have seen some crazy-looking flies in my life tied by anglers who think a little too much and come up with perfect imitations of whole kernel corn flies or Purina trout flies. A yellow Wooly Worm is a good corn imitation and a Pheasant Tail looks pretty similar to hatchery food.

Fall Fly Selection

FALL FLIES ARE VERY CLOSE to summer patterns with a few exceptions. During autumn dry-fly fishermen should always have some size 14, 12, and 10 Orange Caddis or Orange Stimulators as well as sizes 14 and 12 olive, tan, yellow Caddis. Sizes 14, 12, and 10 large Mayflies tied skinny in tan, yellow, olive, and brown work well also. Stick to the same streamers as summer. Chad Williams, who used to work with me and is now at Smoky Mountain Angler in Gatlinburg, ties an orange nymph he calls the Downtown Special that is deadly on stocked fish. Chad is one of the finest fly tyers in East Tennessee.

Winter Fly Selections

SOME OF THE BEST TROUT FISHING I have ever experienced both guiding and fishing on my own has been on Gatlinburg water in the winter. I like small black flies. Dry-fly selections include sizes 18 and 16 Black Caddis, gnats, and stones, as well as Bluewing Olives. Smaller nymphs, such as sizes 20 and 18 Black and Brown Midges and sizes 18 and 16 bead head Pheasant Tails are good any time. Peacock herl, a bead head, and a bit of Flashabou can work wonders on stocked trout. Remember also that large fish abound in Gatlinburg waters during the delayed-harvest program and the colder water turns these fish on. Always choose your tippet diameter to match the size fly you are fishing. I try to land these fish as soon as possible, and I release them with my hemostats without touching or lifting the fish from the water. If you want a picture, wet your hands and gently lift the fish out of the water, but only for a few seconds. As a rule, I do not net any fish I release. A net removes the protective slime from fish, which eventually kills them. Wet hands are the way to go if you must touch a fish. In the event a fish swallows the fly or hook, cut the line as close to the mouth as possible. Bronze will rust out quicker than you think; it's better to lose a $3 fly than to kill the fish.

Spring Fly Selection

THE ROBINS ARE BACK; the turkeys are gobbling; the forsythia, redbuds, and dogwoods are blooming; and the trout are everywhere. You can keep a mess as well. Spring dries include sizes 16, 14, and 12 Caddis, mayflies, and stones. Early on go with neutrals—tan, brown, olive, and pale yellow. Large March Browns and Adams in size 10 are my favorites. Big fish are still in the water through May and will crush a dry. The delayed harvest program has forced these fish to fend for themselves, and they turn half wild. They know what flies are hatching and have depended on them to simply survive. April will give way to the pale yellow of May, so work your way to sizes 14 and 12 light Cahills or Caddis. Nymphs include sizes 18, 16, 14, and 12 Pheasant Tails, Prince, Gold-Ribbed Hares Ears,

Tellicos, and Caddis Pupa. Pellet imitations, wet or dry, also work well. My streamers remain the same with sizes 8 and 6 olive, black, and brown Wooly Boogers and Muddler Minnows. I fish 8 foot and 9 foot two-piece fly rods from 4 to 6 weight. Seven-and-a-half-foot leaders in 6x5x4x. Our fish are not leader shy, so long leaders are not needed. Fishing the Smokies can be a humbling experience. Fishing Gatlinburg, Tennessee's stocked water can certainly save a fishing trip and could easily become one of your best days ever on a mountain stream. Just smile and take a bow for all those tourists who'll applaud your fine display of angling skill.

chapter 30

Pigeon Forge/ Sevierville:
Fly-Fishing for World-Class Stream Smallmouth

by Greg Ward

THOUSANDS OF MILES OF BLUE-RIBBON trout streams abound in southern Appalachia. From the wild trout streams in the Great Smoky Mountains to the tailrace rivers such as the Clinch, South Holston, and Watagua, fishermen can expect to catch large rainbow trout and even larger brown trout. But the true world-class fishing in eastern Tennessee has nothing at all to do with salmonoids. We are blessed with the finest stream smallmouth bass fishing in the world, an untapped resource that I discovered at the age of 12.

When I was 12 years old, my family moved to a new home in Pigeon Forge. So I went from fishing the trout-laden bubbling brook of Roaring Fork in Gatlinburg to fishing the meandering West Prong of the Little Pigeon River in Pigeon Forge. We lived on the highest point in our neighborhood, which saved us from the floods that plagued many of our neighbors when the West Prong overflowed its banks. I could look out my window and see the river snake through the cornfields that bordered my backyard. One day when the urge to fish hit (and trust me, it hit often), I grabbed my trusty rod and reel that had landed thousands of trout and raided my dad's tackle box and found a 4-inch-long black Creme worm threaded with two hooks, a couple of beads, and a propeller at the eye. Minutes later I was standing at a beautiful hole on the stream, less than 100 yards from my house; I spent a lot of time over the next five years casting into that honey-hole. That day, I cast toward the upper stretch of the pool and set my rod on a forked stick. Within moments, the tip of my rod began bouncing and a quick hook-set

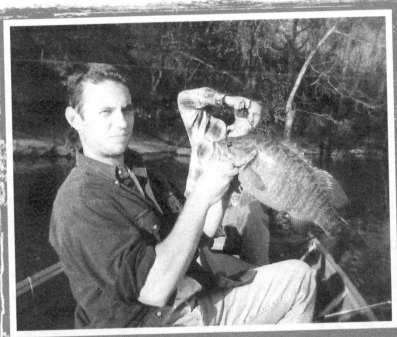

The lower reaches of the Little Pigeon River in Sevierville and Pigeon Forge offer world-class fishing for smallmouth bass.

later, the fight was on. That fish ran me all over the hole, executing leaps and jumps that would make a rainbow trout jealous. It pulled like a freight train and was so big that I had a hard time lipping it. Finally, I hefted the fish from the water and ran back home with a brown bass hanging from my rod. My dad informed me it was smallmouth bass and a nice one at that. At the time, I had a 20-inch rainbow and a 22-inch brown in the freezer waiting to be mounted so I asked if I could add my bass. My dad said okay, and the smallmouth bass became my first trophy bass. Needless to say, I was hooked on smallies after that. As a matter of fact, I still am. I have pursued the "bronzeback" fish through eight states and Canada, fishing the top smallmouth waters. I can tell you straight up that the West Prong and the Middle Prong of the Little Pigeon River in Pigeon Forge and Sevierville, Tennessee, offer some of the best stream smallmouth bass fishing in the country.

In order to conserve this unique fishery, in the late 1990s I spent a lot of time and money to get a law passed to protect it. I spoke to audiences in Memphis, Chattanooga, Nashville, Knoxville, and Gatlinburg, urging the Tennessee Wildlife

Commission to write and pass a law that would protect these fish for generations to come. My efforts paid off in 1998; one fish over 20 inches long is the rule in all of our waters. The days of seeing fishermen drag stringers hung with 4-pound-plus smallies along our riverbanks during the spring spawn are over.

The law has definitely helped conserve and preserve a tremendous resource. My spin fishing clients expect to catch a few 4- to 6-pound smallies and often do. I have been close to retirement on more than one occasion—a world-record smallmouth bass is worth millions. My best smallmouth weighed 9.5 pounds, but I've lost much larger fish that I know (had I landed them) would have broken the world record. In the late 1990s, I caught a 28-inch fish in March that would have matched the Dale Hollow record had she had been fed up. We have the genetics, water quality, food supply, and growing season to produce a world record. Our streams have a great year-round population of smallmouth, and every stretch holds one or more big fish. The numbers explode in the spring during a spawning run that adds at least a 10-to-1 big fish ratio. The West Prong runs 7 degrees warmer than the Middle Prong, so we actually have two runs. I normally get on large numbers of big fish in mid-March through mid-June.

Tackle-wrecking bronzeback action is available to young and old alike.

When the fish go to bed on the West Prong, I leave them alone and switch to the Middle Prong. I focus on transitional fish heading to and coming from spawning grounds. I try not to stress spawned out fish.

Fly-fishing for these monsters is quite an experience, and I've only landed a handful of 5-pound-plus smallies on my fly rod. The types of baits you use will dictate the size fish you catch. I use a 8.5 foot 7 weight with a 2x to 0x leader when I'm after the big boys. An 8-to-9-foot-long fly rod designed to cast a 5- or 6-weight fly line tipped with a 3x leader works well when fishing smaller flies and popping bugs.

December to February

WINTERTIME SMALLIES CAN BE A BLAST if you know where to find them. I have experienced some very productive outings while SUVs pass by, luggage racks stacked with skis and snow boards, heading to the ski lodge in Gatlinburg. The fish hole up in the deeper holes and are somewhat lethargic. A deep hole can be 3 to 4 feet deep or 20 feet deep, depending on the stretch of water. Try casting large crayfish imitations and strip them along the bottom. Big stream smallies love a crayfish lunch during winter. Fishing at mid-day with the sun overhead is very productive. A bluebird high pressure, a fisherman's term I learned years ago used to describe the bright, clear blue sky that accompanies a winter high-pressure system, will up your odds—and remember, shadows are your best friend when fishing winter smallies.

March to Mid-June

OUR SPRING SMALLMOUTH BASS FISHING is excellent. Thousands of world-class fish choke our streams on their annual spawning run. Fly-fishermen can expect to hook 20-inch-long-plus smalllies with little effort, but landing these fish is quite a different story. The fish are not leader-shy so use 2x to 0x leaders if you want to land a big one. An 8-foot, 6-inch 7wt or 8wt rod is a must. My favorite big fish streamers are size 4 or 6 Muddlers and White Wooly Boogers. Large popping bugs and Dahlberg Divers are best on the surface. Nymph fisherman cannot go wrong with large hellgrammite and crayfish style imitations. You can drift hellgrammite patterns, but you need to strip crayfish creations.

If big fish are not your priority, and you are after sheer numbers, I recommend an 8-to-9-foot fly rod engineered to cast 6 weight fly lines sporting a

3x leader. Fish sizes 8 and 6 streamers. White, black, olive, and brown Wooly Boogers and Muddler Minnows are great. Nymph fishermen should stick with hellgrammite patterns but size down to match their tippet. Sizes 12 and 10 Prince, Pheasant Tails, and Black and Brown Stone Flies are hard to beat. Popping bugs work great on the surface. I like to strip popping bugs on the surface and streamers below.

Mid-June to Late September

SUMMER FISHING IS MUCH the same as spring fishing. The numbers of fish drop off, but we have a good population of resident fish that rival the most popular smallmouth streams in the country. Warmer water and lower oxygen levels will push the bass in to the white water, so fish close to the riffles. I speed up my presentation to trigger a strike. My fly selection stays the same with the exception of terrestrials. Dry fly-fishing hoppers and cricket patterns can be a blast if the smallies can beat the panfish to your offering.

Late September through November

NOW IS THE TIME TO FISH your most colorful flies. The fall smallmouth run is much smaller than the spring run, but these fish are here to eat. Our waters are teeming with multitudes of minnows, insects, darters, crayfish, amphibians, and much more. Smallmouth are feeding up for winter and can be extremely aggressive. I am after large fish and use the same larger white Wooly Boogers and Muddlers, although I add some red, orange, and yellow to the streamers. I use more colorful popping bugs as well. The leaves that choke the National Park also fill the West, Middle, and Little Pigeon proper. Once the canopy begins to fall, I switch most of my attention to bear and deer hunting.

Access to our smallmouth bass streams is easy. Sevierville has a nice, scenic river walkway along the West Prong that extends from Sevierville City Park for several miles. RV parks and motels dot the banks of the Little Pigeon proper, and managers of large, retail stores do not mind if you park in their lots as long as you ask. The Middle Prong is a little harder to access, but there are some pull-offs along Highway US 411 and 416. Within the Pigeon Forge city limits there are excellent smallmouth holes that actually transition with trout. Catching a 4-pound smallmouth and a 4-pound trout from the same waters is a goal of more than a few of my clients. Pigeon Forge has a river walkway with ample parking.

Greg Ward with a trophy-class brown trout taken from the lower reaches of West Prong, downstream from Gatlinburg.

The many hotels, motels, condos, cabins, and RV parks along the West Prong of the Little Pigeon in Pigeon Forge can offer a great day fishing while the wife is shopping or enjoying a trip to Dollywood.

Next time you plan a trip to the Smokies bring your 9-foot, 4-weight fly rod to test the 800 miles of pristine wild trout streams. if you want to tangle with some of the finest river bronzeback fishing in the world, do not forget to bring along an 8-foot, 7-weight fly rod and some big flies and popping bugs.

chapter 31

Cherokee Indian Reservation Public Trout Fishing

*T*HE PUBLIC TROUT-FISHING STREAMS of the Eastern Band of the Cherokee Indian Nation in western North Carolina, adjacent to the Great Smoky Mountains National Park, rate among the most intensely managed waters in the United States. A total of 30 stream miles designated as "Enterprise Waters" by tribal leaders flow through the Qualla Reservation and provide thousands of fishermen with fun and trout annually.

Enterprise Waters are stocked twice weekly during the regular season (April through October) and weekly during the winter season (November through February). Creel-size (8 to 12 inches) rainbow, brook, and brown trout constitute the bulk of the Cherokee's regular stocking efforts. However, just to keep things interesting, each week trophy-class 3- to 12-pound trout are released in all these waters. The present North Carolina state record brook trout, a 7-pound, 7-ounce beauty, was taken in 1980 from the Enterprise Waters portion of Raven Creek.

In addition to offering excellent fly-fishing for all three species of trout, the waters of Qualla Reservation also hold a bevy of large smallmouth and tons of hand-size rock bass. These fish are exceedingly common in the lower reaches of the Oconaluftee River as well as downstream from its mouth at the Tuckasegee River.

Trout fishing at the Qualla Reservation gets very high ratings. Summer creel limits are liberal: ten trout per day. Bait restrictions during this popular time slot are also virtually nonexistent. Naturally, the creation of such a worm-dunk paradise bears a price tag.

Gatlinburg has become well known for stocking trophy-size trout during its winter catch-and-release fishing season.

Visitors are charged daily and seasonal user fees, but presently anglers fishing here are exempt from needing a state fishing or trout license. All things considered, the cost of fishing at Qualla is a red-hot bargain, especially if you're fishing for the frying pan or a trophy trout.

The tribe's three ponds account for six surface acres, and are located beside Big Cove Road, approximately 5 miles upstream from the town of Cherokee. They are encircled by well-manicured fescue grass, and are heavily stocked twice weekly. The three ponds are both productive and popular.

Fly-fishing is remarkably good here. Higher fertility results in better hatches of aquatic insects than in the national park. The presence of the some-times pesky "stockers" does not adversely affect the resident population of trout, which is in surprisingly good condition according to tribal fishery experts. Fly patterns and techniques outlined for fly-fishing national park waters work ex-tremely well on these tribal waters.

Streams presently under the Qualla Reservation's Enterprise Waters designation include: Raven Fork downstream from its confluence with Straight Fork; Bunches Creek downstream from where it passes under the gravel road; the Oconaluftee River from its entrance into the Qualla Reservation, down-stream to its boundary at Birdstown; and Soco Creek downstream from its con-fluence with Hornbuckle Creek, to its mouth at the Oconaluftee River. All of these flows are tributaries of the Oconaluftee River and, with the exception of Soco Creek, all begin within the pristine confines of the Great Smoky Mountains National Park.

Raven Fork

SIZE: Medium to fairly large

FISHING PRESSURE: Extremely heavy

FISHING QUALITY: Very good for stocked trout, outstanding odds for trophy-class trout

ACCESS: Big Cove Road

USGS QUADS: Smokemont, NC; Bunches Bald, NC; Whittier, NC

RAVEN FORK LEAVES THE GREAT SMOKY Mountains National Park as more than a mountain rill; it rates as a small, fast-flowing river in its own right. This is one of the more popular "put'n'take" streams, but one that, surprisingly, hosts a smart native population of rainbow and brown trout, which many anglers over-look for the easier-to-catch food hatchery trout.

Raven Fork's upstream Qualla Reservation reaches are reserved for en-rolled members of the Eastern Band of Cherokee Indians, but public fishing is welcomed downstream from the creek's confluence with Straight Fork.

Big Cove Road, which begins at its junction with US 441 in the town of Cherokee, quickly traces alongside Raven Fork from its mouth at the Ocon-aluftee River to the starting point of the Enterprise Waters at the mouth of

Straight Fork, a distance of approximately 8 miles. Big Cove Road is an excellent paved highway, with a liberal scattering of commercial campgrounds and stores along its route.

While Raven Fork is a moderately wide, fast stream with an abundance of medium to shallow riffles, it also sports a large number of cascades and corresponding deep plunge pools. Around 90 percent of Raven Fork (and other Enterprise Waters) flows very close alongside roadways that lend easy access.

Raven Fork possesses a fair number of such remote, steep-banked gorges, that require considerable effort to get into. These areas are not usually stocked, but they hold amazing concentrations of sizable trout, particularly angler-wary browns.

Personally, I am uncomfortable fly-fishing in a crowd, or for that matter being in any crowd, be it in a liquor store or on a trout stream. Solitude is available on Raven Fork's off-the-beaten-path reaches, but do not expect easy pickin's because Cherokee's trout streams receive considerable angling pressure, and you are probably not the only fisherman who's drifted a night crawler along a difficult-to-access reach recently.

Bunches Creek

SIZE: Medium to small

FISHING PRESSURE: Heavy

FISHING QUALITY: Excellent

ACCESS: Bunches Creek Road, (a four-wheel-drive-only gravel road)

USGS QUADS: Bunches Bald, NC

BUNCHES CREEK IS A MEDIUM-SIZE tributary to Raven Fork, and flows into the latter at the junction of Big Cove Road and Bunches Creek Road, a rough, four-wheel-drive-vehicle-only gravel road that connects Big Cove Road with the Blue Ridge Parkway, then on to US 19. That section of Bunches Creek downstream from the creek's last contact with the road (approximately 3.6 miles from its mouth) to its junction with Raven Fork is open to the public as Enterprise Waters.

Bunches Creek is one of Cherokee's most overlooked little trout-fishing hotspots. It is a small creek, but a very lovely bit of moving water. A constant overstory of hemlocks and hickories and a lack of crowds make this one ideal for fly-fishermen seeking a bit of elbow room.

Bunches Creek has several noteworthy tributaries, most of which begin within the National Park, although not all by any means. These include Indian Creek (shown as Redman Creek on older maps), which begins at more than 5,000 feet in elevation west of the Heintooga Overlook on the western slopes of the Balsam Mountains in the park, and enters Bunches Creek approximately 1.3 miles upstream from its mouth. An old jeep road traces alongside Indian Creek, but under present tribal regulations, this stream is not open to public fishing.

Heintooga Creek, another high-elevation park flow, enters Bunches Creek approximately 2.4 miles upstream. This stream begins in the craggy area between Horsetrough and Heintooga Ridges on the Balsam Mountains range. It is a pretty hop-across stream, which enters Bunches Creek at an elevation of almost 3,000 feet. Although the regulations given out by the Qualla Reservation Game and Fish Management Enterprise do not show this stream, it is restricted to tribal members only.

Oconaluftee River

SIZE: Large

FISHING PRESSURE: Extremely heavy, but rarely crowded

FISHING QUALITY: Superb, particularly for large trout

ACCESS: US 441; Big Cove Road

USGS QUADS: Whittier, NC; Bryson City, NC

FISHING THE RESERVATION'S REACHES of the Oconaluftee River is a treat, and would be so even if it were not intensively stocked. This is one of the great brown trout streams of the eastern United States, and one that shells out huge, full-finned "resident" trout with as much regularity as many Western streams.

The Oconaluftee River is large enough to float fish from a canoe or johnboat during most seasons, although surprisingly few anglers use these crowd-beating methods. Most float trips occur downstream from the river's US 19 bridge.

Upon leaving the national park, the Oconaluftee River bisects the bustling tourist town of Cherokee, the Qualla Reservation's tribal center. Although you might be casting a Light Cahill in the shadow of a hamburger emporium, this does not really matter when the fish are biting. The river's roar and the delight of fishing bury all thoughts of civilization.

Fishing pressure is most intense where access is easiest: upstream from the US 19W bridge to the park boundary. Therefore, the most intensive stocking occurs there, and fishing is always excellent. Incredibly fantastic fishing for smallmouth bass is found in this river and the Tuckasegee River, especially in the lower reaches of the 'Luftee.

ACCESS: US 441 traces alongside the river's eastern bank from the park boundary downstream to the river's confluence with Soco Creek. Big Cove Road lends access to the river's eastern bank downstream to where this road has a junction with US 19W, which lends additional access to the Oconaluftee River downstream from the town of Cherokee to the reservation's boundary at Birdstown. Access to the river's other side is provided by a roadway known as Old #4.

Soco Creek

SIZE: Small to medium

FISHING PRESSURE: Heavy

FISHING QUALITY: Excellent

ACCESS: US 19W

USGS QUADS: Sylva North, NC; Whittier, NC

SOCO CREEK IS THE ONLY SIGNIFICANT streamshed beginning within the confines of the Cherokee Indian Reservation. Its origins are between mile-high Soco Bald (5,440 feet in elevation) and Waterrock Knob Mountain (6,292 feet in elevation), which form a steep-walled series of ridges that divide Oconaluftee and Maggie Valleys. Unlike its sister peak to the west, Soco Mountain is home to many people, despite its rugged character and steep terrain.

Compared to other Qualla Reservation streams like the Oconaluftee River or Raven Fork, Soco Creek is quite small. Its headwater reaches are pleasant and tree-lined; however, its final 3 miles, though adequate and providing good fishing, lag behind other Cherokee streams in aesthetics. Soco Creek's headwater reaches are small, but a generous helping of cascades and pools amidst the shade of towering streamside hemlocks and dense-growing laurel make it appealing.

Upstream from Soco Creek's junction with Hornbuckle Creek, approximately 10 miles upstream from its mouth at the Oconaluftee River just downstream from the town of Cherokee, this stream is restricted to tribal members. Although Soco Creek is fed by two impressive feeder streams, Wright and Jenkins Creeks, these flows are not open to public fishing under the Enterprise Waters program. It is also worth noting that a very small section of Soco Creek downstream from the US 441 bridge to that point where the creek again flows adjacent to the reservation, in places is partially under tribal control, while one section of approximately 50 feet is under the control of the state of North Carolina. This area is well-marked, but pay attention to which section of the stream you are in when choosing to fish there.

ACCESS: Access to Soco Creek is excellent, with US 19W providing the bulk of this access. This federal asphalt way closely follows the stream's course for approximately 8 miles to the second bridge just upstream from the town of Cherokee. There, the creek makes a 1.4-mile loop around a sloping ridge, skirting under US 441 before merging with the Oconaluftee River. No roads provide access to this loop area, but enough anglers explore it to keep a footpath open along this reach.

US 19W follows Soco Creek very closely in most sections, although it does lose sight of the creek in places. Numerous side roads lend additional access to those areas away from this highway, and because Soco Creek, like all Enterprise Waters, is heavily fished, well-worn footpaths trace the creek's course.

Index

DEAR CUSTOMERS AND FRIENDS,

SUPPORTING YOUR INTEREST IN OUTDOOR ADVENTURE, travel, and an active lifestyle is central to our operations, from the authors we choose to the locations we detail to the way we design our books. Menasha Ridge Press was incorporated in 1982 by a group of veteran outdoorsmen and professional outfitters. For many years now, we've specialized in creating books that benefit the outdoors enthusiast.

Almost immediately, Menasha Ridge Press earned a reputation for revolutionizing outdoors- and travel-guidebook publishing. For such activities as canoeing, kayaking, hiking, backpacking, and mountain biking, we established new standards of quality that transformed the whole genre, resulting in outdoor-recreation guides of great sophistication and solid content. Menasha Ridge continues to be outdoor publishing's greatest innovator.

The folks at Menasha Ridge Press are as at home on a white-water river or mountain trail as they are editing a manuscript. The books we build for you are the best they can be, because we're responding to your needs. Plus, we use and depend on them ourselves.

We look forward to seeing you on the river or the trail. If you'd like to contact us directly, join in at www.trekalong.com or visit us at www.menasharidge.com. We thank you for your interest in our books and the natural world around us all.

SAFE TRAVELS,

Bob Sehlinger

BOB SEHLINGER
PUBLISHER

About the Authors

Don Kirk

DON KIRK HAS BEEN A FULL-TIME writer and editor for parts of five decades. He has written several books, been the start-up editor on dozens of magazines, hosted television and radio shows, been a consultant, and published more than 10,000 articles on fishing and hunting. A native of east Tennessee's Great Smoky Mountains, Don is the best-known fly-fishing expert in the country on southern waters, especially the trout streams of the Great Smoky Mountains National Park. His fishing guidebooks to the Smokies have sold more than 100,000 copies. He is currently publisher of *Southern Trout Magazine* (www.southerntrout.com), the first-ever publication devoted exclusively to fly-fishing for trout in the Appalachians Mountains (from northern Virginia to northern Georgia), plus southern tailwater trout rivers as far west as Arkansas.

GREG WARD IS A LIFELONG RESIDENT of Pigeon Forge, Tennessee. Since his teens he has guided hunting and fishing clients and operated a fishing shop in the Forge. Ward is a well-published outdoor writer with the good fortune of having a wife with a PhD in English. He is quite well known as an expert on Smoky Mountains fly-fishing throughout the county. Additionally, he is an entertaining, animated speaker.

Greg Ward